D1609980

# The Daily Telegraph
## SOCIABLE
## COOK'S BOOK

If ever you have wondered what sort of food you would get if you dropped in on Bon Viveur, this Sociable Cook's Book gives the answer.

But it is not only a collection of recipes for favourite dishes that Fanny and Johnnie Cradock serve to their family and friends. It is also a gold-mine of kitchen knowledge.

As in their previous *vade mecum*, THE DAILY TELEGRAPH'S Cook's Book, which was written at the request of readers who enjoy Bon Viveur's weekly cookery column in THE DAILY TELEGRAPH, the authors again pass on the kind of kitchen know-how that makes all the difference between success and failure.

Like the Cook's Book, this sociable sequel is meant to be read as much for pleasure as for profit.

*Winifred Carr*

Book designed and illustrated by William Farrow
Drawings on pages 371 to 392, by Frank Missen
Original manuscript edited by Alison Leach

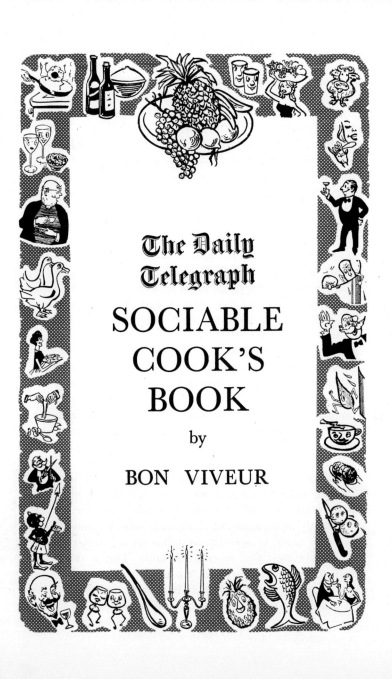

# The Daily Telegraph

# SOCIABLE COOK'S BOOK

by

BON VIVEUR

If you are one of the great majority today by whom everyday cookery and simple entertaining has to be done single-handed; or with hired help which keep drawing your eyes to the kitchen clock as the cost piles up— THIS BOOK HAS BEEN WRITTEN FOR YOU.

More and more we are conscious of the need for planning and presenting meals for almost every occasion which match the increased pace of our own and other people's lives. Of course, there are times when nearly all of us plan special meals in advance and then, after a good deal of thought, cook them with loving care. In the main, however, our daily lives are made up of trying to fit a quart into a pint pot and when it comes to modest entertaining, we more often than not find ourselves having to provide and present a meal for guests as an extra to a full working day. Then of course cooks flash round their kitchens flat-out with only just enough time to sling on presentable clothes and skid into the drawing room a split second ahead of the first guest.

Nevertheless the word "cook"—unless it is prefixed "drudge"—must be a synonym for "ambitious" and for "experimental" too, for the whole essence of the perennial fascination of good cooking is in the trying out of dishes with a difference—anything in fact which has not been attempted before.

Now do not get us wrong. We would neither of us be so foolish as to imagine that we are going to come up with this our second book of Cook's Chat and fill all the pages with recipes none of you know. All we do say is that we are constantly experimenting, constantly finding things that are new to us, or making variations on a familiar theme which are then well received at table. This is when we rush to our typewriters and record what we have done in the hope that one day we may be able to pass them on to you and that some of them may add a little to the things you already know. This book is nothing more than an edited version of our current culinary notebooks, with occasional harkings-back to cherished recipes which have pleased so many people in our own home that we make so bold as to submit them for your consideration. We have compiled it as nearly as we can manage in the way that we would explain it to all of you if you and we were gossiping and experimenting together in the privacy of our own kitchen. The subject is limitless; the fascination knows no bounds.

If we unashamedly fluctuate between the grand and the very simple, this is because it is how we live, for above all we only write about the things which we have done. So we have slipped in some rather grand dishes. There are occasions in everybody's lives when they come down heavily for a touch of grandeur. We have laid quite a bit of emphasis on what some of our young call "dressing up simple things to turn them into blissy party dishes", so that the simple things can do double duty in the home by featuring on day-to-day menus and on celebrant ones as well.

Above all we have produced this book in grateful acknowledgement of the tremendous support you gave to the first Cook's Book and—if we are to be completely honest—because this is the way we most enjoy writing about our work and our discoveries.

BON VIVEUR

First published 1967

Published by
The Daily Telegraph and Morning Post, Fleet Street, London, E.C.4

Printed by
Vandyck Printers Ltd., 32-34 Great Peter Street, London, S.W.1

# Contents

Please read this before going any further

All the recipes given in this book are
marked in the margins, but as we have
found it absolutely necessary to refer to a
number of recipes already published in
THE DAILY TELEGRAPH'S
COOK'S BOOK, we have saved you the
bore of repetition by marking all these
with an asterisk.

*Bon Viveur.*

# Chapter 1

# *Which are you?*

Are you a Sociable Cook? Or a Secretive Cook whose rites and rituals are strictly reserved for the members of your family? Neither category excludes you from being a careful cook, or an economical cook, or a wildly extravagant, obsessional cook or any other kind of cook you can think of. But whichever other kind you are, you will be either Sociable or Secretive.

What is a Sociable Cook? Well, for a start, a member of any income group from the most heavily endowed to the shortest pursed; someone who is completely unruffled by unexpected extra mouths to feed. The Sociable Cook never thinks of extra mouths as "guests", does not feel herself forced to do something special for them and is therefore absolutely serene and composed by their turning up, simply because to him/her what is good enough for the family must surely be good enough for anyone else. The Sociable Cook is a sharer, not a show-off, and always expects the turner-upper to slip naturally into an extra ("Never mind if it is odd, it's comfortable") chair at the dining hall, dining room, dining alcove or kitchen table.

9

The Sociable Cook takes it for granted that turner-uppers are there because they want to be and not because they want to criticise. This results in people being **glad** to drop in, being **glad** to take "pot luck", **glad** to eat and drink whatever is available **because the whole atmosphere is so warm, relaxed and natural.**

The Secretive Cook on the other hand is one on whom no one "pops in." The Secretive Cook "entertains" on set occasions and by numbers . . . out with the Crown Derby coffee cups, on with the lace tablecloth and add in at least two courses and two more wines than ever would be put out for a family occasion. If anyone is so foolhardy as to compliment the Secretive Cook on a dish, the inevitable result is a swiftly assumed, tight-lipped expression not wholly without cunning and a brusque "one of my dear mother's recipes, I'm so glad you liked it."

In the same case the Sociable Cook beams happily and offers, "Would you like to have it? I'd be glad to write it out for you."

We know a lot of Sociable Cooks. Some of them are so slap happy that their methods appal us—but only afterwards when something we are doing sends us off into fits of giggles at what she or he did to poor old *Petits Pots de Chocolat* or how there was nothing in reserve and the can opener flashed when four more were landed on him/her five minutes before supper. But those very giggles are warm with the recollection of a very happy time, slosh-it-up regardless though it may have been.

One of our favourite "Sociables" is pretty rich by most standards today—her staff are numerous, but she is so kind to them that they never seem to be there when visitors drop in. Then it is all hands on deck to prepare a salad, help lay up for sixteen on the big kitchen table—and listen, as we dig out the cartons of potted shrimps and cut the brown bread and butter for her, to delicious chatter and solicitous enquiries about personal problems which we have forgotten but she never!

Another "Sociable" is flat broke—and "You'll just have to manage with bread and jam ... Fanny, cut up those loaves for me; Johnnie, will you please carry the tray?" is the prelude to an unfashionable and fattening tea session, which is warm, witty and delightful, although the home-made jam has not set properly and China tea is too costly to serve. This one makes perfect scrambled eggs—and knows it, so you take down a little pot of cream and some mushrooms or truffles when you "drop in", she accepts them delightedly and you have party scrambled eggs instead of that pretentious attempt at a *soufflé* which never quite comes off.

If you can corner her for long enough from feeding the dogs and cats, shooing half the neighbourhood's children to hand-washing before tea, settling the affairs of W.I., W.V.S., Red Cross and the fund-raising Old Time Music Hall at the village hall, she is quick enough to digest any time or labour-saving trick you pass on—and mad keen to add recipes which really work to the dog-eared ledger in which she rams newspaper cuttings, notes on envelopes, everything—but who relegates to the guest rooms cookery books which do not dot I's and cross T's for her ... "I haven't the time to wade through dozens of recipes to find one which really works."

Both these women are currently facing a wedding (daughter, so they are stuck with everything) and twenty-firsts ("This is such a lovely house for parties we must have it here"); they "entertain" incessantly but never in their wildest dreams would they lay claim to being blueprint Cook-Hostesses. The husband of one has become a superb omelette maker since we stayed at Christmas, gave him a pan and took down extra eggs for private sessions in case supplies should be embarrassingly denuded. The other is dizzy with delight because she has found our recipe for *choux* paste "really works" and now it is *choux* paste with everything until she gets around to finding time to test something else.

These are the cooks for whom this book is written. Loving and lovable people who have great demands upon their time and are neither exceptionally brilliant nor show-off, but who are ambitious about raising the standards of everyday meals and equally ambitious about the "spreads" they mount for their friends.

# PHILIPS
## in the kitchen

## Sharp knives & Super meals

Philips Electric Knife Sharpener—
that's the modern way to sharpen
all kinds of knives and scissors
in seconds. Such a big help in the
kitchen . . . *and* when it's time
to carve the Sunday joint. Yes,
Philips Electric Knife Sharpener
is a terrific time-saver — and it's
tremendous
value at **79/11**

You've another big time-saver in the
Philips 3-Speed Food Mixer. It
mixes everything from milk shakes
to rich fruit cakes—fast. It's
light in weight—yet amazingly
powerful. And simple controls give
the right speed—and eject the
beaters for cleaning — at the touch
of a finger.
All this for **£5:17:4**

*Chapter 2*

# Sauce for the goose

If there is any difference at all between the food we cook for ourselves and the food we cook when we are entertaining, we think the standard is just a shade higher in what we do for each other. Certainly it should be true that what is good enough sauce for family geese should undoubtedly be good enough for guest ganders. One of the best examples of this was given to us by that splendid eater, Sir Gerald Kelly. When he was a very young man, he took his great friend, the late Mr. Somerset Maugham, back to his mother's home to family supper. On leaving, Mr. Maugham complimented Mrs. Kelly on the excellence of her ham. After his departure Mrs. Kelly turned to her son and said with great astonishment, "What a very strange young man! He praised my ham. As if I should have given your father a bad one."

One of the great fallacies is that dishes for guests and dishes for family meals fall into two strictly separated categories.

Now do not get mad with us before we include **out** of that sweeping generalisation dishes which no housewife in

15

her senses would make to feed growing children, or the man of the house home from work. Of course quails in aspic, *caviar bouchées*, *bisques* and *biscuits glacés* are as remote from family meals as Waterford tumblers and Crown Derby coffee cups are from nursery tables.

But there is a point at which party and family foodstuffs converge to become one and the same thing.

Consider the case of scrambled eggs—a good example, we think, because we often hear people, who freely admit they know next to nothing about cookery, claim, in the same breath, "But I make splendid scrambled eggs!"

Well, if they do, they have an in-built asset without which no cook can succeed—the infinite capacity for taking pains— because scrambled eggs do not make themselves and badly made ones are disgusting.

Better a good dish of properly made scrambled eggs than a more pretentious dish which falls far short of perfection because ambition has been allowed to outrun experience.

scrambled eggs

**Scrambled eggs** are breakfast food but they can very swiftly become main everyday and party food. The additional requirements are simple—a little more money to spend on the dish and the RECIPES. Either way, of course, you need to allow 2 eggs per person and one for the bowl to every 6. These must be whipped with a dessertspoonful of milk to each egg and seasoned with salt and pepper. Then you must dissolve enough butter to cover the base of a very thick pan. When the butter is melted and bubbling, you must pour in your egg mixture and stir, stir, stir unremittingly with your spoon. Indeed this is one of the few jobs for which the sharp edge of a metal spoon is far better than the blunt edge of a wooden one. Once the spoon begins hauling up creamy flakes from the base of the pan, you are nearly home. Stop while the mixture is still very moist and creamy. Never forget that **eggs go on cooking** even on a warm plate and the synonym for "dry" in scrambled eggs is "ruined"!

On to hot, freshly made, buttery toast goes the mixture and away it goes to the table and that is the end of breakfast. But it is only the beginning of the scrambled egg story.

oeufs
brouillés
aux cèpes

oeufs
brouillés
aux morilles

oeufs
brouillés
forestière

oeufs
brouillés
aux truffes

Use only 4 dessertspoonsful of milk to 8 eggs, replace the remainder with 4 dessertspoonsful of thick, rich cream and add whichever member of the fungus family you can obtain and afford with, of course, seasonings. Thus you obtain **Oeufs brouillés aux Cèpes, Oeufs brouillés aux Morilles, Oeufs brouillés Forestière** (with mushrooms) or **Oeufs brouillés aux Truffes.** All good enough for an opening course at a feast, so we give you the stockists of the various fungi on page 367.

Try thinking this example out in all culinary directions and you will see the point we are trying to make.

In the Cook's Book we gave you a recipe for Irish Stew—but what an Irish stew! The late, great Erwin Schleyen, who made the Mirabelle Restaurant in Curzon Street, served this—his—version at a *semaine gastronomique* in Paris when he took his entire (British) kitchen brigade over to show the

French what could be done with English food. The Parisians went mad for "*le Irish Stew à l'Anglais*" which the most argumentive could scarcely claim was recognised food for visitors.

Pancakes* are family food when served with lemon or orange and soft brown sugar, made in advance of course so that Mum eats hers in peace with the family. But because thin, fine ones can be made and stored, they are ideal guest material too, with such fillings and sauces as we have given on pages 225-227.

"Mashed Potatoes" are certainly family fodder. Even so—and if these are made properly in the first place, it is no great chore to transform the mixture from a rather gloomy, forked up, grey-white hump, which looks like a Saxon burial ground, into *pommes duchesse** or good, golden *pommes croquettes**.

Similarly, IF you can make a good egg custard (confectioner's custard*) to serve with casserole-cooked fresh or tinned, bottled or frozen fruits, you can most certainly make any one of a number of the cream puddings called *bavarois* (page 250).

Our culinary thinking is always dominated by French cooking—about which there has been a plethora of misconception. We like to think that a high proportion of our receipts fall into the category of *Cuisine Familiale* quite frequently the best of all French cooking, and based on closely guarded receipts handed down from one generation to the next. Like French home cooks, we base our all on the great classic tenets and then we create, adjust, taste, discuss and finally incorporate into our repertoire. Of course there is one big difference—we do not guard them jealously, and we are happiest when we can pass them on to you.

So we make no bones about talking to you about "simple everyday types of *pâté maison*" because thousands of you have written asking for these recipes. Simple *pâtés* are quick to put together and they take care of themselves in the oven. Then they sit happily in refrigeration for some time, ready to be whipped out, given time to get back to room temperature (otherwise flavour is lost) and served for that most admirable light summer lunch for work or playtime . . . *pâté*, gherkins, fresh bread or toast and butter followed by a cheese board and fresh fruit. Give that to your hot, exhausted women friends instead of an elaborate, cream-enriched luncheon which they praise lavishly and eat reluctantly (because ninety per cent of women do not want to eat fattening foods) and you will be sure of sincere appreciation.

After succeeding with the family *pâté* do not flinch from the more elaborate special party versions, which are only extensions of the simple ones—**just embellishments of basics in fact.** Indeed do not be afraid of serving the family version as the opening course for a **French meal.**

## Pâté Familial or Croûte Familiale
(page 79)
## Truite en papillote aux Aromates ou aux Amandes*

---

## Escalope de Veau Natur ou à la Crème
(page 193)

---

## Salade de Saison

---

## Fromages Assortis

---

## Fruits

Let us break this menu down and see what it entails. Get your chosen *pâté* made and out of the way days beforehand. The trout, cleaned but with the heads left on can be put in their kitchen foil parcels (see **Salmon Trout** page 134) the night before and then slipped into the oven for 30 minutes just before your guests are expected (then turn the oven down to lowest). While the trout cook, you can make the chosen *escalope* dish and keep that on the lowest shelf of the turned-down oven. That is all there is to do except make a brew of really good "*filtres*" (page 367).

If you want to show off, put a selection of fruits in individual baskets for each guest on a few vine, Virginia creeper or angelica leaves. Set out the assorted cheeses on a board covered with a split straw wine bottle cover, labelling each cheese neatly on a little cocktail stick and paper "flag". But serve

bread, **not** biscuits, with cheese for a French meal. Advance-make the *vinaigrée** or *vinaigrette** and turn the salad in it at the table, thus avoiding the service of vegetables with the veal. If you must have them, they should be served as a separate course **after** the veal. Nothing will be wasted from this meal. The cheese, *pâté*, fruit, butter, bread and gherkins can all be eaten up afterwards. Allow one 8 oz. trout per person and one 4 oz. very thin *escalope*.

Now let us try the same thing with a delicious but plain **English bill of fare.**

**Potted Salmon** (see below)

**Oxtail, Creamed Swedes and Pommes Croquettes***

**Fruit Fool with Jersey Cream**
(fruit dependent upon season) page 22

**Stilton Cheese and Celery**

There are several things about this meal which make it particularly interesting. The **Potted Salmon,** of course, can be put up and refrigerated days ahead. It is made by substituting 1 lb. of salmon for the given $\frac{1}{2}$ lb. of cod and herring roes in **Our Fish Pâté** (page 85). It should be served with **hunks** cut from base and topknot of a cottage loaf and this should be heated through before cutting, in a **loose** wrapping of kitchen foil at gas 1 (290°F). The butter will be best in a classic round pat with an acorn stamp on the top (stockists, page 365).

**Oxtail** (page 186), like any casserole, actually improves with re-heating, thus allowing it to return to gas 2 (310°F) the next day until piping hot again.

The **swedes**—so sorrowfully unappreciated by the majority—also re-heat leaving only the golden **pommes croquettes\*** for the cook/host/hostess to make just before the meal.

fruit
fools

As for the **fool**—made with fresh, bottled or frozen fruits—it will always be good if the fruit ($\frac{1}{2}$ pint) is **sieved dry** then sweetened and the cream is thickly whipped double Jersey (beaten in) with a night's rest before eating to allow it to settle down. Sling some ice into the celery jug after washing and before overnight refrigeration and see how exhaustively guests will think cook has expended her energies!

Both these meal examples can be dreary beyond belief if tinned salmon, cream substitute, cheap butter or bought *pâté* are allowed to creep in.

There are countless examples of simple but memorable meals—everyday in fact in their content. The only rub is that everything used must always be of fine quality—pure and fresh. You can never succeed with the ersatz.

Let us not deceive ourselves. It is much easier to make an elaborately sauced dish palatable with substitutes than to cook simple foods perfectly although of course the claim is baseless that sauces were intended to mask inferior flavours! The true function of saucing is to flatter the basic item into yielding its maximum flavour. If a sauce is strong enough to eclipse the flavour of the subject, **it is wrong.**

We always feel the sad remark made to us at our own table by the late Mr. Somerset Maugham is an excellent guide to simple folk on how to entertain the extra-privileged. We were discussing food and wine intently when suddenly he said, "Of course I love rice. I love nursery rice pudding. But nobody ever gives me nursery rice pudding any more . . . I suppose I'm too grand."

The moral to this is that the humble—when prime—is suited to the most eminent guest.

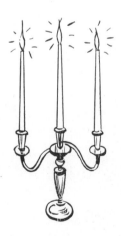

# Chapter 3

# *How not to be a Thomas Lipton*

*Question: I have been given a set of silver fish knives and forks for a wedding present. My grandmother says I cannot use them as they are vulgar—can you advise me?*

*Answer:*

Fish knives and forks were a Victorian *"nouveau riche"* innovation, like little silver tongs for picking up asparagus! Our grandparents ate fish with two plain silver forks, which we find jolly uncomfortable so we teach that fish knives and forks are incorrect, yet we have them and we use them— because they make fish eating easier!

Really the keynote to "correct eating" is **comfort.** This puts the little silver asparagus tongs right out of court. Instead, just (a) pick up asparagus stalks in the fingers, (b) dip the fingers into a finger bowl and (c) wipe them on a table napkin—which, by the by, is never a *"serviette".*

No one knows these little conventions unless they have been taught them, so there is always some young person somewhere who is made uncomfortable and embarrassed at not having been told exactly what to do with some item on their plate.

It is nearly always possible to hold back and see what everyone else does then copy. But never shall we forget **our** embarrassment at watching a young man struggling to swallow the hairy "choke" of a globe artichoke because he did not know that this should be removed and discarded.

Few of us have the aplomb of King Edward VII who, when Sir Thomas Lipton picked up his finger bowl and drank from it, promptly did likewise. In short it is much simpler to know.

| | |
|---|---|
| jacket-roasted potato | So much of good manners at the table is dependent upon good treatment and presentation by the cook. A **jacket-roasted potato** is absolutely ruined if it is split and plonked on to the same plate as a main course serving of meat and other vegetables and sauce. It belongs on a small side plate which, like salad, is always laid to the left of the cover so as not to get in the way of the wine glasses on the right. If a teaspoon is provided, the potato can be buttered, salted, peppered and kept dry by being safely out of contact with any sauces. Then, openly, in family circles, the potato-denuded skin can be re-spread with butter, seasoned and enjoyed last, as the very best part of all! |
| cob corn | A knowledgeable cook drives wooden cocktail sticks into each end of **cob corns** before sending them to table with a sauceboat of melted butter. A knowledgeable eater either picks the cobs up by their sticks and gnaws from end to end, or—if no sticks are provided —grasps each end of the hot buttery cob firmly and attacks it. |

**globe artichokes**

**Globe artichokes,** when properly presented, (see the diagram on page 392), have the offending "chokes" removed. The little top tuft (pulled out from the top in order to get at the inedible "choke") is inverted, like an upside down dunce's cap, scattered with chopped parsley and used as mere "top garnish" or "presentation" for this delicious *hors d'oeuvre* vegetable. The classic accompaniment is *sauce vinaigrette\**—the one with herbs in. This is poured into the central cavity. Then the leaves are pulled off singly the flesh half-sucked, half-nibbled off the fat stem end of each one which is then discarded to a small extra plate or piled around the rim of the artichoke plate until all are denuded and the *fond* or artichoke bottom is revealed. This is then eaten with a knife and fork . . . another dish which should be indivisible from a finger bowl.

**prawns**

**Prawns** can be a problem too. If you practise a bit in private first, you will find that if you pick up an unshelled prawn and push head and tail firmly towards each other, this breaks the body shell apart and the tail shell will come away easily. Then dunk the exposed flesh into the mayonnaise which is usually provided, holding the prawn by its head, and once again eat from your fingers.

**"finger foods"**

Other **"finger foods"** include **gulls' eggs,** which you just shell and dip into salt, pepper, cayenne, paprika—or a sauce and nibble like a mouse; just as you would eat **celery sticks, radishes, spring onions and**

27

**quails.** These tiny little birds are simply insulted by "refained" eaters who slice off their minute breasts and give up the unequal (knife and fork) struggle with the succulent little carcasses. Pick 'em up in your fingers too, like **lobster claws, crab claws** and **oysters.**

mussels

Similarly, a bowl of mussel soup, or **mussels** in a glorious pond of wine, herbs and cream, is not wholly tackled with a spoon. Tear off the empty half shells, pick up the half shells with the mussels in, eat them off the shell and use each shell to scoop up and drink mouthsful of the liquor (more finger bowls). Now we must pursue that glancing quail reference to bones-in-fingers. Queen Victoria picked up a chicken's leg and nibbled it, thereby earning herself a reproof from a four-year-old at her table who told that intimidating monarch, "You piggywig, you suck your bones!"

Crying defiantly, "What's good enough for Queen Victoria is good enough for us," we nibble all **cutlet bones, bird bones** and **spare ribs**—if there is no finger bowl, the table napkin just goes for a Burton!

caviare

pâtés,
terrines
pâté de
foie gras
or foie gras
truffé

Once we saw a little mound of superb Russian grey **caviare** being chased around a plate with a knife and fork. The correct way is to eat **caviare** like jam—spreading a little at a time on to hot toast—and once again **nibble!** This jam-spreading method is also far and away the best method of eating and enjoying **pâtés, terrines** and that glory of

28

gastronomy **pâté de foie gras** or **foie gras truffé,** using French bread instead of toast.

melon

If **melon** has been Spanish-cut (page 64), it is much pleasanter to eat with a knife and fork; but if it is just slapped down in a crescent, then one hand to steady one end and the other to scoop out the flesh with a spoon is perfectly *de rigeur.*

grapefruit

**Grapefruit** really cannot be eaten decently by anyone **if** it has been wrongly cut with a grapefruit cutter in such a way that bits of flesh are spooned up with bits of skin clinging to them and the halved grapefruit itself. The chin suffers, the table suffers. Learn to use a grapefruit cutter **properly** so that you run it round each fleshy segment which can then be picked up comfortably in a teaspoon, leaving a cage of skin in the grapefruit, not hanging half out of your mouth!

When we were young and dessert appeared unfailingly at every formal dinner party, the "difficult" fruits were always handled by the man sitting on left or right of the woman— depending on which way she had "turned" as this last course appeared. In those days you "turned" with each course. The man would peel the pear, peach, or nectarine, cut a truss of grapes from the bunch with the standard silver grape scissors and crack and shell any kind of nuts with the always provided sufficiency of nutcrackers. Both the "turning" and these graceful male attentions are relatively extinct today so it behoves every

male and female to know how to take care of
their own fruit for themselves.

banana

The ungainly practice of spearing a **banana**
on a fork and holding it aloft while paring the
skin down with knife and thumb is as point-
less as it is clumsy. Put the banana on the
dessert plate parallel with your own body.
Put the fork into the left hand, tip and lift
the (always) silver knife with the other hand.
Make a straight cut from one end to the other
along the top. Fold back the skin with both
knife and fork down the whole length and
then cut off small segments to pop in the
mouth. This process fulfils the three rulings
for table manners. It is clean, it is easy and
it is comfortable.

grapes

Curiously enough there are two ways of
eating **grapes** correctly. In France the rule is
fingers only, and the finger bowl provided by
the English, is used to swirl each truss of
grapes and cleanse them before nibbling
them off the stem, pips and all.

In England it is fingers too but in this case
the fingers do not merely hold the stem. They
pick the grapes off singly and if the eater is
anti-pips, these are neatly popped out into
the hand and thence on to the plate.

peaches
nectarines
and pears

In the higher echelons of elegant behaviour
the thumb is not used to shove against the
side of **peaches, nectarines** and **pears** so
that the skin can be peeled down with the
knife. The easier and, therefore, better way
is to steady the fruit on your plate by driving
the fork in as near the base as possible, peel

the skin back down to fork level with the knife, turn the fruit over, push the fork into the peeled end and remove remaining skin from the base. Now you simply halve the fruit, remove the stone and polish it off in exactly the same way as you would cut small pieces of meat or other flesh.

strawberries The **strawberry** is very tiresome because we think the best way of eating them is to hull them, squash them down in a bowl and stir them up like a dog's dinner, with lashings of cream and sugar. This alas, is not formal dinner party behaviour!

When the strawberries are unhulled, each berry is held by its stem, dipped into cream and sugar, which are put in two separate blobs on the plate, and then the fruit is nibbled off its stems. Alternatively, and if they are served hulled, then the sugar and cream may be put over them, for eating as a pudding with spoon and fork, but here again, squashing is out.

pineapple If you are faced with a whole **pineapple,** your hostess should be shot. It is, however, perfectly correct for you to confront what appears to be a whole pineapple standing upright with its tuft on top, provided that it has had its base cut off, has been sliced, skin and all, and subsequently re-shaped for service. Take a slice, drive a fork into the centre, cut the skin off all round in a neat ring, put it on the side of the plate and then eat the fruit with a knife and fork as, say, eggs and bacon.

| | |
|---|---|
| cherries | **Cherries** are easy—stalk in hand, bite off, suck stone off in mouth, eject (see grapes). If you encounter a bowl of fat **dessert** |
| dessert | **gooseberries,** you again use your fingers. |
| gooseberries | Just pull the tiny stalk end back on each so that a scrap of flesh is exposed, put this way on into the mouth, squeeze and suck without any bathwater noises. |
| | |
| cape | The **cape gooseberry** very rarely appears |
| gooseberry | on English tables other than as a *petits fours*. When bought or picked each little orange coloured berry is enclosed in what appears to be a beige Chinese lantern of bracts. These are peeled back by hand, pulled to the top of the fruit, twisted round to make a stem and dipped from this stem into *fondant*, or *glacé* icing (page 293). Therefore all you have to do at table is pick up the stem, bite off the fruit—it has no stone—and put the stem on the plate. |
| | |
| nuts | It is obvious to everyone that when **nuts** have been cracked with nutcrackers and the shells pulled away, the nuts are eaten with the fingers. The only sin here is one of omission when salt is not made available, because nuts taste far better when they are dipped into the salt. |
| | |
| figs | Regrettably **figs** cannot be sucked either. Spear the base of a fig with your dessert fork so that the fig is held upright on the plate. Cut from stem to within $\frac{1}{4}$ inch of base. Repeat crosswise, so that the unskinned flesh falls into four neat petals. Cut the flesh |

from each in a whole section (halve if these are large) and eat with knife and fork.

oranges    The great problem fruit is **oranges,** which we maintain should not be served unless they have been prepared in waterlilies (page 375). If they are not, we suggest you copy Miss Matty and her stickler-for-good-be-haviour elder sister. Take a couple of lumps of sugar, retire behind a screen, shove in the sugar and suck.

pome-    As for **pomegranates,** their pippy flesh
granates    makes them completely anti-social, so grab one and retire to the garden or the bathroom to chew, suck and spit in decent isolation.

Problems do not however begin and end with fruit.

There are some very fishy concepts about how certain fish should be eaten. Consider

oysters    the **oyster.** This bivalve has either to be devoured live or else cooked with great celerity. Yet time and again we see oysters slain in restaurants. Firstly the service savagely rules they should be opened on to beds of ice. This ensures that they come to table half frozen. Then the eater picks up a fork and drives it through each one, thereby finishing it off.

An oyster should be eased from its deep shell with the flat side of the oyster fork—if, of course, it is still attached. Then it may be lifted underneath with the fork by the pernickety. The *savant* merely picks up the shell and swallows the oyster whole, then brazenly uses a small piece of brown bread and butter to mop up any of the exquisite juices which remain.

But there is a little more to it than that if, in these days of declining standards, you are to ensure yourself against being served stale oysters in some large restaurants. The blue-print for perfect service can be seen at the Savoy where the oyster opener brings his trolley to your table and opens the oysters as Mr. Weller might have said "before your wery eyes." He, it was, you will recall, who lived during the oyster eater's paradise, since he was known to have observed, "it is a wery remarkable circumstance that oysters and poverty always seem to go together."

Not only are they high priced today but some big establishments who know for certain before a meal session that they will serve x dozen, **open them up in advance before the rush begins.** Just bear in mind for your own protection they always open on to the deep shell, not the flat one, and unless you know or can see the oyster service in any establishment, say this when you order, "I will have mine on the flat shell if you please, unbearded, without ice and please do not detach them." By this little bit of trickery they are sunk and must open yours freshly. If you wish to impress with your knowledge, do not even permit the waiter to put that horrid assembly on the table of Tabasco and vinegar and other lethal sundries and if you want a bit of first-class one-upmanship you just murmur to your companions, "I do so agree with the great André L. Simon who once said, 'Even a drop of lemon juice is the thin edge of the wedge of heresy'."

whitebait     **Whitebait** are easy—just a fork—but if, as you should do, you get half a small lemon and not two or three of those useless little bits, pick it up in one hand, drive the fork into it with the other, squeeze and turn gently on to the fork. You can see the pips as they pop up, put them on one side and control the run of juice over your portion.

sole          Now let us suppose you are confronted with a whole, skinned **sole.** Do not pick at the top with the knife and fork. Use these to push the sole to the farther side of your plate. Then run the knife straight down the spine-bone. This is the division between the two upper fillets. Stroke the knife under the flesh against the invisible bones underneath and you will find that you can turn each fillet over the fork straight on to the empty part of your plate and eat it comfortably. Enjoy the second upper fillet in the same way. Then, starting at the tail end, slip the knife under the completely visible spine and bone cage, ease it away from the base flesh and eat the two under fillets in equal comfort.

sprats        The same applies in miniature to **sprats** because we think that the heads and bones, unlike whitebait, the Continental *petite friture* and sardines, are disagreeable.

35

**lobster**

It is really odd but some of the most luxurious foodstuffs are traditionally and classically badly served in good restaurants. Take the case of the **lobster.** Assume it is served cold. If it is not wet and milky, it is certainly not worth eating. Nor will it be fresh because after taken from the sea a lobster subsists on its own moisture until it is so dried out it dies. But when it is fresh, even the small claw flesh can be excavated easily. Yet what happens? With a flourish of silver service the waiter removes the main tail to neck piece of white meat to put it on your plate. He then breaks off the large claw, cracks it or gives you a pair of nutcrackers and **whisks all the rest into the kitchen** to be turned into *soupe de poissons* or stock for a fish sauce. We will not allow this.

We insist our half lobsters are put unassaulted on our plates, then with lobster prongs (a common metal meat or kebab skewer is a very good domestic substitute) the nutcrackers and finger bowls, eating and excavating continues until there is not enough left to take the edge off the appetite of a well-fed cat!

This does not apply to a hot lobster because the existence of sauce ensures retention of shell. It is merely more messy to eat so the table napkins that are used must be replaced with fresh ones for the remainder of the meal. Indeed there is a lot to be said for the very practical and amusing practice of tying bibs around guests before serving them with rich and messy shellfish dishes.

trout       The most important fact about **trout** is that they must never be headless since under the gills lie two very tiny pearl-shaped collops of flesh which are regarded by gourmets as the *bonnes bouches*. The gill is lifted with the tip of a knife and the little pearl pushed back. It pops out quite easily. Then the movements are precisely the same as with a sole on the bone except that a trout is much easier and when the spine bone is removed, the head comes away with it.

scampi       Fried **scampi** served with mayonnaise, *Hollandaise* or *mousseline* sauces are easy enough to eat because they are just little curly bodies out of their shells. You impale each one on a fork, dip into the sauce and eat; but when scampi are sauté-ed in butter and there is lots of lovely juice on the plate, you must either leave the juice or choose between two methods. Most people in this island are not as thick-skinned as the Cradocks who will unashamedly wipe a piece of bread around the plate.

The only alternative is to break up small pieces of bread, drop them into the sauce, impale the scampi on a fork as before and then use the little bit of bread—craftily concealed underneath—to soak up a little of the buttery juices. Only thus can you get the best out of the dish.

snail       The **snail** in culinary parlance is a fish, presumably a land fish since the largest farm we have ever seen is on the Route

Napoleon, a good hundred miles from the Mediterranean, well removed from any river and inhabiting the hedgerows. It is still a wretch to eat because *escargots* scissors, until you are used to them, are difficult to open and close; these should always be provided for holding the hot little snail shell. Then a very slender *escargots* fork (substitute —one of those Victorian ivory handled tea forks) is driven in with the other hand and the snail hauled out whole. Lift the shell by the scissors and pour the juices into your mouth, or pour them on to the indented *escargots* plate and mop them up with that ubiquitous piece of bread.

kebabs    Whether a **kebab** is made of fish, flesh or fowl, it still turns up in private houses on its skewer unless a trained waiting staff is kept. Hold the head of the skewer in one hand through your table napkin (or you may regret it), slip the prongs of a fork just behind the head, pull the skewer handle with one hand, push the back of the fork in the opposite direction with the other hand and thus clear the skewer and align its contents neatly on to its bed of rice below. With a bit of practice you can push a single fork prong through the "head" and push off the contents with a knife.

boiled    There has been more trivial discord stirred
egg       up in homes by the simple matter of how to eat a **boiled egg** than the subject deserves. "Don't behave like a kitchen maid", snarled

an old uncle of ours to a junior member of the family who was tapping away at the top blunt end of his egg and picking off the bits of shell with his fingers.

"Slice the top off neatly", he snapped at the bewildered sinner, "and be sure you do so with one neat movement".

Well, there it is—that is the ruling, but we can find no possible cause for offence in the shell-picking method except perhaps that it is confoundedly finicky.

fried
and
poached
eggs

Even more finicky was the **fried** or **poached egg** treatment used by a young man we once knew very well. Bits of bread or toast were torn up and packed round the egg on its *croûton* or toast in order that not one single drop of yolk should reach the plate. If it did, he pushed it away and refused to eat it.

The clever thing, if you are not a bread wiper, is to so apportion the bacon or toast on the same plate as to get up every scrap, including the delicious bacon fat, by the time the last mouthful is popped in. Otherwise you will have to wipe, or leave good stuff on the plate. Teaspoons should be used for *oeufs en cocottes*, and forks for *omelettes*—whether Belgian *soufflé*, classic French, Spanish *tortilla* or Basquaise *pipérade*.

duchess
potatoes

If a cook makes **duchess potatoes** so loose and flabby that they flop off the fork when the knife apportions them to it, no one can be possibly be expected to eat them tidily. The only way of conveying this sort of mush to the mouth is by turning the fork over, prongs uppermost, and using it as a sort of scoop, which is frowned upon as not very pretty or in good taste.

game
chips

**Game chips** can be little beasts too unless you throw discretion to the winds and pick them up in your fingers like *pommes pailles*, those crisp hair-thin *juliennes* of potato, which simply explode all over the place like the seeds of a spitting cucumber if you try to drive a fork into them. Their larger cousins, *pommes allumettes*, and those blatant old **chips** are conversely only eaten with the fingers from newspapers with that lethal old malt vinegar, so we can dismiss them very sharply, but should you be lucky enough to be able to make or to be served with *pommes soufflées*, always use your fingers. These tiny, golden brown achievements which look like baby pillows can only be appreciated this way and because of the heat of the oil in which they must be fried for the second time, they are innocent of grease within seconds of being lifted out.

poulet
à la
Kiev

A real menace if you have not been fore-warned is that great chicken dish which the late papa Vecchi of the Hungaria brought to England—**Poulet à la Kiev.** A properly made *Kiev* looks like a brown, crumbed giant tadpole on your plate; inside is chicken and **inside that** is melted butter. If you shove a fork down the fat middle of it, you will get a squirt of butter in the eye and possibly all over your clothes as the know-all actress did when she ate one on stage

40

with us. We asked her very politely if she knew how to eat it or would like to be shown, to which she snapped, "Of course I know," and got her dress smothered in butter for her pains. The trick is to slit the top of the *Kiev* lengthwise from end to end and while slitting to use the back of the fork, prongs uppermost, to press gently—this way the butter oozes over the portions instead of erupting and the dish eats perfectly.

If you are ever confronted with a vegetable which looks like little bits of frilled, green crêpe paper with stalks on, pick each one up and eat it like miniature asparagus in your fingers, The name—**asparagus peas.**

asparagus
peas

Once again we make a distinction between family behaviour and formal dining when it comes to **salads.** Tossed green salads are either served *à la française* or else put on a side plate without any implement whatever. Then the torn leaves are picked up in the fingers when in the bosom of the family. When on your best behaviour use a fork.

salads

If anyone is dotty enough to serve a *papillote* of anything without a Dish for Dumping, the only thing you can do is to split the top open with your knife, if it is made with paper or parchment, or unfold it with your fingers if it is made with kitchen foil and then eat whatever is inside as best you can from the opened container. Of course, if a discard dish or plate **is** provided, you get rid of the case and eat in comfort.

papillote

puddings

In the matter of **puddings,** these are always either that or cake—leave the word "sweet" to the catering trade! All the "puddingy" puddings like steamed ones with sauces should be eaten with a fork, which is impossible with English fruit tarts made with water—both pond and pastry must be tackled with a spoon and fork at no great benefit to the eater. Proper pies without ponds are easily eaten with forks only.

Loose creamy mixtures should be served in individual containers and, therefore, eaten with a teaspoon. Firm ones like *charlottes, bavarois* and *mousses* also only need a fork; but if you want to be a roaring stickler, you must use a spoon **and** fork whenever a dessert spoon is necessary.

spaghetti

We have saved the worst till the last—**spaghetti**—for which a dessert fork and spoon should be provided. If these are not provided in a restaurant, request them—firmly. The only thing to do with the increasing prevalence of messenger-boy-waiters and kitchen-porter-chefs is to teach them by the old law of demand and supply. Help yourself to sauce and/or cheese, and mix well together with fork. Keep the fork in the right hand, take the spoon in the left, place the bowl of the spoon on the far side of the plate so that the inside of it is towards you, drive the fork down into the spaghetti very nearly vertically and twirl it in your fingers so that the prongs are against the spoon. Once you have tried this, you will find that you can wind up yards in seconds and convey each coil to your mouth without slapping yourself over the left ear with a long hot dangling strip.

There is just one more point. If you are host or hostess you do what a vulgar son of ours described to a girl friend as "grab your irons first" because then everyone else will start. If for some reason you see that one of your guests is employing a slightly eccentric method, you must always do the same.

*Chapter 4*

# *Saving graces*

*Question: Do you have a list of small hints for cooks which you think everyone should know?*

*Answer:*

The small change of culinary experience is as much concerned with pre-cooking and safety as it is with the job itself. We know, alas, by bitter experience that even the most experienced cooks make fatuous mistakes from time to time because of that dreary old human handicap—fallability. So before we list some more of the odds and bits which we have found it is helpful to know, we must—with a nice burn scar apiece to remind us of our own carelessness—START WITH SAFETY.

**DO** turn the handles of all pans inwards at your cooker until they are flush with the sides, not projecting beyond them. Otherwise, sooner or later, some unobservant scuttler will hurry past, catch a pan, overturn the contents, maybe burn themselves and possibly even cause a fire!

**DO** make sure, when deep-frying, that no hot oil container is ever filled to more than slightly under half its overall depth with oil. Otherwise one of these days you will forget to dry a wet frying item, in it will go, up the oil will seethe to ooze relentlessly over pan rim on to cooker, you, or both. IF this should ever happen to you, snatch out the frying basket and the seethe will subside. Then you can ladle out some of the surplus oil and save the day. But LADLE out the hot oil; never try lifting up the whole pan of the dangerous stuff until it has cooled down beyond the point where it can burn you.

**DO** come to terms with the inescapable fact that super cooks have loose wrists and cool hands. IF your's are not always cool, cool them under the tap or in a bowl of iced water when doing delicate palm-of-hand jobs with almond paste or any other moulding or handling item.

**DO** a classic wrist-loosening exercise. All the folk we train are made to do it every morning before starting work. Clasp your hands together in front of you with the fingers and thumbs completely overlocked. Pull your elbows down while maintaining the hands in these positions. Now let one wrist sag completely, then sag the other one. Do this slowly, gradually increasing speed, sag left wrist, sag right one, until you are rattling your interlocked hands like a pair of castanets. When Fanny was studying to be a violinist many years ago, this was the morning exercise given to her by her master to ACHIEVE LOOSE WRISTS.

**DO** test the validity of our claim that cooking is a cleanly and creative art and not a grubby chore, and that an apron is (to us) a mark of shame. Stand square on to a cooker, feet planted apart, mime something splashing . . . you will find that as you pull back, you curve your front to the splashes—and catch them. In fact you are convex as you react. Now stand anglewise in the Third Ballet Position. Grasp a pan handle in one hand, a spoon in the other. Mime stirring. Bend right over the pan and you will find that this way you are **concave** instead of convex; that you

46

have a far greater range of movement to left, right or behind you instead of being locked in by that square-on position; that in fact unless you are in an advanced state of being a future Mum, nothing could fly out far enough to reach you.

This is how we always stand. This is why we never mark our clothes when cooking. We tackle students this way. We say, "Here is an apron. Wear it always until the Saturday you can produce it **unmarked** after a week's cooking, then chuck it out and forget it."

Chefs always wear spotless white. They never mark themselves. IF they did, where would they be when a valued client sent for them during a luncheon or dinner session to compliment them and ask them to take wine with them? There is no time to change. One does not keep valued clients waiting if one hopes to succeed in the catering trade!

**DO** sit down for 5 minutes before tackling the cooking. Make a brief list of the food you intend preparing. Then you can see at a glance **where to start,** so that you do not hang round the kitchen nursing the last dish long after everything is finished, NOR do you pop off to do something else, put down the pinger you are carrying and burn Tail End Charlie!

**DO** make a list before a shopping foray. Hours are wasted by women who lean dithering against the counter, muttering, "Now was there anything else, I wonder?"

**DO** make special Don't Forget lists before your final pre-Christmas shopping expedition. Here are our two *aide memoire* lists which may bring to mind some forgotten item for you:

**Johnnie's List:** soft drinks for children and teetotallers; beer or lager for late **night thirsts; ingredients** for mulled wines and punches; cigarettes, tobacco, cigars; pipe cleaners; candles; matches; oil; fuse wire; dog, cat and bird foods; orders for coal, coke and wood; spare electric light bulbs; wine glass and tumbler replacements; de-frost refrigerators; get new corkscrew; theatre tickets; check fairy lights and pot and wrappings for tree; buy Alka Seltzers; book overseas telephone calls; check fire extinguishers; fill up all refrigerator ice trays; order ice for bath tub for buffet party; get small money for children to give carol singers; new money for their stockings and not nearly so small in envelopes for tradesmen's Christmas boxes.

**Fanny's List:** Biscuits and books for spare bedrooms; spare bedding and pillows in rolls with towels and toothbrushes for unexpected stranded guests; buy stamps for bread and butter letters; check cake and tree candles; buy things for children's stockings like sugar mice, chocolate money, giant lollies, popcorn, liquorice allsorts, candy floss, barley sugar, fruit and nuts, puzzle games, those terrible joke things like sausages which make rude noises, jigsaws and comics to keep them quiet in early morning and after meals; get Silent Night record to play when tree is lit; don't forget crystallised fruits, nuts and raisins; brandy and vodka for flaming pud; sort out and press Christmas clothes; get a face pack; wangle a last minute hair appointment.

**DO** resolve to try at least one new recipe every week and file the to-you-outstanding dishes in your own "Cook's Book."

**DO** resolve to start a store-cupboard or add to your existing one **immediately.** Decide on the amount you can spare for reserves from the weekly housekeeping budget. Once begun, it is amazing how quickly a store-cupboard accumulates (see p. 355).

**DO** add **bush basil** to your annual sowings and when you prick out or thin these seedlings, pot up a few, leave them out all summer and increase their length of cook's service by bringing them in at the end of September and keeping them on a sunny windowsill (if of course you have no warm glasshouse).

**DO** damp a cloth and stand a cake tin on it for a few moments if a **cake** stubbornly refuses to slip out. This way it will be forced to yield.

**DO** try making your own **port wine colouring** with red rose petals, just cover them meanly with water. Simmer them until they are purged, strain off the fluid and reduce it strongly by re-simmering down to a tablespoonful or two. The more you reduce, the stronger the colour.

**DO** make your own **green vegetable colouring** by dry-cooking masses of spinach, wringing it out in a treble fold of muslin, re-straining the liquor and simmering this down as far as you dare without it getting cloggy.

**DO** put a bit of charcoal into a jug or jar and invert **cut cucumber** in this mixture. It will keep so much better. In the port-wine Douro of Portugal, stem-ended tresses of grapes are kept for months as decoration before eating by driving half the stem through the cork of a jar filled with water and charcoal. The nourishment seeps to the grapes and keeps them alive indefinitely.

**DO** remember that if you can grow **hothouse cucumbers** at all, you can grow them **all the year round.** We start picking our January sown crop in May, and finish in late September by which time June sown seeds of (coincidence!) Telegraph Improved are well on the way to fruiting.

**DO** include **dill** among your annual kitchen rows of rotated radishes, spring onions and lettuces. This frondy beauty is enchanting as decoration and does wonders to a bit of frozen Pacific salmon besides being useful with any number of other fresh and salt-water inhabitants. Sow in rotation—it is short-lived at least in our experience.

**DO** try the contradiction in culinary terms taught us by a brilliant French cook, Madame Mado Poncellet of Le Crotoy. She startled us by claiming that she was as famous for her **eggs and bacon** "*à l'Anglais*" as for any of her great French dishes and then startled us even more by her method of cooking the eggs, but it works superbly. Melt enough butter in an iron or Pyrosil frying pan to cover the base. Break in as many eggs as you wish, slip into the oven one shelf above the centre at gas 6 (400°F). In approximately 6 minutes the eggs will have set and be cooked to perfection, while you frizzle No. 3 cut back bacon on the grill rack (low position) with bits of toast underneath to catch the fatty drips.

**DO** use lemon juice and water in preference to vinegar and water when **poaching eggs.** The vinegar acidulates the water and makes the eggs taste of it, which is unpleasant.

**DO** remember that lemon juice squeezed over **fruit salad** segments of **banana, pear and apple** will stop them blackening.

**DO** store **flapjacks** in an earthenware or china container—they dislike being kept in tins.

**DO** try using a piece or two of ordinary tissue paper to **separate the grease from liquid** at speed. It works far better than any skimmer! Just slide the tissue paper in from one side of the pan or pot and allow the grease to flow into it. Then you can gather up the corners, lift out the paper pocket of grease and throw it away.

**DO** make sure you have some black tissue paper in the house before tackling the two stages of **herb-drying and storage.** First you bunch the herbs and hang them, head downwards, in a slightly draughty position. Then as soon as they are dry and slightly crisp, you wrap them in black tissue. Make a few air-holes with a skewer to offset danger of moulding, and thus protect the herbs from the otherwise inevitable dust-accumulation during long storage.

**DO** dip inner **jam covers** into a saucerful of brandy before adding top covers if your storage space has the slightest bias towards dampness. This effectively delays mildew.

**DO** take heart over **curdled mayonnaise.** There is an even surer way to restore the separated mess than with water. Let it settle. Pour off as much oil as possible. Start again with 2 more egg yolks. Whip these until they are very thick indeed. Then drip back the sediment left from the failure batch. Finally re-whip in the poured-off oil.

**DO** dip your **meat batter** (or old flat iron used as a substitute) into cold water before each flattening blow. This way the surface of the meat, fish, game or poultry will remain unbroken and smooth. Bashed with a dry implement the flesh splits up and breaks.

**DO** boil a "skin" of water in the base of a **milk saucepan** before pouring in the milk. This way you avoid that base coating of scorched milk bubbles.

**DO** confine **mint** in the garden. Plant it in a worn-out bucket with plenty of holes in the bottom for drainage and then plant the bucket in the ground—the only way you can curb this obstreperous herb's rampagings.

**DO** try using a loop whisk instead of a wooden spoon when making large batches of **sauce or custard.** Chefs always do. They grasp the whisk firmly and work it back and forth across the pan **far more than around and around.** Once mastered this is both quicker and more effective.

**DO** try adding a teaspoonful of softened bitter chocolate to the **sauce or gravy** which you make from the sediments in a baking tin after butter-roasting a chicken. It gives a tremendous fillip to the flavour.

**DO** remain unruffled when a **roux-thickened sauce** shows you have used too much of any kind of fat by having a greasy fringe on top which starts separating. Let the sauce cool. Then press the back of a spoon into the middle and thus force the surplus grease into the spoon. Two or three minutes of patient pressing and spooning, a quick rebeating and the sauce can be heated up and served satisfactorily.

**DO** spare time to peel the inner white skin from **egg shells before using them to clear stock.** With the skins on, the shells do not function properly.

**DO** try lining an oiled, greaseproof paper lined sponge tin with **lemon verbena leaves** before pouring **in a sponge mixture.** The flavour is even better, we think, than when this is done with **scented geranium leaves.**

**DO** try to have three tins or jars of **fragrant sugars,** not just the one with vanilla pods buried in it. Save thinly pared skins of oranges and lemons. Dry them till they are crisp in a low oven. Bury them in castor sugar and have **lemon sugar** and **orange sugar** ready flavoured for your use.

**DO** save orange and lemon peel even when you have an ample supply of orange and lemon flavoured sugars. You can turn it into such excellent *petits fours.* Cut the pith away from the skin. Cut into 2½ inch to 3 inch long strips,

$\frac{1}{4}$ inch wide. Boil up three times in three lots of fresh, cold water, straining after each boiling. Then simmer in a mixture of 8 oz. granulated or loaf sugar dissolved in $\frac{1}{2}$ pt. water. Give three 10 minute simmerings, allowing everything to become completely cold between each. Then dry on a rack and either roll in 4 oz. sifted icing sugar sifted with 1 heaped eggspoonful cream of tartar and store in an air-tight tin or, after drying, dip completely into softened cooking chocolate or chocolate chips (page 365).

**DO** give **hot-house flowers** bloodheat water to drink when you cut or buy and bring into the house. That is what they are used to! Icy water will give them the purple sulks.

**DO** split the stems of **forsythia, lilac and syringa** to help them get enough to drink. Otherwise down will go their heads like naughty children.

**DO** pack scraps of sopping wet cotton wool into **hollow-stemmed-flowers.** This doubles their lives in water thereafter.

**DO** give **laurel leaves** a coating of colourless varnish before using them on tables or in vases in winter. Then they will shine delightfully in firelight and curiously enough this helps them to last. Take the varnish well down over the leaf-stalk join where it meets the stem.

**DO** burn the stems of those great **Papaver Orientalis**— the big poppies which are so flamboyant they are almost the No-Better-Than-They-Should-Bes of horticulture. This is the way to make them last in winter with half an aspirin or a penny dropped in, or with the new crystal reviving and sustaining powder which has recently come on to the English market (page 365).

**DO revive wilted violets** by putting their heads into

water. Violets drink through their faces. Turn each bunch upside down, leave overnight and in the morning they will be all sprightly once again.

**DO** give your deep freeze a chance to freeze vegetables really well and do make sure that you only use prime quality vegetables.

## WHAT TO SOW FOR FREEZING
### (Home Gardeners Only)

**Asparagus:** Conover's Colossal; Tetra.
**Beetroot:** Housewives' Choice; Detroit Dark Red; Crimson Globe.
**Broad Beans:** Harlington White Windsor.
**Broccoli:** 9 Star Perennial.
**Brussels Sprouts:** Jade Cross; Noisette.
**Carrots:** Early Nantes Improved; Amsterdam Forcing.
**Cob Corn:** Kelvedon Glory; Spancross.
**French Beans:** Tender Pod; Super Metis.
**Peas:** Petits Pois Gullivert.
**Runner Beans:** Goliath.
**Spinach:** Monstrous Viroflay.
**Tomatoes:** Roi Humbert Italian Long; Market King; Outdoor Girl New; Hundredfold.

## HOW TO PREPARE THE PRODUCE

**Asparagus:**

Grade carefully to matching length and thickness. Trim, wash, scrape lightly if desired, **steam** 2-4 min., according to thickness, chill, pack and store.

**Beetroots:**

Pick small, round ones. Wash very thoroughly. Boil until skins will just rub off. Chill, skin, pack and store.

**Broad Beans:**

Pick when young and small. Wash in pod. Plunge into boiling water. Boil 5 min., plunge into cold water, remove beans from pods, pack and store.

**Broccoli:**

Remove large leaves and tough stalks. Wash thoroughly and pack head downwards in suitable container. Cover with salt and water: 4 rounded tablespoonsful salt to 8 pts. cold water. Leave 30 min. Remove, drain and split larger heads lengthwise into halves. Steam 5 min. or boil 4 min. Pack and store.

**Brussels Sprouts:**

Pick when tight and small. Remove all blemished leaves. Trim off stem ends. Wash thoroughly. Plunge into boiling water. Boil 3-5 min. according to size. Chill and store.

**Carrots:**

Choose short, stumpy and young ones. Trim, scrape and wash thoroughly. Treat as Brussels sprouts—boiling time 5 min.

**Cob Corn:**

Remove husks and silk. Trim off stems. Wash, treat as Brussels sprouts. Boiling times: 7 min. (small), 9 min. (medium), 11 min. (large).

**French Beans:**

Pick when very slim. Top, tail, wash. Boil 2 min. Treat as runner beans.

**Peas:**

Discard under and over-developed peas. Wash, boil 1 min., chill and store.

**Runner Beans:**

Only non-stringy ones! Wash thoroughly. Cut off tips and edges. Slice or use whole in convenient lengths. Plunge into boiling water. Boil 3-3½ min. according to size. Chill, pack and store.

## Spinach:
Remove stalks carefully, taking away all stem on large fully developed leaves. Wash, **steam** 2 min., chill, pack and store.

## Tomatoes:
Choose firm, ripe and small tomatoes. No cooking required. Remove stalks, wash thoroughly, pack and store.

Store in either strong polythene bags with instant closure strips or double folds of aluminium foil for long storage. If polythene is very thin and liable to crack, outer-wrap the bags in the stockinette used by butchers for delivering stock bones.

**DON'T** waste the top space of your cooker when it is not in action. Turn it into a working surface by covering the top with a slip board of laminated plastic.

**DON'T** pile baking sheets, Swiss roll tins, etc. on a shelf. Turn part of a kitchen unit into a cook's filing cabinet with ply uprights for partitions. Then you can file them, see at a glance which one you want and pull it out with ease instead of scrabbling like a mad thing under a tottering pile.

**DON'T** have one huge kitchen table and tear round it all day like a demented fly round a jam jar. Instead buy two small tables with laminated plastic tops and draw leaves at each end. Then they can be folded up or opened out at will, always leaving a space between for you to go **through** instead of **round!**

**DON'T** have a shelf for saucepans. Bag the wall space inside a cupboard, cover it with pegboard, slip in hooks and hang up dozens, easily.

**DON'T** store **almond paste** items until 24 hours after making. Leave them to "sweat" out on a wire tray.

**DON'T** boil **beetroots.** Put them in a casserole (after scrubbing) cover with water and cook them slowly gas 6 (400°F) under a lid. That was Escoffier's way.

**DON'T** despair because the **brandy** always goes out when you have lit it over the **Christmas pudding.** Use equal quantities of brandy and vodka. This latter has a very high alcoholic content. Heat both together in a small saucepan until they are too hot for your dipped-in (clean) finger, then light and while carrying to table, shake dish slightly all the way. The draught ensures continuous burning.

**DON'T** throw away the hard cores of any kind of **cabbage.** Use the coarsest grater to grate them and add them to the cabbage in the pot.

**DON'T** despair if you slip up with any **cake mixture and it sinks** in the middle after baking and when cooled on a rack. Cut out the goo from the centre. Then either fill with fruit or fruits and cream for sponges or almond paste for rich fruit cakes and ice as desired or just top dust with sifted icing sugar.

**DON'T** panic when a **cheese fondue** curdles. Dissolve a teaspoonful or two (according to quantity) of potato flour (*fécule de pomme*) in wine, water or kirsch. Pour on, stir like mad and the mixture will come together again quite happily.

**DON'T** be fobbed off by naughty grocers who sell you Emmenthal for Gruyère. These are easy to distinguish. **Gruyère** is full of small holes and is the aristocrat; **Emmenthal** is full of large holes and is the poor relation. There should be quite a wide price difference between the two or you are being stung!

**DON'T** use very **fresh eggs for whipping whites stiffly.** Egg whites are far better when mature! Once separated and foil-covered they keep in refrigeration for several days without any deterioration. Then they whip like mad.

**DON'T** let all your violets, acacias and marrow flowers wilt on their plants and die. All can be scalded, wiped, dipped into **Fruit Fritter Batter**\* to make delicious fritters (*beignets*).

**DON'T** despair when a turned-out **gelatine mould** bounces like a little rubber ball. Just cut it all up, put it in the top of a double pan over hot water and allow it to dissolve slowly. Meanwhile make up another quarter batch of the original recipe if very rubbery, or another eighth if only fairly rubbery. Just remember to stop short of adding any gelatine to this lot! Stir this into the dissolved mixture in the pan. Re-oil the moulds. Pour the mixture back again and this time it will be SET FAIR.

**DON'T** let it worry you if a **gelatine mould** wobbles and splits itself while being turned out. If it is a collapser, dissolve a $\frac{1}{4}$ oz. gelatine in a spoonful or two of warm water where the original given quantity was 1 oz. If only just wobbly, add a mere $\frac{1}{8}$ oz. gelatine to the re-dissolved mixture, treated exactly as for an over stiff mould.

**DON'T** **casserole meat** until it has been floured and sealed by brisk frying all over before putting in the pot. Otherwise the liquid will contain all the flavour and the meat will be like tasteless old bits of bath sponge.

**DON'T** store **meringues** in tins. They keep much better in glass jars with well-fitting glass lids, or in good old earthenware casseroles with first coverings of foil and then their own lids.

**DON'T** pour hot vinegar on to **pickled onions**—that is what makes them go flabby—fast! Use it cool.

**DON'T** try making **pastry** in an emulsifier. This is a splendid aid if restricted to the jobs it can do properly. But not for pastry as a reader found to her cost.

**DON'T** buy **pie and cutlet frills.** Make your own from 6-inch strips of 2 inch wide plain or coloured tissue paper, up to 15 inches long and 5 inches wide strips for ham bones or giant legs of pork. Fold each strip lengthwise. Snip even $\frac{1}{4}$ inch apart cuts through the fold to within 1 inch of the two edges to make looped fringes. Now just reverse the fold. Do not press down. Coil over one, two or three fingers according to required size and secure with a scrap of Sellotape.

**DON'T** peel and boil **potatoes.** Scrub and steam in their jackets. Then the skins come off easily and you keep all the flavour.

**DON'T** use table salt for cooking. Use **Maldon salt**—the only sea salt produced in Britain or the French *gros sel* (page 369). These are held in the highest esteem by serious cooks.

**DON'T** try **skinning tomatoes, peaches, nectarines** and similar items until you have first dipped them (in a sieve) into (i) boiling water, (ii) iced water. Then the skins roll back like baby carpets.

**DON'T** try hit or miss **sugar cookery.** This calls for absolute precision. You need two saccharometers, one for measuring the degrees of sugar to produce results ranging from "small thread" through to "caramel", which we gave in the Cook's Book. The other should be one which gives you a density reading, for which we have produced this table:

| To make: | Ingredients | Density meter reading |
|---|---|---|
| Water ices | 1 lb. sugar, $32\frac{1}{2}$ fl. oz. water or fruit pulp or fruit juice | 17 |
| Fruit compôtes | 1 lb. sugar, 25 fl. oz. water, for pears, apples or peaches | 20 |
| Babas, savarins | 1 lb. sugar, $22\frac{1}{2}$ fl. oz. water | 22 |
| Stock sugar syrup* | 1 lb. sugar, $12\frac{1}{2}$ fl. oz. water | 28 |
| Candy | 1 lb. sugar, $7\frac{1}{2}$ fl. oz. water | 33 |
| Liqueurs, bonbons | 1 lb. sugar, $6\frac{1}{4}$ fl. oz. water | 34 |
| For glazing fruits | 1 lb. sugar, $6\frac{1}{4}$ fl. oz. water | 38 |

In each case place ingredients in clean thick pan over very low heat. Allow sugar to dissolve and clear until saccharometer registers the required degree.

*Stock sugar syrup is used to soften fondant, make *pâté à bombe*, and sweeten fresh fruit *compôtes* not specified above.

**DON'T** throw away **cold tea.** Use it to cook prunes, apricots and other dried fruits. It gives them a tremendous lift in flavour.

**DON'T** throw **lees of wine** away. When you are not using them for saucing or any other immediate cookery, you need to have two wine bottles, one labelled "White" and one labelled "Red". Sling in the lees. Set in a sunny window all summer long and by autumn you will have a bottle of red and a bottle of white wine vinegar. Remember the name "vinegar" derives from "*vin aigre*" which just means . . . sour wine!

# IT'S SUPER-SEALED

## TO KEEP A LITTLE LONGER

# Chapter 5

# *Beginners on stage please!*

Melon Boats
Prosciutto e Melone
Melone e Figue
Citrus Fruit Salad
Gherkin Tassels
Prawn Cocktail
Smoked Eel
Anguilles au vert
Horseradish Sauce
Cheese Custard Tart
  (egg yolks only)
Hot Baked Grapefruit
Bagna Cauda
Pickled Eggs
Champignons Kandaourow
Choux au Caviar
Choux au Foie Gras
Beignets Périgourdine
Pâté à frire

Petits Pots d'Escargots
Petits Pots de Moules
Crevettes chaudes
Pâté Chaud
Pâté Familial
Croûte Familiale
Pâté de Canard
Pâté de Ris de Veau
Raised Pie Paste (English)
Raised Pie Paste (French)
Taramosalata
Our Fish Pâté
Crêpes Mediterranées
Savoury Lemon Sauce
Croûtes Mornay
Madeirenses Avocado Pears
Gazpacho Apéritif
Banana Crisps
Coconut Strips

*Question: My husband says the first course is not really very important. He maintains it is the main course which makes or breaks a meal. I have an uneasy feeling he is wrong. Will you give us your ruling?*

*Answer:*

You are right and your husband is wrong. A meal which begins badly is handicapped from the start. Conversely, a meal which has created a good impression with the first course, can bear the strain of a near-failure later on. Moreover, *hors d'oeuvre* or "openers" give boundless scope for attractive garnishes and the eye should always be pleased before the appetite is appeased and the digestion satisfied.

In the matter of human judgement a running controversy persists in this household. Johnnie says that although he has often gone against his first impressions, they have always proved right in the end. Fanny says that some of her most abiding friendships have been launched with acrimony; but there is no difference of opinion in the matter of first impressions at the table.

We are quite prepared to go on record saying that we have never in our lives had a good meal either in a restaurant or in a private house which started with luke-warm soup or a wedge of melon just dumped on a plate. Luke warm soup is an abomination—it must be either scalding hot or icy cold. There is nothing wrong with melon, but the cook who cares shows her hand very plainly by the way she presents it.

melon boats

Try the Spanish-cut **Melon Boats** presentation. Cut a sixth or a quarter from a melon according to its size and then with a sharp knife cut the entire flesh away from each section in one piece and as close to the rind as possible. Now cut vertically from one end to the other through the flesh to make either 7 or 9 pieces. Straighten them up if they have slipped at all, push the first one away from you so that a third of its length juts beyond the rind, push the next one towards you in the same way and repeat alternately to the opposite end. You will then have something which looks rather like a barge with the oars sticking out, but much more attractive.

You can put a *glacé* or maraschino cherry in each of the spaces on either side, or tiny little rolls of the raw Italian ham called Parma ham or *prosciutto*, in which case this becomes **Prosciutto e Melone.**

*prosciutto e melone*

If you want to serve melon with figs—**Melone e Figue**—use the ones with the pink flesh. Sever the melon flesh from the rind and cut as for Melon Boats. Put one on (ideally) a pink or white plate and put one, two or three prepared figs—according to size—in line beside the melon. To prepare the figs, cut almost in halves through the stem end to the base without quite severing, reverse the knife and make a cross cut down thus dividing it into four sections or petals, which are still held at the base. Press these outwards so that each fruit resembles a flower, set them in position and you have yet one more way that this modest "opener" proves you care.

*melone e figue*

Half a grapefruit with a cherry stuck in the middle is just about as depressing as a British Railways Hotel breakfast room, If, instead, you peel any number of grapefruit and double the amount of oranges, so thickly that you cut away both the skin and pith leaving the naked flesh exposed, you are well launched into making a very clean, refreshing **Citrus**

*citrus fruit salad*

65

**Fruit Salad** or *hors d'oeuvre*. What you must next do is remove all the segments from each citrus fruit without any pith, which you can only do with a very sharp small knife. Slide the blade between skin and flesh to make the first cut, then turn the blade scooping slightly as you do so and come up the other side. This action jerks the little segments out and you go on doing it all the way round until you are left with a juicy skin-skeleton. Squeeze this over the segments. Choose coupes or wide mouthed goblets. Dip the rims in cold water and press them down lightly into caster sugar. Pile in the fruit segments alternately, layer of yellow, layer of orange. Mix the juice to taste with a little caster sugar and a few drops of maraschino and top-decorate each with a crystallised mint leaf* and leave in refrigeration until the moment of service.

You will doubtless have observed for yourself by this time that this is both an *hors d'oeuvre* and a perfect replacement for a rich pudding after a very lush main course, which is heavily creamy or a mite on the indigestible side, like duck or goose. The only difference is that when you are serving it as a pudding, you pile the layers into a crystal bowl, dredge with sifted icing sugar and moisten with a few drops of green Chartreuse.

On page 79 we deal fairly thoroughly with *pâtés* and *terrines*. Before we get down to real cooking recipes, we want to elaborate a little on the prime importance of the psychological eye appeal in "openers". A slice of good *pâté* is just that—a slice of good *pâté*, but if it is set on heart of lettuce and the top is decorated with one or two tassels of gherkins (which are the classic accompaniment to *pâté* or *terrine*) and the accompanying Toast Melba slipped into a water lily folded napkin, you are off to a flying start with something that could otherwise look rather dull.

gherkin
tassels

**Gherkin Tassels** are very easily made. Choose the straightest ones you can find in a jar, lay each on a board, hold the tip of the stalk end firmly in one hand and slide the knife from the opposite end to within $\frac{1}{4}$ inch of the tip so that you are splitting the gherkin lengthwise without cutting it right through. Then starting $\frac{1}{4}$ inch from the stalk end, make as many vertical cuts to the tip end as the width of the gherkin will allow. This produces the tassel effect which can be developed into a fan if you ease the little strips out widely as you lay them on to mayonnaise, aspic, or other coating agents.

prawn
cocktail

One of the most sordid little offerings is the ubiquitous **Prawn Cocktail** with a good old ground padding of lettuce cut with a knife and darkening at the edges, a tired prawn drooping disconsolately over the edge of the glass like a debutante at the end of her first ball and its opposite number—a piece of lemon tasting of the knife—clutching the opposite side of the rim like a seasick passenger against a taffrail during a rough Channel crossing. This kind of presentation almost invariably confirms that the mayon-

67

naise will be that bottled stuff, further
sharpened by bottled tomato sauce, that the
incidence of prawns will be low, of overcooked diced potatoes high, whereas if we
have not put you off them for life by this
time, Prawn Cocktails can be delicious.
Start by tearing crisp heart of lettuce and
using the pieces to line the base and sides of
a glass or bowl, so that when the prawn
mixture is filled in all the lettuce does not
have to be excavated from the base. Then
make up a mixture which comprises 4 oz.
fresh, freshly shelled shrimps or prawns
(halve the latter), 2 oz. small diced hothouse
cucumber with the skin left on, 2 oz. real
mayonnaise* perked up with a few drops of
Tabasco and an additional teaspoonful of
strained lemon juice—and absolutely no
potato salad at all.

Mix the given ingredients in a bowl with 1
tablespoonful thick whipped cream and add
the merest flick of sherry or dry Madeira to it.
Place about 3 dessertspoonsful in each portion
on the lettuce. Sprinkle the top first with
paprika, then with chives and drive a single,
shelled prawn with the head left on, tail end
downwards, into the centre so that the head
can be lifted out by the diner, the flesh
nibbled off and the head discarded easily.
Now fringe the glass all round the dome with
very thinly sliced unskinned cucumber
rounds in overlapping lines and place a very
small lemon basket (see diagram page 371)
at the side of the glass on the plate, on which
you will send it to table. Then the lemon

68

basket can be picked up easily and additional lemon juice squeezed over as desired without getting your fingers in a filthy mess.

These lemon baskets should be used when serving **Smoked Eel.** You either buy the eel ready to serve in slender skinned fillets or by the pound unskinned. If you choose the latter, you then make an incision with a small sharp knife around the head of each eel and then pull the skin back towards the tail. It comes away quite easily. After the skin is removed you will be able to ease the four fillets away from the spine bone, cut them into neat, short lengths and arrange one or more per portion on beds of lettuce hearts.

smoked
eel

Serve with brown bread and butter and if you wish, hand fresh **Horseradish Sauce** as well. This should not be a vinegary, bottled mush but simply washed, peeled horseradish root, grated and mixed with cream and freshly milled black pepper. Some think it too strong for the delicate flavour of eel—and you may be among them, as indeed we are; but if we do not refer to it in this context, you will probably write and bully us for the exclusion!

horseradish
sauce

The British eel has somehow or other gone class-conscious on itself and while the discerning East End Londoner revels in it, it is snubbed by the more high faluting. Prove to yourself how foolish this point of view is by using eels from our waters for making a very attractive version of Belgian **Anguilles au Vert.** Should you be squeamish; get the fishmonger to cut a generous 1½ lb. of eel into 2½ inch lengths. Soften 1 oz. butter in a frying pan, add 1 oz. oil and slide the eel pieces in, over a fairly brisk heat, turning them carefully until they are "stiffened". You will see the flesh contract so the frying action will explain visually what we are saying. At this point you really need a parsley mill (page 369). These can be bought at most good ironmongers today for a very few shillings. They are invaluable. Mill up bit by bit about 4 sorrel leaves with stems removed, the same of spinach, 2 small tarragon heads, 6 sage leaves, enough burnet to yield a small rounded teaspoonful and enough parsley to yield 2 rounded table-spoonsful. Season the eel pieces with salt and (preferably) milled black peppercorns. Place into a square or rectangular heat resistant glass dish. Stir all the herbs into about ¾ pint of dry white wine, pour over the eels, add a bay leaf, cover with a lid or scrap of kitchen foil and cook in a pre-heated oven at gas 4 (355°F) for 15 minutes or until fish is cooked but still firm. Remove bay leaf, lift eel pieces out. Add about 1 lb. eel trimmings to the liquor, cover and cook again at gas 2 (310°F) for about ¾ hour. Lift out all trimmings. Pour off herb-laden liquor. Wipe dish. Replace eel portions neatly. Cover with the unstrained herb and wine liquor and when this has stopped steaming, put into refrigeration until set to a delicate pale green jelly. Serve with canelled slices of lemon or the lemon baskets already explained (page 371).

(page 371)

We were experimenting recently with ways of using up surplus egg yolks and we discovered a really excellent **Cheese Custard Tart.** The case is made of savoury short paste\*, in an 8-inch diameter flan ring or Victoria sponge tin. Then you scald 5 fluid oz. milk and 5 fluid oz. single cream with a generous pinch of both salt and pepper. While it is scalding, beat 4 egg yolks lightly in a bowl. Pour on the milk-cream mixture and pour back and forth from bowl to pan **three times.** Then stir in 2 oz. of either grated Gruyère or Emmenthal cheese, pour into raw pastry case and bake at gas 3 (335°F) one shelf below centre until the mixture is set and the top is a pale golden brown. This is most marvellously creamy and delicate. Moreover it has the great virtue of being quickly and simply made, so you are left free to get on with something else while it is baking.

**Hot Baked Grapefruit** has the same virtues. There are two ways of doing it, and we will start with the plain one which can be served either for breakfast or as an opening course for teetotallers. Select large, firm, thin-skinned grapefruit. Halve them and cut them properly with a grapefruit cutter (page 368). Turn them upside down in a deepish container and leave them for 30 minutes so that the surplus juices drain away. Drink the juices—they are

slimming! Turn the grapefruit halves cut side
uppermost again. Cover each with soft brown
sugar ("pieces") and sprinkle lightly with
powdered cinnamon and nutmeg. Dot several
small flakes of butter on the tops and bake
for 15 minutes at gas 5 (380°F). Serve immediately.

The second version which we think exceptionally good merely requires you to add
a teaspoonful to a teaspoonful-and-a-half of
Marsala or Bual or Malmsey Madeira to each
grapefruit half before baking. Curious as
it may seem the grapefruit swell when baked
and therefore appear much larger than when
you started.

If you want to follow Scandinavian custom
and have your openers before going through
to the dining room, you might like to try the
very astringent, hot aperitif appetiser of Italy
called **Bagna Cauda.** First you assemble a
miscellany of fine lettuce leaves, endive sprigs,
chicory leaves, celery sticks, watercress sprigs,
spring onions, radishes on stalks, heads of
corn salad (romaine), salsify sticks, strips of
red, green and yellow pimento, whole young
spring carrots and the little flying saucer
shapes of tinned water chestnuts (page 370).
Then light a spirit stove or gas ring and make
your Bagna Cauda.

Put ½ pint olive oil into a fondue pot. Add
6 peeled, halved garlic cloves, 1 smallish tin
of anchovy fillets, a generous thread of saffron
and a small flat teaspoonful of freshly milled
black peppercorns. Stir over the heat until

*bagna
cauda*

the brew bubbles. Gather round and dunk salad segments in the sauce; but pray remember this is not a good opener for a meal destined to be accompanied by fine wines.

One of the things we always have on hand is a jarful of that good old English standby, **Pickled Eggs.** Rehearse with raw eggs in shells by filling them into your chosen jar to see how many it will contain. Hard-boil these (by putting them into cold water over strong heat, and maintain at a steady simmer, for an overall time of 8 minutes). Then slide them into cold water, shell them and return them to the jar with thin layers of very finely sliced raw onion packed between and two little sprigs of rosemary driven in down the sides of the jar.

Prepare the pickling fluid by mixing 1 pint of tarragon wine vinegar with 1 gill garlic wine vinegar and 1 gill dry white wine. Add 1½ pints cold water, 24 peppercorns, 2 raw medium onions sliced finely and 2 very small hot red peppers. Bring the whole thing to the boil. Remove from the heat, pick out the onions and pour over the eggs when the mixture has cooled to just above blood heat. Then cover and store. After careful testing, we have proved that these will keep for at least one year!

Serve whole or split lengthwise into petals arranged on beds of torn cos lettuce leaves and hand **Sauce Tartare** separately. You scarcely need a recipe for this as it is simply classic egg yolk mayonnaise with plenty of finely chopped chives stirred into it and we have **not** made a mistake! If you check us in "Larousse Gastronomique" (French edition!), you will find that unlike the English version which sharpens the whole thing lethally with chopped gherkins, **it should be chives.**

sauce
verdurette

Alternatively you might like to serve **Sauce Verdurette** with your Pickled Eggs. This is our old friend, French Dressing or *Sauce Vinaigrée*, to which you add to every ½ pint, 2 finely chopped hard-boiled eggs, 1 tablespoonful each of chopped chervil and tarragon, 2 level tablespoonsful of chopped parsley, and 4 heaped tablespoonsful of chopped chives. Please do not try making this in the winter. All the herbs must be fresh, otherwise it is very nasty indeed.

A dish of tinned artichoke bottoms will not come amiss as an "opener" either if you heap each little bottom or cup liberally with *Sauce Verdurette* and arrange length-wise cut quarters of Pickled Eggs in between.

cham-
pignons
Kandaourow

While on the subject of tins let us share with you a little *succès fou* recipe of our own which we christened **Champignons Kandaourow** because we created it for Princess Beris Kandaourow, the possessor of a very educated palate! Her father employed Madame Jeanne, the great French *cordon bleu* who cooked for Escoffier in the last few years of his life. So Mme. la Princesse was exceptionally well trained!

74

First take a large shallow copper frying pan and cover the base to a scant ¼ inch depth with Marsala, then add about the same quantity of cold water, bring the two to a gentle simmer. Then slide in enough de-stalked, medium-sized mushrooms to cover the base completely. Cook through on both sides at a steady simmer, lift them out and set them on to a flat dish cupside uppermost. Then simmer the liquor down to a mere 2-3 tablespoonsful and spoon a few drops of this dark brown glaze over each prepared mushroom. While these cool, prepare the filling by whipping 1½ gills double cream to a peak and folding in 1 small jar of the inexpensive Danish type caviare (page 367), with a teaspoonful of strained lemon juice and a generous seasoning of black pepper. When the mushroom cups are quite cold, place this filling in a nylon icing bag with a wide crown pipe, and pipe a little rosette of caviare cream into each mushroom.

choux
au caviar

We subsequently used this identical filling for another favourite—**Choux au Caviar.** Just pipe ordinary water *choux* paste mixture* into small cork shapes on an oiled baking sheet. Bake at gas 7½ (435°F) one shelf above centre until a strong golden brown—25-30 minutes according to size. Cool on a rack. Split, fill with the caviare cream mixture and dust the top of each lightly with powdered paprika before arranging on a flat serving dish.

With the same kind of choux buns you can use the contents of another tin to make **Choux au Foie Gras,** in which case your filling is composed of one 2½ oz. tin of *pâté de foie gras* or substitute with 1 gill of fairly stiffly whipped cream, 1 tablespoonful of medium sherry and 1 teaspoonful of brandy mixed together, and filled into the cold buns. These too can be scattered with paprika powder before serving. *Pâté* can be used to make an impressive little hot *hors d'oeuvre*— **Beignets Périgourdine**—but this time you will have to roll the *foie gras* into very small balls about the size of large cherries and put them in refrigeration until they are extremely cold and therefore firm. Then you drop them into *beignet* fritter batter mixture\*, lift them out with a teaspoon and scrape them off the spoon with the tip of a knife into slightly smoking hot fat so that they puff up and turn a good golden brown.

choux au
foie gras

beignets
Périgour-
dine.

pâte
à
frire

We suggest you use the **Pâte à Frire** of Carême, it is a beauty! Dissolve 2 oz. butter in ½ pint water and let the water boil. Toss in 6 oz. flour, turn off the heat and beat very thoroughly indeed. Add a generous pinch of salt, 2 teaspoonsful of brandy, marc or Armagnac and gradually beat in 2 stiffly whipped egg whites. Remember, this is not a paste which can be kept standing about. You can assemble all your ingredients beforehand but you **must** make it and use it straight way.

Conversely you can make two very "different" and succulent hot *hors d'oeuvre* and keep them in refrigeration overnight for re-heating thereafter. They are a closely related pair and the first **Petits Pots d'Escargots** is made with tinned snails. In France these are served in tiny little coloured pots about the size of small egg cups. But buying six egg-cups per portion is a bit impractical in England, so we suggest for the average household that it is better to serve one larger portion per person in small ramequins, with three large "sugar cubes" of bread on top of each instead of the single bread cube which tops each one of the six-per-person French service. Agreeably for us all they are easily made, although people ponder and debate as to their contents when they taste them.

Take a tin of snails and strain away the liquor. Halve the (approximately 24 per tin) snails. Then, in a separate bowl place 2 breakfastcupsful fine soft crumb of brown bread and add sufficient melted butter to hold the crumbs together in a paste.

Add $\frac{1}{4}$ teaspoonful of salt, the same of black pepper and 2 ozs. of coarsely chopped, skinned, blanched almonds. Now add the snails with 2 crushed garlic cloves, stir well together and put the mixture into the ramequins. Place 3 crustless bread cubes on top of each ramequin. Just before serving bake at gas 5 (380°F) until the bread cubes are well-browned on top. These are best served on a small plate and eaten from the ramequins with teaspoons.

77

petits pots
de moules

The second version is **Petits Pots de Moules.**
Everything is the same as in the previous
recipe except that the snails are replaced by
mussels. Allow 36 mussels instead of 24
snails. Scrub, beard and steam them in a
colander or steamer over hot water until they
are all open. Remove the mussels from their
shells. Cut them up roughly and fold them
into the given crumb mixture. Bake as for
**Petits Pots d'Escargots.**

crevettes
chaudes

Whenever we return from a trip to France
via Le Touquet/Lydd we indulge ourselves
at an excellent small restaurant in Le Touquet
with the **Crevettes Chaudes** we mentioned
in the Cook's Book. The grey shrimps of the
Pas de Calais area are a local speciality and
with the sea just down the road, it is easy for
local chefs to obtain the sea water in which
they are cooked. But so it is for us when we
are by the sea in England. Our shrimps are
equally good—though different in flavour—
so we thought you might like to have the
recipe tucked into a corner of your memory
for when the chance comes.

To a quart of freshly-caught shrimps allow
3-4 small bay leaves, about a dozen peppercorns and plenty of sea water. Before you
start cooking them, wrap a crusty loaf
(cottage English if French *flute* is not available) loosely in kitchen foil and put on the
centre oven shelf at gas 4 (355°F) to get hot.
Bring the sea water, peppercorns and bay
leaves to a good simmer, slide in the raw

78

shrimps and cook them just until they turn bright pink. Drain, tip into a lidded casserole and eat in the fingers with plenty of hot bread and butter. Of course you do not shell each little shrimp! You just hold head and tail together, bite off the body and discard the remainder.

There are also very good **Pâtés Chauds** which you serve as first course specialities. The chosen mixture for these is cooked in individual ramequins or casserole pots. The best way is to make a simple **Pâté Familial** to cook in the standard manner, and just steal some of it to make the individual **Pâtés Chauds.** As this is a variation of any standard *pâté* recipe, you can choose whichever one you prefer from the following old friends.

First, let us study a simple **Pâté Familial,** for which the butcher can do quite a bit of the work. Get him to mince you 10 oz. of raw unsalted pork fat, 8 oz. of lean veal, 8 oz. of lean pork and deliver with it ½ lb. pork sausagemeat. Mix minced meats and sausagemeat together. Crush 2 garlic cloves and toss them in. Grate 1 medium onion finely and add it to the mixture, juice and all, with a level teaspoonful of mixed spice, the same of salt and about ¾ of a level teaspoonful of black pepper. Then work up the whole lot together with a small ladleful of strong stock, 4 tablespoonsful of sherry or Madeira and 3 tablespoonsful of cooking type brandy. Line a heat-resistant glass pie dish, a *soufflé* mould or, ideally an earthen-ware *terrine* with neat strips of the fat and lean of No. 3-4 cut back bacon. Press in the mixture, cover with a piece of kitchen foil, put the lid on top and stand in an ordinary meat baking tin two-thirds filled with hot water. Place in the oven one shelf below centre and cook at gas 4 (355°F) for about 1 hour or until a skewer driven into the centre oozes the very palest pink moisture. Replace the foil and put heavy weights on top. Then leave till cold in ordinary domestic refrigeration.

If you want to go one step further you can then pour on a $\frac{1}{4}$ inch layer of melted pork fat. If you fancy taking **two steps,** then extract the sausagemeat from the recipe and also the ladleful of stock. Mix up all the other given ingredients as explained and line your chosen container with the sausagemeat rolled out on a lightly floured board like pastry. Then add the strips of bacon and fill in the mixture.

croûte
familiale

Should you fancy a third step then turn this into a **Croûte Familiale** by lining the container with the raised pie paste (page 83), then adding the rolled out sausagemeat, then the bacon, then the remaining *pâté* mixture and covering overall with a lid of paste. In this case you cook uncovered with foil or lid. Bake at gas 6 (400°F) for first 20 minutes, then reduce heat to gas 4 (355°F) and continue cooking for about 1 hour.

We have still not quite finished with the

variants on this simple dish because with all or any of the suggestions we have made, you can sink four hard-boiled eggs into the *pâté* after half of it has been pressed into the container and then cover with the remainder. Incidentally, there is an excellent mincer on the market which makes the job of producing fine, medium or coarse grated items ludicrously easy (page 369).

When we want to make **Pâté Chaud** from any of this group, we choose the **Pâté Familial** without the sausagemeat but with the ladleful of stock. Then we work into it 2 heaped tablespoonsful of ground almonds and the same of soft brown breadcrumbs. Half fill individual heat-resistant containers with this mixture, cover each with foil only and cook as already explained, in a meat baking tin of water at gas 4 (355°F).

pâté de canard

Now let us assume the occasion is a more special one and you need a grander *pâté*. You can really show off with **Pâté de Canard.** Cut an 8 oz. piece of lean bacon into small dice and do the same with 8 oz. of raw unsalted pork fat. Take a duck of average weight and tear off every single scrap of skin. Chop off the legs and cut off all the remaining flesh from the carcase. Dice this flesh and put it in a *terrine* with the prepared bacon and pork fat, 8 tablespoonsful of brandy, a level teaspoonful of salt, a scant ¾ level teaspoonful black pepper and a slightly rounded eggspoonful of mixed spices. Leave to steep, turning it occasionally for 2 hours. Meanwhile take all the meat from the duck's legs and mince it with 6 oz. lean bacon, 10 oz. raw unsalted pork fat and 8 oz. of lean veal. Add 2 whole eggs and a liqueur glass of brandy to the minced mixture. Pound in a pestle and mortar and then rub through a sieve. When the 2 hours is up, mix the mixture in the *terrine* into this meat paste. So far you have not used the liver of the duck so now chop it up finely, stiffen it by frying in $\frac{1}{2}$ oz. bubbling hot butter for 1 minute and stir it into the prepared mixture. Turn this into a *terrine*, cover with kitchen foil, stand in an outer pan two-thirds filled with hot water and bake in the oven at gas 4 (355°F) for at least 1 hour 15 minutes or until a pushed in skewer gives you a very faintly pink oozing of juice. We cannot fail to observe that of course the addition of a tablespoonful or two of chopped truffles or truffle trimmings is a very good thing indeed, but they are murderously expensive so we shall be entirely sympathetic if you leave them out.

As this is a fairly complicated recipe you will find it consoling to know that once you have mastered it, you will then know how to make pigeon (3), pheasant (1 cock), partridge (3), grouse (brace) or sweetbread (2 lb.) *pâtés* by merely replacing the duck with any one of these items. We only need to remind you that the sweetbreads must be blanched, skinned and carefully divided before using.

Blanching in this context is different from the blanching used for vegetables and salads.

pâté
de
ris de veau

82

For about 2-3 lb. of sweetbreads, which **at their price** is about the limit that any of us will ever run to, you will need 3 heaped tablespoonsful of any flour, a quart of boiling water and enough cold to mix the flour to a smooth thin paste in a basin. Pour the boiling water on to the paste, stirring all the time. Turn it into a large saucepan, sink in the sweetbreads, allow them to simmer with extreme gentleness for 5 minutes only, then remove from the heat and let them become cold, gradually, in their thin wallpaper paste. Finally rinse them under cold water, pat them dry with a clean cloth and painstakingly separate the little bits of skin and gristle from the costly "breads" themselves. This is a maddening task and the only consolation that we can give you is that the *pâté* tastes superb.

Before we leave this meat and poultry *pâté* subject we must give you two mistake-proof raised pie pastes in which you can use any of the given mixtures to make a casket or **Pâté en Croûte.**

English
raised
pie
paste

**English Raised Pie Paste** is made with 15 oz. of sifted flour, 2¾ fluid oz. of water, 2¾ fluid oz. of milk and 4½ oz. of **pure** lard. Put lard, milk and water together in a small thick pan and bring them to the boil slowly enough for the lard to be dissolved by the time the fluid is boiling. Remove from the heat, stir in the flour, beat vigorously to a smooth thick paste, turn the dough on to a floured board (wood, remember, not marble

83

—this is a dough which has to be kept warm) and knead until it is smooth. Use immediately, keeping trimmings warm under a cloth for top and decorations. When needed, brush decorations with cold water to hold securely.

French
raised
pie
paste

The **French Raised Pie Paste** is entirely different. You use 17½ oz. sifted flour to 4½ oz. butter, 5½ fluid oz. of water and a generous pinch of salt. First sift flour and salt together. Then sift them on to a marble, not wooden, surface this time, and push the flour out to form a ring border. Place the butter in the centre and work up with two small table knives, one in each hand, adding water gradually and drawing flour in a bit at a time until all ingredients are absorbed. Then knead the dough on the well-floured surface until quite smooth and always, repeat **always,** store in a lightly floured cloth in mild domestic refrigeration for 24 hours before using.

Now let us turn to fish *pâtés*.

taramosa-
lata

One of the most popular is the Greek **Taramosalata** for which pike roe is particularly good; but as pike is regarded as a coarse fish in England—although in France it produces one of the greatest of the great classics *Quenelles de Brochet*—you will either have to snatch the roe from the unwanted fish after the fisherman in your family has enjoyed fishing her, or else liaise with a local fisherman. Otherwise use cod's roe.

The generally accepted method is to cook it in a pan with salt, onion, wine and water or just water, but we find a better result is obtained by steaming; so try putting 8 oz. of cod's roe in a steamer with a medium, quartered shallot or onion and with cold water in the base pan, allow this to come to the boil, then cook for 7 minutes, turn off the heat and remove the steamer, leaving the fish to cool under the lid before attacking it. When you do, discarding the onion, either work classically with a pestle in a mortar or use a modern emulsifier. Put two thick slices of crustless white bread into a basin. Moisten with flicks of water until it is sufficiently spongy for you to squeeze to a pap, discarding the surplus water. Add the roe and work up with the bread pap to a well-blended mixture. Now toss in 1 egg yolk and start working this up, adding 1 very small teacupful of olive oil in a thin stream. Follow with half a small teacupful of lemon juice, season to taste with pepper and, if you are like us, add a tea-spoonful of anchovy *purée*, or 4 anchovy fillets which have been thoroughly pounded before-hand.

Having dealt with this, you may like to try **Our Fish Pâté** which we think is more exciting. Steam 8 oz. of smoked cod's roe with 8 oz. of soft herring roes for maximum of 15 minutes. Cut and trim the crusts from 2 thick slices of brown bread. Moisten with white wine, pound to a paste, and also pound 6 large or 10 small boned anchovy

our
fish
pâté

fillets. Scoop all the steamed cod's roe from the terra cotta skin which encloses it, and put this and the herring roes with the anchovy and bread pastes into a mortar or emulsifier. Start pounding. Pound in gradually the strained juice of 1 medium lemon and $\frac{3}{4}$ of a teacupful of olive oil with a crushed garlic clove blended into it. Work this up finally with a generous seasoning of black pepper and pack into as ornamental a *terrine* as you can muster.

This is only one way of serving Our Fish Pâté. It can also be filled into little *choux* paste buns—as we have already suggested for our caviare cream (page 75).

It can be piped, decoratively, on to fancy-shaped *croûtons* for which the additional "fancy" touch is to use a fish-shaped cutter, and then sprinkle the piped *croûtons* with finely chopped fresh chives and or parsley.

crêpes
Mediterra-
nées

savoury
lemon
sauce

It can be turned into a dish of **Crêpes Mediterranées** if you spread it into pre-made pancakes*, roll them up, align down a buttered heat-resistant dish and cover with a **Savoury Lemon Sauce.** We blatantly pinched this from a Greek lemon soup recipe and adapted it to our tastes and needs! First you must make a little fish stock, by putting a pound of fish heads, tails and trimmings into a pan with water to cover, 1 bay leaf, the thinly peeled rind of half a lemon, 3 peppercorns, two parsley stalks and a quarter of a medium shallot or onion. Simmer until the fish trimmings look flabby and purged (about 35 minutes). Strain and reduce by re-simmering to $\frac{3}{4}$ of a pint. Add the strained juice and grated rind of 1 lemon and bulk up to 1 pint with dry-ish white wine. Thicken with a heaped teaspoonful potato flour (*fécule de pomme*), pour over the prepared pancakes and bake at gas 4 (355°F) under a light covering of foil for 20 minutes before serving.

If the idea of such a clear and transparent sauce displeases you, then increase the amount of potato flour to make the sauce slightly too thick and thin it down with top-of-the-milk or cream to the required consistency. This will do absolutely no harm whatever to your culinary reputation more especially so if you are serving anyone who inhabits the sea front from Marseilles to Athens!

We sit down eleven at minimum to kitchen family luncheons these days and hot from several grills at one of these sessions come **Croûtes Mornay**—an exciting way of using either a home made *pâté* or the bought one we recommend to you on page 369. We used our recommended bought puff-pastry (page 371) for it too, rolled this out to a mean $\frac{1}{4}$ inch thickness, cut it into rectangles and bake at gas 7 (425°F) until puffed and lightly top-coloured. Split each rectangle in two. Cover the bases with slices of *pâté* ($1\frac{1}{2}$ slices of the bought *pâté* cover a good-sized rectangle to make a filling portion). Cover each with its puff pastry "lid", put on heat-

croûtes
Mornay

87

resistant plates, swill liberally with *Sauce Mornay\** and if made with hot, freshly-baked pastry, just put each portion under a strong grill to bubble and brown like Welsh Rarebit. If made with cold pastry cook in the oven at gas 2 (310°F) until heated through and then "finish" under a grill.

It is quite impossible to finish an *hors d'oeuvre* chapter without some reference to avocado pears, even though everyone knows the *vinaigrette* and shrimp versions backwards. It is just possible, however, that everyone does not know the delicious treatment given to these fruit in Madeira. **Madeirenses Avocado Pears** are simply split, de-stoned and heavily scored with a silver knife. Then you pour in enough Madeira wine to moisten the scores thoroughly. Some people prefer the sweeter types, either Bual or Malmsey, but you may like to experiment with our choice, the drier ones, Sercial or Verdelho.

*Madeirenses avocado pears*

No one ever seems to think of special non-alcoholic drinks to be served as a complement to *hors d'oeuvre*, so we have come up with one which is keeping our emulsifier working overtime—everyone likes it so much. It is a Spanish family recipe for a **Gazpacho** served well iced in tall glasses. For 8 people take 2 oz. white or brown crustless bread. Soak in cold water and when it collapses, tip it into an emulsifier with an extra gill (¼ pint) of cold water. Add 1½ lb. of rough-cut, ripe tomatoes, 2 crushed garlic cloves, ¾ lb. of chopped, unskinned cucumber, 2 chopped-up

*gazpacho*

88

hard-boiled eggs, 6 generous tablespoonsful of olive oil, 3 tablespoonful of wine vinegar and 2 split, chopped, de-pithed, de-seeded, large raw pimentos. Churn the whole lot up until sufficiently pulverised to rub through a sieve. Then correct the seasoning strongly with salt and milled black peppercorns. Stir in 1 heaped teaspoonful of celery salt. Make icily cold in refrigeration and serve in tall glasses over at least 2 heaped tablespoonsful of crushed ice.

At the time of writing this we had just returned from a holiday in the Caribbean where *l'heure de l'apéritif* was enhanced by the unfailing appearance of **Banana Crisps.** These are a splendid bit of one-upmanship. They are very easily achieved. Choose the most under-ripe bananas you can obtain. Slice them very thinly indeed. Toss them into slightly smoking hot oil and let them turn a good rich brown. Dredge them out with a slice and set them on a bit of absorbent paper. **They will be flabby.** Do not worry. Within moments they will crisp up. Sprinkle them with salt, pepper and (optional) powdered paprika. Remember to make plenty because they vanish at the speed of fish under an attack by cormorants!

Purists will like to know that plantains are used more frequently than bananas in the islands of Barbados and Grenada; but, as we knew plaintains were difficult to obtain except in areas where there is an incidence of green-grocers catering specifically for West Indians, we experimented with under-ripe bananas and found they were perfectly successful too.

If anyone returns from a local fairground armed with a coconut or if you find some in the shops during the winter months, try serving **Coconut Strips** at your next drinks party. Bore holes in the coconut where the three little brown dimples show on the outside. Drain off the milk and halve the nut. To do this easily, wind a piece of strong string or wire, tourniquet tight around at centre. Then tap with a hammer on to string or wire and the two halves will fall apart. When you have excavated the flesh and cut away the brown part, slice the flesh up to the thinness of sliced whole citron peel when you use it for the top of a Madeira cake. Toss them into a light brine (1 heaped tablespoonful coarse rock salt or *gros sel* to 1 pint cold water), stir until the salt is dissolved and let them rest for 30 minutes. Then fish them out, pat them dry in a clean cloth and either serve them *cru* or brown them in a slow oven gas 1 (290°F) before putting in a folded table napkin.

Both these last recipes are typical examples of how to make a little of inexpensive items go a very long way while enhancing your culinary reputation among your friends.

# High Speed Gas gives you the upper hand

## and a big hand from your guests

*heat that obeys you*

FARROW

# *Wot! No Stockpot?*

Bone Stock

Basic Fish Stock

Veal Stock

Soupe Paysanne

La Petite Marmite

Soup for Slimmers

Cabbage Soup

Pot-au-Feu

Poule-au-Pot Family Style

Purée St. Germain

Chiffonade

Tomato Soup

Crostini

Purée Alsacienne

Crème de Betteraves

Bortsch

La Cotriade Bretonne

Velouté de Saumon

Petits Frits de Saumon

Crème aux Amandes

Crème à l'Oseille

Velouté aux Moules

Velouté au Crabe

Beef Tea

*Question: You wrote about soups in The Cook's Book under the title "Not a Stockpot in the House." Does this mean you think stockpots are out of date, because you don't seem to suggest cubes and packets in their place? I dislike them anyway and this seems to limit the range tremendously.*

*Answer:*

All we set out to do in the Cook's Book was share some of the excellent soups which can be made without a stockpot. We are never without them and always have one, two or three on the go. We think they are indispensable as we never use cube or packet substitutes! Come into our kitchen unheralded and you will be certain to find a bone stockpot anyway, if not a fish one, a game one and a vegetable one as well—except the day before we are going off on a trip to some Far Flung Bit.

93

Incidentally, Fanny was inculcated into the inestimable value of the stockpot at a very early age by her mother. **Her** stockpot predelictions were so marked that on one occasion when a neighbouring landowner mislaid a couple of peacocks some wit's solution was round the county in a flash, "Look in Bijou's stockpot!"

bone
stock

Now do not get us wrong. We do not put the scrapings off everyone's plate and old, chewed bones into a dirty great iron pot which goes on simmering for months. We make a weekly pot of bone stock and this, after first making, is ritually re-simmered daily for a minimum 25 minutes. Nor do we think it is a very good idea to mix poultry, game, white and red meat in the same pot. Stick to one variety—veal bones, beef marrow bones, or, if you like, mix pork and veal together and let mutton keep to itself—always.

Say you are using beef bones. The ideal container is a vitreous enamel lined iron pot—oval in shape, two handled and with a light lid which is easy to take on and off. Cover the bones liberally with cold water. Drop in a large Spanish onion stuck with a few cloves. Hook the string loop of a *bouquet garni* or faggot of herbs\* over one handle, and when possible add the cleaned outside stalks of a head of celery. Let the water reach boiling point, when it will almost certainly acquire a head of rather nasty froth. Skim this off with a round, flat, perforated spoon-slice sometimes called a "skimmer" and sometimes a "spider". Sling this scum away. Pour on an additional tumblerful of cold water. When the liquid re-boils, put on the lid, reduce it to a steady simmer—that is with just a thread of steam escaping—and maintain for at least 2 hours. Now chill the stock, after which it will generally have a thin top-crust of pallid fat. Cut this away and set it aside as it is good enough for everyday shallow frying jobs. If when you remove it in sections and turn one over, you find that the underside is coated with nasty little bits, scrape them off and throw them out. The rest is stock, ready to be strained and simmered down to a quarter its original bulk if a concentrated flavour is required for sauces, or to be used as it is for making family soups.

basic
fish
stock

For a **Basic Fish Stock** you start off with the trimmings of skin, spine bones, head and tail of such fish as sole, plaice, turbot, halibut and whiting. We often add a whole whiting or two, but this is optional. Cover this lot with cold water or with three quarters water and a quarter inexpensive dry white wine. Add the thinly peeled rind of 1 small lemon, 2 bay leaves, a sprig of fresh fennel (when available), an onion stuck with cloves (these we faithfully recommend and always omit because we loathe them and they only remind us of toothache!) several parsley stalks, if possible with a bit of root and half a dozen peppercorns. Simmer this collection for 1 hour only. Then strain immediately. This sort of stock should never stew in its own juices and bits and pieces. What you can do is re-boil it after straining and then simmer daily for at least 3 or 4 days, provided that you do so for long enough to ensure it being protected against souring (30 minutes minimum). Further guarantee this for yourselves by keeping the reserve jugful in mild refrigeration.

These are the very bare bones of the bone stocks because there is no use in us going on about elaborate versions which are beyond the means of the average Sociable Cook. There is a charming one of Escoffier's which recommends the use of a pheasant, two old grouse and a partridge or two with a litre of claret, a couple of pounds of lean veal and a few other inexpensive sundries! There is another of Carême's that would give you the Culinary Twitch and set you back for about one week's housekeeping money! We are merely trying to exemplify the kind you can draw on regularly for family meals and increase in flavour thereafter by reduction plus wine and other flavourings.

veal
stock

A good **Veal Stock** is obtained by using 6 lb. of veal bones, two pig's trotters (unsalted please), a couple of sprigs of rosemary added to our standard *bouquet garni\**, and the onion, celery stalks and parsley already mentioned in other stocks. If simmered for long enough, after straining, this will "jell" itself thanks to the pig's trotters. These are just modest extensions of those we mentioned in the Basics we have already given you*. Now let us use them to make some exciting soups.

96

We will begin with the very old **Soupe Paysanne** which the Madame Jeanne we spoke of in the previous chapter served to Escoffier in Monte Carlo during his retirement. Just remember that it is **not** at all the same thing it you try to make it in winter with huge carrots which have developed a hard central core, rather stringy old turnips and enormous leeks. The vegetables must be young as well as fresh. Mince finely 10½ oz. young scraped carrots, 8 oz. young peeled turnips, the white of 2 leeks and 1 celery heart (put those stalks in the stock pot). Dissolve 2 oz. butter and 2 fluid oz. of oil, or ideally 4 oz. of either goose or duck fat, in a thick pan. When whichever you have chosen is piping hot, slide in the vegetable pulp, cover with a lid and cook gently for 10 minutes giving the pot an occasional vigorous shaking without removing that lid! Then pour on 5 pints of veal stock and simmer for 1¼-1½ hours.

Meanwhile make a plain *béchamel* using 2 oz. butter and 2 oz. flour for the white *roux*\* and then thin this *roux* down gradually with 2 pints milk. Then stir 1 lb. of shelled cooked, sieved peas into the *béchamel* mixture. Correct the seasoning to taste and serve with oven-browned rounds cut from a stick or *flute* of French bread. You can, if you like, hand a dish of grated Parmesan or stale mousetrap cheese separately.

Use beef stock to make a brew of **La Petite Marmite.** You will need 1½ pints of this stock to cook a quarter of a very tight white cabbage until it is tender. Before you use this, you will have to assemble the following ingredients: 1 lb. lean stewing steak, 1 large marrow bone, the necks, pinions and gizzards of 3 fowls (your poulterer will oblige), 2 quarts of water, $\frac{1}{8}$ oz. salt, 3 medium carrots, 3 medium turnips, $2\frac{1}{2}$ oz. white of leek and 1 small celery heart. Begin by tying the marrow bone in a piece of muslin. Place steak, necks, gizzards, pinions and salt in a large pot. Cover with 2 quarts of cold water, bring to the boil and skim carefully as a scum forms on the top.

Just remember it is no use blaming us if you either omit this process or skim carelessly and thereby obtain a cloudy and imperfect consommé! Simmer under a lid very gently for 2 hours. Now add the carrots, turnips, leeks and celery heart and simmer again for a further 1 hour. This is when you strain the cabbage liquor into your main pot. Finally you strain the whole potful and correct the seasonings.

For service you then dredge out the marrow bone in its muslin wrapping. Unwrap it, scoop out the marrow from the bone, spread on hot fingers of crustless bread and serve it with the soup, together with the cabbage cut into small pieces and put into a separate dish.

For many years now we have fought desperately against increasing weight. Neither of us have any leanings towards being two little thin characters struggling to escape from a mountain of excess poundage, so every spring we slim on a ruthless diet of citrus fruit juices and salads on which we lose weight and stay fit because the supporting **Soup For Slimmers** provides the necessary roughage. Slice 1 small, tight, white cabbage as thinly as possible with the white and green of 3 washed, trimmed leeks, 1 celery heart and 2 large onions. Place in a pan with clear veal bone stock to cover. Add 1 small level teaspoonful of celery salt, 1 small level teaspoonful of kitchen salt, 2 bay leaves and thyme, parsley, marjoram and sage to taste. Bring this mixture to the boil. Skim if any vestige of scum forms on the top. Refresh with 1 small tumbler of cold water, raise to and maintain at a gentle simmer until vegetables are tender. Season with pepper to taste.

If, like us, you are determined to be anti-social, this soup is considerably improved by the addition of two small crushed garlic cloves. You may also replace part of the quantity of white cabbage with grated Brussels sprouts or red cabbage. Remember to stir very well when reheated so that each serving has a proper proportion of the vegetable contents.

You can also make a less austere **Cabbage Soup** which is good, filling, family-stuff on an economical level. You begin by softening 1 oz. butter and 1 oz. oil in a casserole. When these are bubbling, add 4 shallots or 1 large Spanish onion sliced thinly, 6 No. 4 cut rashers of streaky bacon de-rinded and diced and 1 or more crushed garlic cloves. Allow them to cook without colouring, giving an occasional stir, for about 4 minutes. Then add 1 very small tight white cabbage cut into rough dice and blanched. To do this pour a kettle of boiling water over the prepared cabbage, leave for 5 minutes, drain, refresh in cold water and sling into the pot. Cover liberally with strained bone stock, bring to the boil, cover with a lid and cook for $\frac{3}{4}$ hour, one shelf above centre at gas 2 (310°F). Toss in 2 oz. diced French beans. Replace the lid and return to the oven, reducing the heat to about gas $1\frac{1}{2}$ (300°F) for 1 hour. Add a heaped tablespoonful of milled parsley and of chopped chives when possible. Hand small rounds of toasted French bread and grated cheese as accompaniments.

pot-au-feu

Now let us tackle an aristocrat among French family soup recipes—the **Pot-au-Feu** which Escoffier describes as "*le symbole de la vie familiale.*" This is a particularly useful recipe as in a sense it is a basic, which you will see for yourself as we go along. Put 10 oz. beef flank, 8 oz. beef bones and $3\frac{1}{4}$ pints of cold water into a stockpot. Bring to the boil, skim, pour on a further $\frac{1}{2}$ pint of cold water, re-boil and simmer for $\frac{3}{4}$ hour. Now add $\frac{1}{2}$oz. salt, 3 peppercorns, 1 small head celery, 1 turnip, 1 carrot, 1 sprig chervil, 1 bay leaf, $\frac{1}{2}$ leek split downwards, 1 small parsnip, 1 small onion stuck with 2 cloves and slightly browned in a little very hot dripping, 1 small well-washed lettuce (preferably cos), 1 garlic clove and ½ a small firm cabbage heart which you have previously blanched (see previous recipe) and tied up like a parcel with fine string. Replace the lid, regain boiling point, adjust heat to achieve a steady simmer and continue until vegetables are tender. Strain. Place the meat in a large soup tureen. Chop all vegetables except the cabbage. Untie the cabbage, cut into small wedges and add to the mixture in the tureen. Skim the fat from the liquor and re-boil it. Either pour over the contents of the tureen or serve in a jug putting some meat and vegetables in each person's bowl and filling up with the soup. This, too, should be served with rounds of French bread baked in the oven at gas 4 (355°F) until pale golden. Of course if you can be persuaded to add the lights and liver of a fowl, the soup will benefit considerably!

poule-
au-pot
family
style

Let us go on and turn this into a related classic called **Poule-au-Pot.** You go along with the *Pot-au-Feu* recipe until you reach the point where we ask you to simmer for ¾ hour. Then you will need a small fowl, which you will stuff with 2 oz. finely chopped lean bacon, 2 oz. brown or white bread-crumbs, a quarter of a small garlic clove well crushed, the chopped liver of the bird, a scant teaspoonful of chopped parsley, a tiny head of tarragon chopped fine, ½ an eggspoon-ful of grated nutmeg, 1 level teaspoonful of salt, ½ a level eggspoonful of milled black pepper and 2 oz. of minced bacon fat. Mix the whole lot together, stuff into the bird, sew up securely with fine string and truss it well. Plunge into the simmering pot. Add the ingredients given at this stage for the *Pot-au-Feu*, cover and simmer steadily until the bird is tender and vegetables are cooked. Now remove the meat and the chicken into a large tureen, toss 1 small teacupful of rice into the stock-pot and simmer until this is cooked. Then proceed exactly as for *Pot-au-Feu*.

If you want to turn this soup into a dinner party "opener", you serve the clear, strained liquid only, to which you add tiny dice of chopped chicken breast and you hand separately rounds cut from a narrow French bread *flute*, which you first dip in white wine and then fry in pure butter in a shallow pan. Naturally the remainder is eaten up for a family meal after and so has no bearing on a recipe we once saw given on French television when the chef began work on a goose and ended up by throwing the goose away and only using the neck!

purée
St.
Germain

Too few people realise that the difference between a **Purée St. Germain** made with second rate peas and one made with sweet, young garden peas strikes an almost exact parallel with the difference between butter and margarine. So for this one please begin by shelling delicate little peas until you have $1\frac{1}{4}$ pints. Put them in a thick pan with $1\frac{1}{2}$ oz. butter and 1 oz. of something called **Chiffon-**

chiffonade

**ade** which is shredded lettuce heart, preferably cos, cut with a knife. (This is the only permissible knife-cutting exercise ever done with a lettuce but this time we really want it to bleed). When all are tender, pass through a sieve, add 1 pint of clear, rich white stock, taste, correct seasoning and re-heat slowly adding a further 1 oz. of butter, a scrap at a time as you stir. Finish this soup with $\frac{1}{4}$ pint of single or "coffee" cream.

For sheer perfection cook $\frac{1}{2}$ lb. of young peas in white stock, strain them and add a spoonful or so to each serving, or float a blob of whipped cream in the centre of each bowlful and sprinkle some of the extra peas on top.

While on the subject of vegetables let us reflect a little on tomatoes. English tomatoes are at their best when eaten like apples, but when it comes to Italianate dishes of pasta, or to *Ratatouille*, and indeed all Provençal dishes, these are hopelessly inadequate. We bridge the gap by growing Roi Humbert Italian Long tomatoes and the French ones that look like tired waiters' feet—all bulges!

tomato
soup

We have no hesitation however in giving preference to the English ones for making our own, much prized, real **Tomato Soup.** First slice up the white and green of young leeks to give yourself 10 oz. Put these in a pan and cover them generously with cold water. Add the giblets and neck of 1 fowl and simmer all together until the leeks are just tender. Now introduce into the pot 2lb. of rough-cut, unskinned English tomatoes, 8 small heads of lemon thyme and 2 heaped tablespoonsful chopped chives and simmer again with a further 1½ pints water until tomatoes are tender. Fish out the giblets and neck, rub the remainder through a sieve and correct the seasoning with salt and pepper. At this stage this soup can be cooled, refrigerated and "finished" a day later for service. This is when you pour in at least ¼ pint of double cream and re-heat, gently, until piping hot.

crostini

A most delectable union can be achieved between this soup and something called **Crostini** which we first encountered by the lake at Torre del Lago. This remote little place, tucked away behind Viareggio, boasts an inn with a chef proprietor who produces some very pretty dishes. For his *Crostini* he passed 2 inch squares of crustless bread through raw beaten egg and milk (¼ pint to 1 egg) before deep frying them in slightly smoking hot oil. Then he spread them out on a heat resistant dish, covered them with a thick *béchamel** with finely chopped mushrooms in it, sprinkled them liberally with grated Parmesan, moistened the tops with melted butter and baked them at gas 6 (400°F)—high shelf—until the cheese bubbled and browned.

When you are NOT serving your *Crostini* with a tomato soup, you can add chopped chives and crushed garlic to the *béchamel* but it is a bit much for our soup!

Given a chance, we say, the humble spud can turn itself into a very reasonable filling

brew called **Purée Alsacienne.** You will
need 1½ lb. of diced peeled potatoes and ½ lb.
sliced onions, which you then mince and put
into a pot with 3 pints of boiling stock (beef
or veal) and a level teaspoonful of salt.
Bring to the boil and simmer for 30 minutes.
Then stir in ½ pint milk and 1 oz. butter in
small flakes. Correct the seasoning with salt
and pepper and sieve rather coarsely. Add a
generous tablespoonful of chopped parsley
and serve with new crusty bread from a
cottage loaf torn into rough pieces and heated
until lightly brown in the oven at gas 4
(355°F).

Very few people appreciate that beetroot
makes a good soup or if they do, then at the
drop of a hat they say *Bortsch*. We also say
**Crème de Betteraves.** You begin by
peeling 2 medium raw beetroots and grating
them on the coarse side of the grater. Put
them in a pan with 2 pints of chicken stock,
a sprig of basil, 1 celery heart split lengthwise and 1 very small shallot, juice and all
after grating coarsely. Bring this mixture to
the boil and then simmer until all the contents are tender. Rub through a sieve.
Correct the seasoning. Add 1 oz. butter in
small flakes and re-heat slowly, stirring in
¼ pint of double cream.

Of course we do not intend for one moment
to infer that **Bortsch** is not exciting. It is
a most wonderful soup when properly made
but there is no use embarking upon it if you

are going to take short cuts and make little economies. Grate a dozen very small raw beet-roots. Put in a stock-pot with 4 small, coarse-grated turnips, 1 teacupful coarse-grated white cabbage heart, a head of celery chopped small with the stump coarse-grated, a large, grated French onion, a *bouquet garni** and 2 lb. breast of beef. Cover completely with a good clear beef bone stock, bring to the boil, skim, refresh with a tumbler full of cold water, remount to boiling point and steady off at a good simmer, which must be maintained for $2\frac{1}{2}$ hours. Strain the mixture which should be the colour of thin red wine and simmer it down to only two-thirds of its present bulk before correcting the seasoning with salt and pepper. Add 1 generous tablespoonful of milled fresh parsley and 1 small finely chopped sprig of fennel. Serve very hot or icy cold with sour cream to be handed separately.

Now we will turn our attention to using some fish stock. For the leek soup with eels called **La Cotriade Bretonne,** take 2 pints of fish stock with wine (page 95). Add to it 1 lb. trimmed, finely sliced leeks, the strained juice of 1 lemon and a really plump eel cut into $1\frac{1}{2}$ inch pieces. Bring this mixture to the boil and then simmer very gently until leeks and eel are tender. Taste, adjust the seasoning with salt and pepper and stir in 1 teacupful of thick cream just before serving with small toasted rounds of French bread spread with garlic butter*.

Now for special occasions, we are going a bit
grand with a soup which we created when a
member of the family asked "Why don't
cook books have any soups made with
salmon?" So here it is—**Velouté de Saumon.** Hard work but definitely worth it!
Begin by steaming 1 lb. of Pacific salmon—
save your good Scotch salmon for the fish
course—separate the flesh from all skin and
bone, flake up and pound with a pestle in a
mortar until the fibres are well broken down.
Dissolve 1¾ oz. of butter in a thick pan, stir
in 1¾ oz. flour, blend to a smooth thick paste
and keep stirring over a low heat while
cooking for 2 minutes. Pour in 3 fluid oz. of
dry white wine, beat until smooth, add a
further 3 fluid oz. of the wine, beat again
until smooth and add ¾ pint of milk gradually,
beating well between each of these additions.
Pour this sauce slowly over the pounded
salmon, pounding with one hand and pouring
with the other until you have achieved a
thick smooth paste. Rub as much as possible
through a fine sieve. Understand before you
start that there will be a heavy residue. This is
correct and need cause no anxiety. Scrape
the sieved mixture back into a saucepan.
Add ¼ pint of double cream. Taste, correct
the seasoning with salt and pepper and serve
piping hot.

Being obsessionally opposed to wastage we
worked enough soft brown breadcrumbs into
the residue from our *Velouté de Saumon* to
make a fairly dry paste, added a dessert-

spoonful each of chopped chives and chopped parsley, a whole raw egg and salt and pepper to season. When you have done likewise, you will find the mixture is still fairly flabby. Put it into the refrigerator for $\frac{1}{2}$ hour to firm up. Roll in small balls in sifted flour, pass these through raw beaten egg and then coat them thickly with fine soft brown breadcrumbs. Chill again in refrigeration until needed. Just before serving, slip them into slightly smoking hot oil to turn a good rich brown, heap them on a white paper-doyley covered dish, surround with sprigs of fried parsley (page 138) and watch these **Petits Frits de Saumon** vanish at speed. Hand *Sauce Tartare* (page 73) separately.

petits
frits
de
saumon

Let us go on a little longer indulging ourselves on the luxury level with **Crème aux Amandes.** Long ago this soup was featured by Voisin, the great little Paris restaurant, of which anyone who knew it still speaks with bated breath. Put $1\frac{1}{2}$ pints of the very best milk into the top of a double saucepan over hot water with a quartered onion, a sliced celery head and 6 oz. of sweet almonds milled finely. Cover and leave to poach for $1\frac{1}{2}$ hours. Dissolve 1 oz. of butter in a pan, add 1 oz. flour, stir to a thick paste and continue stirring for 2 more minutes. Add the almond mixture, having removed the celery and onion and rubbed the rest through a sieve. Remember to add it gradually with careful stirrings between each addition. Taste, correct the seasonings with salt and

crème
aux
amandes

pepper, add 1 level teaspoonful of caster sugar and "finish" with ½ pint of double cream stirred in until the mixture reaches boiling point.

In the Cook's Book we gave you a recipe for the greatest of all sorrel soups, *Germiny*. We think you might also like to have a more moderate **Crème à l'Oseille** for serving ice cold in summer. Pick over 6 oz. of sorrel to remove any blemished bits and stalks. Dissolve 2 oz. butter in a pan, add the sorrel and allow it to darken and collapse. Sieve it and stir it into 1½ pints of strongly reduced clear chicken or veal stock. Correct the seasoning with salt and black pepper and gradually stir in at least ¼ pint of single cream. Now ice it, remembering that it will thicken up as it chills, but to what extent we cannot tell you exactly because we are not sufficiently clairvoyant to know the density of your *consommé!* If it is too thick when you want to serve it, toss in a few ice cubes. The soup can stand it.

crème
à
l'oseille

Should you hanker for not quite an aristocrat —say a member of the landed gentry— among fish soups, then we strongly recommend you to try **Velouté aux Moules.** Turn back to page 107 and help yourself to the sauce we gave you for our *Velouté de Saumon*. Instead of all that pounding and sieving that you have to do for the salmon, steam 3 pints of scrubbed, bearded mussels until they open. Sling these into the sauce.

velouté
aux
moules

Stir down to your required consistency with single cream, taste and correct the seasonings. Unlike our salmon soup which is gorgeous chilled, this soup is only really delicious when served piping hot in bowls, not those wretched soup plates.

velouté
au
crabe

The same sauce can again be used for a **Velouté au Crabe.** If you can be certain of buying pure crab meat (page 367), you stir 4 oz. into the given quantity of sauce, correct the seasoning with pepper only and then thin down with single cream.

beef
tea

Just in case all this rich soup gossip has made you feel fragile, let us soothe your interior with a real **Beef Tea.** Escoffier has a delicious expression at the opening of his recipe, "*Pour obtenir une tasse à thé de suc de viande . . .* ". So when you want one, take 1½ lb. of lean beef absolutely devoid of fat, chop it finely, pack it into a large bottling jar and bit by bit add 4 soup spoonsful of cold water which this meat will gradually absorb. Then add 2 grains of *gros sel* or coarse kitchen salt. Close up the jar tightly. Stand it upright on a piece of wood in a large pan in cold water which comes two-thirds up the jar. Leave it to simmer, simmer, simmer for 3-4 hours. Strain off the liquid and that is Beef Tea.

# Busy cooks are Campbell cooks!

Ever tried cooking with soup ? Try cooking with Campbell's Soup and see how much quicker and easier Campbell's can make a busy housewife's life ! Unlike ordinary soups, Campbell's Soups are CONDENSED—come to you thick and rich in the can, with no unnecessary liquid added. So they're just right for cooking. Try the recipe below and see what we mean :

*CHICKEN POT-AU-FEU*

*2 lb. chicken joints; 2 oz. plain flour; a good shake of pepper; 2 oz. butter or margarine; 1 (10½ oz.) can Campbell's Old-fashioned Tomato Rice Soup. ½ soup can water.*
*Dust chicken with flour and pepper, brown in butter in large saucepan, stir in soup and water, cover and cook for 45 minutes over low heat, stirring frequently.*

This is just one of the more-than-150 quick and delicious recipes in the Campbell Cookbook, "Cooking for a Busy Day". If you'd like a copy of this wonderful-value-for-money cookbook (hard washable cover, colour illustrations, step-by-step instructions) just send your name and address and a postal order value 7/11d to Campbell's Soups Ltd. (Cookbook Offer), King's Lynn, Norfolk. Please allow three weeks for delivery.

# *To egg you on*

*Question: Can you suggest some ways of using eggs which are suitable for light luncheon, supper and buffet dishes? My family detest "preserved eggs" and when the hens are in lay I rack my brains for new ways of serving them.*

*Answer:*

You are not alone with your problem. Time and again, particularly at week-ends after the traditional Sunday luncheon, the cry goes up, "What on earth can I give them to eat for supper?" To which, in our house, the short answer is AN EGG. Except for breakfast, a depressing aura of bed-sitting-rooms and women going-to-bed-alone-with-a-book surround boiled eggs—but give them a little bit of a tiddle-up and they become Cook's First and Last Standby, as a number of filling, easy and "special" dishes made with one egg—or twenty!

Our detestation of the ersatz is relatively well known today, so we may as well confess that there is one bought substitute for home-made puff paste which we think so excellent that we seldom make our own (page 369). To get the best out of it, you must cook it high up in your oven at high speed. The minimum—even for beef in puff pastry is Gas 6 (400°F.) but it is happiest at Gas 7½ (435°F.) when it rises and flakes and puffs and tastes delicious.

oeufs en pâte

With a pack or two of this in deep-freeze or refrigerator freezing compartment and a bowlful of eggs, you can put **Oeufs en Pâte** on the table with ease and speed.

For each portion use a saucer to cut out a pair of circles in **very** thinly rolled puff paste. Flour a saucer, lay in one circle and break in an egg. Now add a teaspoonful or two of top of the milk or single cream, seasoning and a little milled or chopped parsley or chives and salt and pepper to season. Wet the paste rim with water, cover with the second paste circle and pinch the edges together very securely indeed. Slide the whole thing into hot fat at a little below the blue haze stage and allow to puff up and fry to a good golden brown. Dust with paprika before serving and everyone will think you terrifically clever.

eggs and rice

When we were children, we doted on a dish of **Eggs and Rice,** which had no name. To copy it, season about ½ lb. of cooked rice, turn into ½ pint of well-flavoured cheese sauce and turn into a wide, shallow bowl. Smooth off the top. Hard-boil 4-5 eggs, halve them and press them down into a pattern on the rice bed. Cover thickly with heated, strained, buttered corn, either from cob or tin—and that's it. Strange nursery food maybe but immensely popular.

oeufs mollets à l'estragon

On a slightly loftier scale there is nothing more alluring on a hot night than **Oeufs Mollets à l'Estragon,** but you must be careful about cooking the eggs. They need to be spooned gently into fast-boiling, slightly salted water and cooked for exactly 4 minutes. Then you must tap the shells lightly and peel them at once under a thin stream of cold water. Remember they are still soft—that is what *"oeufs mollets"* means, so if you leave them, they will be hell to shell and you will probably split them. When shelled, slide each into an artichoke bottom, coat thickly with mayonnaise, *Sauce Mornay** or *sauce chaudfroid** or just seasoned, whipped double cream, flavoured with finely chopped tarragon, 1 level teaspoonful to ½ pint of sauce. Whichever you choose as a coating agent, "finish" each egg with a "vee" made with a pair of tarragon leaves. The substitute is a pair of pointed leaves cut from split, flattened spring onion stalks, in which case you must change the name to *Oeufs Mollets en Gelée*.

tarte aux
oeufs
en gelée

One we find very popular is **Tarte aux Oeufs en Gelée.** Like many of the others in this chapter we have talked of, this can be advance prepared and put into refrigeration to await your pleasure. Ideally you should have a square flan case (stockists, page 370), but of course it can be made in either a round one or a Victoria sponge tin. We always prefer flan rings, simply because it is so much easier to handle the finished item than when it has to be dug out of a tin. Line whichever it is with fairly thinly rolled out Savoury Short Paste\*, then line with greaseproof paper, fill with dried beans, rice, lentils or split peas and bake at gas 6 (400°F). Remove beans. Allow to cool on a rack. Hard-boil 6 eggs for an 8 inch diameter tin. Plunge immediately into cold water, shell and slice neatly. Cover the base of the made flan case with halved, boned sardines, cover with the slices of egg and spoon on aspic at the syrupy stage (page 255) until the eggs are just covered. When set arrange tiny rounds of sliced stuffed olives between the egg slices and lock these in with a thin film of more gently-spooned-on syrupy aspic.

There is also a splendid mixture made with hard-boiled eggs which completely foxes the uninitiated—as indeed it did us for quite a

116

while when a friend gave it to us for the first time. Chop and sieve finely 8 hard-boiled eggs. Season them with salt, pepper and a few drops of Worcestershire Sauce. Then stir in a teacupful of fairly stiffly whipped double cream and put the mixture into an emulsifier to whip down to a perfectly smooth consistency. Pour into a small crystal bowl. Sprinkle chipped chives thickly on top and press these down over the surface. Spoon a "lid" of syrupy aspic (page 255) on top and serve as **Crème des Oeufs** with crustless slices of leaf thin brown bread and butter rolled up like sausage rolls with an asparagus tip in each.

crème
des
oeufs

You can use exactly the same egg mixture, without the Worcestershire sauce but with the cream of course, to make **Creme des Oeufs en Gelée.** In this case you swill just enough syrupy aspic into wetted individual moulds (stockists page 368) to coat the base and sides to a thickness of about $\frac{3}{8}$ inch. When set, place the egg mixture in an icing bag with a $\frac{1}{2}$ inch crown pipe (stockists page 368) and pipe a rosette on to the base of each. See that you make this round for a round individual mould—or oval for an oval one—and pipe in enough to leave only a narrow surround clear of the aspic walls— otherwise you will have too much aspic in the finished item. Bring the rosettes to within $\frac{1}{4}$ inch of the top of each mould. Chill them thoroughly. Fill up with syrupy aspic and serve on a bed of cress with a tiny

crème des
oeufs
en
gelée

rosette of whipped cream piped on to the centre of each, after unmoulding. "Finish" with a minute sprinkling of either paprika powder or chopped parsley.

oeufs en gelée

The classic form of this takes you back to the *oeufs mollets*. You proceed with aspic as already explained for the previous recipe but when making **Oeufs en Gelée** you slip a whole, soft-poached egg into each aspic-lined mould, placing each one very carefully so that there is a tiny space left for the aspic to be poured in all round.

oeufs en surprise

Should you hanker for something more filling with an egg, revert once more to basic *oeufs mollets* and turn them into **Oeufs en Surprise.** Wrap each soft-boiled egg in a de-rinded slice of No. 3 cut back bacon and then enclose in **very** thinly rolled puff pastry. Be careful to moisten this pastry **all over** with raw, beaten egg, so that you can overlap the edges to make a firmly enclosed parcel. Then slide these into the deep fryer with the oil just below blue haze stage (or you will not have time to get the pastry cooked through before its outside is over-browned).

l'omelette du Maréchal

Although we talked at some length about omelettes in the Cook's Book, there are one or two distinguished variants which do merit further attention. A very notable show-off for a special occasion is **L'Omelette du Maréchal.** For it you must assemble 8 separated eggs, salt and pepper to season,

1 breakfastcupful of thick cream, 2 oz. of finely grated Parmesan cheese, $2\frac{1}{2}$ oz. butter, plus, say, an extra $\frac{1}{2}$ gill of slightly whipped cream and about a flat tablespoonful of both grated Parmesan and Gruyère. Heat your dry omelette pan. Whip the 8 yolks lightly with a dessertspoonful of cold water to each one; and make up the cream mixture before whipping the whites. Here is how it is done. First soften 1 oz. of the butter in a small thick pan but for pity's sake do not melt it —just get it hot enough to beat to a feathery cream. Beat in the 2 oz. Parmesan cheese and stir in the breakfastcupful of cream with extreme gentleness until a smooth blend is achieved. Set this aside while you make the omelette. Whip the egg whites. Pour on the yolk mixture and fold in lightly. Melt the remaining $1\frac{1}{2}$ oz. butter in the heated omelette pan. Allow it to become hot and turn brown at the edges. Pour in the egg mixture, still over a low heat, and leave until bubbles break on the surface. Fold it over in the pan with only one fold. It is far too fat and puffy to make a double fold. Turn it out on to a heated, heat-resistant dish. Pour on the cheese and cream mixture, then the extra cream and sprinkle the extra grated cheeses on top. Brown till it bubbles under a fierce grill and rush it to table.

An exquisite variant on this *soufflé* omelette is made by working sorrel into the cheese cream. For this **Omelette Soufflé à l'Oseille** you will need exactly $\frac{1}{2}$ lb. of carefully picked-over sorrel, shorn of stalks and brown bits. Place the leaves in an absolutely dry pan over a very low heat and let the leaves draw, darken and subside, giving them an occasional stir. Rub through a sieve, season and use.

le demi-soufflé forestière

Another exciting one, **Le Demi-Soufflé Forestière,** has the stuffing underneath it instead of inside. Say you use 6 eggs— separate the whites from 3. Place 6 oz. of thinly sliced, unskinned mushroom in as thick pan with $\frac{1}{2}$ pint of milk or $\frac{1}{4}$ pint each of milk and cream, simmer for 7 minutes, strain and set aside. Dissolve 1 oz. butter in a small pan, stir in 1 oz. flour and add mushroom liquid gradually, beating well between each addition to make a smooth creamy sauce. Fold in the mushrooms, season to taste, perk up with about 1 dessert-spoonful of grated Parmesan and Gruyère **mixed.** Then spread over the base of a buttered, heated dish. Keep warm while you make the omelette.

Heat the pan **dry.** Whip the remaining 3 whole eggs and 3 extra yolks together with 2 tablespoonsful of water. Whip up the set-aside 3 egg whites very stiffly and fold them into the prepared egg mixture. Toss in a generous walnut of butter into the hot pan. When dissolved, pour in the whipped eggs and scoop sides to middle, bottom to top, with a spoon, levelling off each time until the mixture is just below setting point. Smooth off, fold over once and slide on to the top of the mushroom sauce. Sprinkle with a few paper-thin leaves of Gruyère, top with a spoonful or two of cream, slip under a fierce grill to bubble and turn golden brown . . . and there you have as delicate a mixture as any cook could with to achieve.

oeufs<br>pochés<br>au vin<br>rouge

Have you ever poached an egg in red wine? The cooking presents no problems but the wine consumption is high, so pause before you embark upon it and decide that you can spare ¾ of a bottle of modest Beaujolais or Spanish Claret.
When you **can,** put the wine in a thick pan and simmer it down to one quarter of its original bulk. Take 4 eggs in shell. Spoon them into fast-boiling water for exactly half a minute. Lift them out **fast,** have the reduced wine ready waiting and at boiling point in a shallow pan and break in the eggs. Pull the pan to one side and leave until the eggs are poached. Lift them out on to round *croûtons* of bread, let the wine plus half its remaining bulk in double cream, simmer hard over a fierce heat until there is just enough thick fluid to spoon over the four portions, and *voilà!* **Oeufs Pochés au Vin Rouge.** Hand lots of French bread please and drink more Beaujolais with them, thereby proving to yourselves that there **are** exceptions to the rule that eggs and wine do not go well together!

cold<br>omelettes

Maybe you have never thought of serving **Omelettes Cold for Picnics?** The French do, the Italians do, the Spaniards do—so why shouldn't we? The fact is that there are far too few British cooks who will steadfastly adhere to the "Mère Poularde" method of making omelettes. There must be eggs—but not one speck of water, milk or any other fluid. Instead there must be softened butter, plenty of it, run through the fingers on to the lightly beaten eggs. Then if the omelettes are made fast in very hot pans over absolutely full heat—and turned out before they are cooked through—**they will eat well cold.** For taking on a picnic it is really invidious to try and improve on the good old French peasant style—make single portion omelettes (with 2 eggs apiece), split pieces of French bread (*flutes*) lengthwise, butter lightly and slip made omelettes between. We like to do this while the omelettes are still hot as this infuses an extra delicious flavour to the bread. You can then add slices of any cold, cooked *charcuterie*. Just abstain from the last authentic touch—a raw onion or clove of garlic, which is eaten like an apple. Even the most Sociable Cook would thus be courting downfall!

Donnish uncles with a tendency to chatter about wines and the advantages of holidays in the Dordogne when it is "nice and cool", react favourably to **Cold Cheese Omelette.** Strictly speaking you should stir 1 oz. diced Gruyère and 1 level tablespoonful grated Parmesan into every 2-egg whipped and seasoned mixture, but obviously you can

cold
cheese
omelette

substitute either mousetrap or a mixture of diced Wensleydale and crumbled cream or cottage cheese. Bear in mind, when widening the arc of cheese experiments, that the gooier the cheese, the creamier the cold omelette. In fact, in the interests of this creaminess it is not at all a bad thing to slide a teaspoonful of thick cream into each prepared 2-egg mixture.

cold
omelette
fines
herbes

If your teenage daughter is going through the stage of being tremendously "with it" over food, give her a cold **Omelette Fines Herbes\*** and remember to say "feens airb" which will keep your end up with your young!

cold
potato
and
banger
omelette

If contending with hungry husbands and schoolboys, give them **Potato and Banger Omelette.** This means you will add 2 oz. diced cooked potato, a pinch of dry mustard and 1 large chopped, cooked sausage, or 3 chipolatas, to each 2-egg mixture, and see that this omelette is slipped inside a very large, split, buttered-and-mustard-spread length of French bread.

cold
ratatouille
omelette

Treat **Ratatouille Omelette** in the same way stirring 1 heaped tablespoonful of cold cooked *ratatouille Niçoise* into every 2 prepared beaten eggs and spread a further thin coating of *ratatouille* over the egg surface before flipping over.

The **Spanish Soufflé Omelette** is another one which eats well cold. Make the filling first. Heat enough oil to skin the base of a small frying pan. When hot, throw in 1 large or 2 small, skinned, chopped tomatoes, 2 oz. finely chopped mushrooms and half a green or red pimento, also chopped. Cook until soft but not browned. Just before they are finished, stir in a quarter of a crushed garlic clove, a generous pinch of salt and pepper and an eggspoonful of strained lemon juice. With your filling ready, you can now separate 4 standard eggs, whip the whites stiffly and beat the yolks lightly **with** 4 dessertspoonsful of cold water. Fold the prepared filling into the egg yolk mixture and then fold in the whites.

To cook this kind of omelette, which is entirely different from the classic French omelette*, you put 2 tablespoonsful butter into a heated omelette pan, which has only a very moderate heat beneath it. Pour in the raw egg mixture, smooth off in the pan and leave undisturbed until minute bubbles begin to break on the top surface, then fold in halves. If you decide to have this hot at home, sprinkle it liberally with milled parsley for service.

If you want to be completely authentic, you will of course ignore our remarks about butter for this particular soufflé omelette and use olive oil instead—and plenty of garlic.

Making a sort of half-way house between omelettes and scrambled eggs is the Basque speciality **Pipérade.** No butter this time. Use enough pre-melted-down, raw, unsalted pork-fat to cover the base of a 7-8 inch frying pan. When this is hot, allow 1 large, thinly sliced, chopped pimento to cook slowly in it until it is nearly done. Then add 2 large-ish skinned, chopped tomatoes and complete the cooking. Add a generous pinch of salt and pepper and 1 small crushed garlic clove. Work away with the mixture, using the back of a wooden spoon until such time as you have achieved a soft *purée*. Step up the heat to medium. Slide in 4 whole raw eggs and immediately stir with the fork until the mixture is delicately creamy.

This can be served three ways: plain; with little rounds cut from a slender French loaf spread with garlic butter and heated in the oven at gas 4 (355°F) until brown at the edges; or on slices of warmed through-in-the-frying-pan Bayonne ham.

Of far more aristocratic quality is **L'Omelette du Curé Menessier** which we learned some years ago from its creator. We pulled up at his restaurant on a bitterly cold day. The place seemed deserted, but on exploring we found Chef in an annexe restaurant on the far side of the garden. Before we had time to say, "This could never happen in England," we were out of our wet shoes, into two loaned pairs of carpet slippers, toasting ourselves in front of a roaring stove and sipping mulled wine while we were told what the Patron had decided we should eat.

Happily this included his famous omelette.
Set the omelette pan dry over a very low heat.
Put 4 oz. flaked, cooked salmon or salmon
trout in a small pan. Moisten with 3 tablespoonsful of Chablis and 2 of double cream,
add a teaspoonful of finely chopped chives
(Chef's came from a row of pots on the window
sill for winter use, please note!) and simmer
gently for 5 minutes. Make the omelette by
beating up 6 eggs lightly with a fork and
sliding in 2 oz. of softened butter in small
flakes. Add a light seasoning of salt and
pepper. When it is cooked at the base but
still wet on top, spread the salmon mixture
over the upper surface. Flip over one-third.
Make the remaining fold as you turn it out
on to a heat-resistant dish. Swill liberally
with double cream and bubble for a few
moments under a very fierce grill. Clearly
M. le Chef was a Very Sociable Cook!

omelette
mousseline

On this level you must also have **Omelette
Mousseline,** to which you can add any
filling you like. Provided you omit the salt,
you can use it for sweet omelettes as well as
savoury. The ingredients for 2 people are
3 egg yolks, 2 tablespoonsful of thick cream,
3 stiffly whipped egg whites, a pinch of salt
and 2 oz. butter. Stir the yolks, salt and cream
together until well blended. Then fold in the
whites and cook exactly as instructed for
Spanish Soufflé Omelette, studiously avoiding
any attempts to serve it cold as picnic food!

Like children saving the best till last, we are
now going to give you something which we

are almost certain you have not had before. Last summer we went to Tunisia and through the good offices of a Distinguished Personage we were received in an equally distinguished Tunisian house.

After the ceremony of drinking the *Thé de Menthe* in glasses with pine kernels floating on the top, which took an hour, with all the complicated refreshing and re-refreshing of the *barrades* (small teapots in blue enamelled metal), we were solemnly given the freedom of his wife's kitchen by our host, where Madame with the help of a fat, small Tunisian maid, showed us how to make **Brics** or **Bricks.**

brics
or
bricks

It took $3\frac{1}{2}$ hours so of course we were (a) late for a dinner engagement and (b) too full of *brics* to eat by the time we arrived.

We gave you the classic recipe in THE DAILY TELEGRAPH but the fact that this excellent item was so impractical for modern European usage niggled and nagged at us. Let us now explain. As it ends up at table, each *bric* is a puffy, featherweight triangle of fried pastry enclosing an egg and assorted savoury sundries, but we wanted one which took less than $3\frac{1}{2}$ hours to make. We experimented until we found it.

The Bon Viveur version can be made up in advance and stored raw in mild refrigeration for up to 48 hours, provided the *brics* are completely insulated from drying out by being enclosed in kitchen foil. Then when somebody says, "Mum I'm starving, " or "Couldn't I just have a quick snack before

I go?" or when you want to give guests something different on an informal occasion, you simply whip out the required number, lower the raw triangles into hot oil at **just below the slightly smoking stage** and fry them until they puff up like triangular feather pillows.

Begin by rolling out home-made or bought puff pastry (page 369) as thinly as if you were going to make *apfelstrudel*. Cut up the paste into 10 inch squares. Now look at the diagram on page 389. Score a light line at A. to show where you will fold. At B. arrange a semi-circular "wall" of leaf-thin sliced Gruyère or Emmenthal cheese. At C. break a raw egg inside the "wall", then just sprinkle lightly with salt and pepper, liberally with milled parsley and add a tablespoonful of thick cream. Brush the edges all round with raw beaten egg, fold over and nip **very firmly indeed,** lest the edges open out during frying. This is something which has enchanted everyone to whom we have served it so far.

You scarcely need us to remind you how easily you can ring the changes on the "wall" with scraps of minced meat, flaked fish, cooked vegetables, cold bits of curry and so on. But, please, we must emphasise two things. If the pastry is not thin enough or the oil is too hot, the eggs will be overcooked by the time the pastry is a good, golden brown. Do not try stepping up the heat either or the pastry will be richly browned outside and as raw as the poor egg inside.

Before we move on to another subject, we want to tie up one or two small points on which we have had a great number of queries. Please remember that eggs go on cooking even on a warmed plate or when left in the heat-resistant containers in which they have been cooked. Therefore if they are to be kept waiting after cooking, you must deduct from 1 minute to $1\frac{1}{2}$ minutes from given cooking times depending of course upon the period of waiting. This is particularly true of eggs cooked in the excellent range of modern oven ware (page 368) which can be put over an open flame, in an oven and thence on the table, as these pans look good as well as work well, but they are extremely heat-retentive. Remember that a soft-boiled egg is one which has been cooked in sufficient fast-boiling water to cover it completely for $3\frac{1}{2}$-$3\frac{3}{4}$ minutes, or from a standing start in cold water, to boiling point and for 1 minute thereafter. Hard-boiled eggs need 8 minutes, after which they must be slung into very cold water, left for about 3 minutes and peeled by tapping the shells lightly all over and easing them off under a thin stream of cold tap water.

Raw egg yolks, placed in mild domestic refrigeration under a close covering of kitchen foil, will keep for 4-5 days without deteriorating or crusting on top. If stored uncovered, they will be crusted and useless in half a day. Raw egg whites will keep for at least a week in mild domestic refrigeration if given the same treatment and, even more important, they will be **better** for using well whipped in *soufflés* and *meringues* than freshly separated ones can ever hope to be. It is sheer nonsense to say that either whites or yolks of reasonably fresh eggs (not necessarily new-laid) can only be kept for 2 days. We proved this point recently by using 10-day-stored separated egg whites, in front of witnesses who disbelieved us, to make a flawless batch of giant *meringue* cases which tasted gorgeous.

Another familiar battle rages over refrigerated eggs. Eggs are porous; refrigerators are enclosed areas which contain a varied assortment of very strong smells and as we do not wish our eggs to be impregnated with smelly cheese, kippers or *ratatouille* well laced with garlic, we **never refrigerate them.** If you think this is a wild asservation, try a small test for yourself. Put 12 eggs, (or 40) into a 7 lb. biscuit tin with 1 raw unwashed truffle. Replace the lid and leave for a week. Now make an omelette with some of those eggs and you will find that it has all the fragrance and flavour of truffles!

# The Bell House

Restaurant

The Bar

HOTEL AND RESTAURANT

SUTTON BENGER NEAR CHIPPENHAM
WILTSHIRE

Telephone SEAGRY · 336

ONE OF BRITAIN'S
BEST RESTAURANT'S

BAR "LE PERROQUET"

BEAUTIFULLY
APPOINTED BEDROOMS

*La Patronne Soigne La Cuisine*

Bedroom Nº7

The Courtyard

*Chapter 8*

# O sole mio

Salmon Trout in Foil
Sauce Hollandaise
Fried Whitebait
Fried Sprats
Fried Scallops
Rissois
Fried Parsley
Our Fritto Misto Mare
Curry Sauce
Goujonnade de Sole (ou Plie)
Baked Goujonnade
Rødspætte Surprise

Bornholmeræggekage
Haddock in Rice Border
Aioli
Bacalhau à la Braz
Pauchouse
Crabe Pilau
Rougets à la Bordelaise
Anguilles Pouyfauçon
Filets de Sole à l'Alsacienne
Sole au Beurre Blanc
Salmon Pie
Filets de Sole en Croûte
Crêpes Bon Viveur

*Question: Which would you say were the most important fish for a home cook to learn how to cook and do you think any kind of fried fish is really important?*

*Answer:*

The fish which swim in the waters encircling this island and those which inhabit our lakes and rivers are all so important that the problem is to know which ones to talk about first. We have the finest fish in the world. This is very probably the key to the poorness of our fish cookery. There is such an *embarras de choix* that everyone just takes the whole thing for granted. Even sloshed into those batter winding-sheets, the fish itself still tastes good—when excavated. It can even stand being boiled and after this scandalous ill usage still hang on to some of its original flavour! This being so, we ask you whether or not it is high time we sought ways of cooking our glorious fishy heritage which would bring out the fullness of its flavours?

salmon trout in foil

Let us begin with the very best of all—**Salmon Trout.** These combine the delicacy of trout with the character of salmon and are unique. The only comparable fish are *omble de chevalier* which are fished from Lake Annecy with almost idolatrous ceremony—or poached with the utmost stealth. They are distant cousins of our salmon trout and need only loving care and foil cookery to bring out their exquisite best. But, wives of fishermen, while you may rejoice when these treasures are excavated from a creel, do stop your menfolk pursuing that sinful tradition of laying out the catch on the lawn, as on a fishmonger's slab, so that all and sundry can see how clever they have been. Sun and air are deleterious to the trout. Get them indoors as fast as possible remembering, as you bear them off, to snitch some of the water grasses from the creel and use these to wrap the fish. Keep in a cool dark place until you are ready to start cooking.

Then take a large rectangle of aluminium foil and rub the inner surface liberally with the very best butter. Season this lightly with real *gros sel*, the true kitchen salt and freshly milled black peppercorns. Lay in a whole, cleaned salmon trout. Lay thin shavings of butter on top. Wrap the parcel up lightly, leaving an air pocket but sealing the edges, top and sides very securely. Set this parcel on a heat-resistant dish and put in a pre-heated oven at gas 5 (380°F). Thirty-five to fifty minutes later the fish (depending on its size) will not only be done to perfection but it will also have retained every single scrap of its succulent taste, fragrance and natural juices. Serve it with these juices strained off into a sauceboat, or go completely against the classic rulings and serve it as we had it only last night with *sauce Béarnaise**.

Pray do not be scared of *sauce Béarnaise*. A lot of mumbo-jumbo surrounds this classic. It is extravagant—yes; but given a small hand electric mixer which can be trailed around the kitchen on a long flex and popped into saucepans at will, *Béarnaise* will always prove your servant and not your master.

There is more, however, to the story than we have yet told you. We long ago stated that we follow the classics whenever possible. Those of you who have heard us on stage and television will also know that we insist that part of our job is to try and cut the corners on time, labour and expenditure, provided always we can do so without taking anything from the finished quality of the dish. So now it is time to confess that increasingly we lift classics out of their correct context in order to discover whether or not they are capable of settling down happily elsewhere. *Sauce Béarnaise* is a typical example, because although you and we know perfectly well it is always quoted as the ideal stable companion to a fillet steak, we have recently discovered (perhaps we should have known years ago) that it is ambrosia with salmon trout.

sauce Hollandaise

Nevertheless we dutifully supply the orthodox **Hollandaise** lest you should prefer to be conventional. We do not give you Escoffier's recipe because it calls for $1\frac{1}{2}$ lb. butter. We have learned recently from a very brilliant cook, Madeleine Stratton of the Bell House Hotel at Sutton Benger, that her far more butter-economical version is bland enough to suit the most pernickety palate.

This is it. Place 3 tablespoonsful wine vinegar in a small thick pan with 2 oz. chopped tarragon stalks and 1 rounded teaspoonful of grated raw shallot (or onion). Reduce by very gentle simmering over direct heat to a mere teaspoonful. Press through a tiny strainer into a slightly larger pan and allow it to descend to blood heat while you beat 8 oz. of butter (slipped into a warming drawer for a few moments to soften) to the creamy consistency of *beurre fondu*. Be careful—once this becomes melted and oily you are sunk! Whip in 4-5 raw egg yolks (depending on size) one by one into the reduced, strained, cooled vinegar mixture. Set the pan over a mere thread of heat. Start whipping and very gradually whip in the creamy butter until the sauce itself is thick and creamy. It takes longer to write than to do and it works every time.

Another new-to-us little trick—this time with fish—came our way recently via the Spanish Mama of a young man who works for us.

fried
whitebait

Her **Fried Whitebait,** treated in the usual fashion, lightly dusted with flour and shaken in a sieve, came to table in a number of tiny fans, looking much prettier than in an indeterminate lump.

Instead of just tossing the floured whitebait a few times into slightly smoking hot oil (so that they do not clog), gather five of them together at a time—by their tails—dip the tail-tuft into cold water—just a mere $\frac{1}{4}$ inch down the fishes—dip in flour, set the resultant "fan" on a slice, (which you have first dipped into the hot oil) and then slide each "fan" down into the oil. The dab of water makes the tails stick together. Not very complicated! But fried like this and arranged in a series of graduated fans around a centrally placed lemon basket, the result is irresistibly appetising.

fried
sprats

You can of course make larger fans using **Sprats** instead of whitebait; but then you must be prepared either to eat the bones as Continentals do, or else to bone each little fish at the table.

fried
scallops

Have you ever tried **Fried Scallops?** They are not cheap, but they are good, just floured, egged, breadcrumbed and fried in slightly smoking hot oil for serving with thin brown bread and butter and *sauce tartare*.

rissois

You might also spare more than a passing thought for the marriage between shelled shrimps and fried pastry. That bought puff pastry we have already mentioned (page 369) is excellent for the little Portuguese **Rissois** which make a very good *hors d'oeuvre* at a dinner. Roll out the pastry extremely thinly. Then cut into 4-inch squares. Score lightly from corner to corner to mark off each square into two triangles without cutting right through the pastry. Mix together in a bowl 6 fluid oz. thick creamy white sauce, $4\frac{1}{2}$ oz. shelled shrimps, 1 rounded tablespoonful milled parsley, a teaspoonful of strained lemon juice and a liberal seasoning of milled black peppercorns. Drop spoonsful of this mixture on to one triangle of each square. Wet the edges all round with raw, beaten egg, **not water.** Flip the uncovered pastry triangles over, pinch the edges very firmly indeed (we do not want the mixture oozing out during the frying time!) and slide the little triangular parcels into hot oil just below the slightly smoking stage. Fry to a golden brown, drain and serve heaped on a paper d'oyley on a flat dish with a surround of **Fried Parsley.**

fried
parsley

A lot of cooks make a tremendous palaver about washing the parsley, blanching it in boiling water, drying it in a cloth and then tossing it into fiercely hot oil. None of this is the slightest bit necessary. Just run the parsley under the cold tap if it looks the slightest bit grubby, put it on a dry cloth to await your pleasure and shed its surplus moisture and then at the last moment fling it into the oil until it crisps up a bit and stiffens. This kind of parsley treatment makes the stuff extremely edible to us as well as rabbits, which is more than can be said for sprigs of raw parsley.

These variants on the standard 'We're Frying Tonite' theme *vaut la peine.* So does an English version (why should the Italians have the exclusive on it!) of **Fritto Misto Mare.** It is only a collection of small fishy bits and pieces fried in batter served with *tartare* or *Béarnaise*\* sauce. On more than one occasion we have had the old winding-sheet treatment dished up to us in the country of its origin. So let us go at least one better.

our
fritto
misto mare

Assemble shelled prawns, tiny rolls of de-rinded No. 3 cut back bacon, tight un-stalked button mushrooms, quartered scallops with their tongues cut off and used separately; mussels (steamed for 1 minute to make them yield themselves up to us) and little ribbon strips (*goujonnades*) of sole or plaice. Dip all these items into (a) flour, (b) raw, beaten, strained egg, and (c) fine soft breadcrumbs. Fry them all singly in slightly smoking hot oil, drain them and heap them on a paper-d'oyley covered dish. Now garnish them with fried parsley and canelled sections of lemon.

Do they need anything else? Indeed they do.

We have served them with a dunking bowl of *sauce Mornay**, with **Savoury Lemon Sauce** (page 86) and with **Curry Sauce** which sends peppery old Generals into ecstasies of delight. Poor old dears, their far-East scorched palates can only be revived by something pretty pungent! And of course, they get no wine with curry flavours—just iced lager, cold beer, or a trivia like *vin rosé*

curry
sauce

because **Curry Sauce** is brutal to a fine wine. To make it, grate a raw medium shallot and scoop both pulp and juices into a small thick pan containing 1 oz. hot butter. Fry the onion gently for about 4 minutes, giving an occasional stir with a wooden spoon. Add the pulp of 2 tomatoes, which have been skinned and de-pipped, and stir in a rounded dessert-spoonful of flour once the tomatoes are soft. When you have worked this up with the remaining ingredients in the pan to a stiffish paste, work in 1 teaspoonful of masala paste (page 369) (curry powder is a very rude name in a serious kitchen). Thin down with a $\frac{1}{4}$ pint of fish stock (use the trimmings from the sole or plaice—there is no reason to leave them with the fishmonger). Then thin down a little further with about $\frac{1}{2}$ gill of top of the milk or single (coffee) cream. This is when you correct the seasoning with salt and a few drops of lemon juice.

goujonnade
de sole
ou plie

Now we must tackle something to which we have only made reference so far, **Goujonnade de Sole** with the reminder that these can also be made with plaice. Cut up your chosen fillets into narrow, ribbon-like strips. Pass them through flour, then through raw, beaten, strained egg and finally bury them in fine breadcrumbs. Lift each one up, twist it and slide it into frying basket sunk into slightly smoking hot oil. They are quick to do, taking only 1½-2 minutes. They look charming. They make the fish go very much further than they will ever do in whole fillets. They can be served plain with salt, pepper and lemon juice, with *sauce tartare* (page 73) *sauce Hollandaise* (page 136), or *sauce Béarnaise**.

You can also make a very little go a long way by using fillets of sole or plaice to ring the changes on a dish called Swedish Herrings*. Butter a small pie dish. Slice 4 oz. of unskinned button mushrooms thinly. Cut 10 oz. of raw potato into slender matchsticks (*pommes allumettes*), and the same amount of sole or plaice into generous ¼ inch widestrips. Layer these three alternately into the prepared pie dish, starting with potato, seasoning each layer with salt and freshly milled black peppercorns. Moisten with top of the milk or single cream and bake until potatoes are tender, at gas 4 (355°F). As these take a mere "glass of sherry time" to cook they are an ideal way of stretching a fish course. The amount of fish intended for 4 portions as baked fillets will serve eight as **Baked Goujonnade.** goujonnade Which is more than we can say for the next dish which is strictly a one-per-portion item.

The Danes use whole plaice for a dish which

141

they call **Rødspætte Surprise,** an extra-ordinarily attractive way of presenting 1 lb. plaice to the family. Clean, top and tail each fish. Lay on a dish, sprinkle lightly with salt and leave for 5 minutes. Turn over and repeat. Then wipe off all moisture and lay the plaice darkside underneath on a board. With a sharp knife make an incision along the spine bone starting and finishing a minimum 1 inch from head and tail. Now pare away the flesh from the bone sufficiently to make two pockets left and right of it. You will then find that you can roll the edges back so as to turn them into wide lips.

Do so. Wedge them open with pieces of raw potato and in this state pass them through sifted flour, raw beaten egg and fine bread-crumbs. Deep-fry in slightly smoking hot oil. Lift out and remove the pieces of potato. The frying will have set the lips apart and you now fill the centres with a left-hand line of piping hot cooked spinach to which you add a nut of butter, a spoonful of cream and seasoning of salt and pepper; a right-hand line of either asparagus tips or cooked sliced mushrooms and a central panel of shelled shrimps tossed for a moment in butter to warm them through. Decorate with pieces of lemon and serve.

Another excellent Danish family dish which is served from the omelette pan in which it is made is **Bornholmeræggekage.** On the island of Bornholm from which its name derives it is always made with smoked herring. We have always found buckling or smoked

*(margin notes)* rødspætte surprise

Bornhol-meræg-gekage

142

kippers quite successful substitutes, more especially if you can obtain the kippers from the Isle of Man. It is a lamentable fact that the great majority of the British public is still unaware that the perfect kippers are Manx. They are an anaemic beige colour—their natural hue—all the rest are merely dyed gingery brown which does nothing for either their quality or their flavour.

So using whichever of the three fishy alternatives we have offered you, begin by putting a dry omelette pan over a very low heat and let it stay there while you do your preparations. Whip 4 eggs and $3\frac{1}{2}$ fluid oz. of milk together in a bowl. Skin and bone 3 smoked herring, or buckling or just skin 6 kipper fillets. Toss a generous nut of butter into the hot pan and allow this to dissolve over a lowish heat. Pour in the egg and milk mixture and stir for about $\frac{3}{4}$ minute, then let it settle. Check with a spatula round the edges as it begins to set. When a firm base is achieved but the mixture is still wet on top, arrange the chosen fish in a star design on top. Let it finish cooking until it is just moist on the upper surface. This is where we stop and serve it. If however you have a fancy for taking it through "*à la Danois*", you then arrange overlapping, very thin slices of unpeeled radishes between the fish fillets and strew the omelette with chopped chives. Naturally you must choose.

If you stick to the rule of fish on Fridays in household and you have a lot of hungry mouths to feed, you may find that your brood reacts as favourably as ours does to **Haddock in Rice Border.** Boil 1 lb. of rice and strain it*. Meanwhile prepare the mixture to be folded into it. This comprises 2 oz. butter and 2-3 oz. sultanas, 1 rounded tablespoonful milled parsley and the same of chives or 2 of either—you to choose—the strained juice and grated rind of 1 lemon, 1 rounded tablespoonful of powdered paprika and a generous pinch of pepper. Once this is done, you make your filling.

Very salty items meet with extreme disfavour in this establishment. If you agree, then put 1 lb. haddock into a pan with sufficient cold water to cover it, bring to the boil, strain and throw the water away. Pour $1\frac{1}{4}$ pints milk over the haddock, bring this to the boil and simmer gently until the haddock is tender. Strain it, pour the milk into a jug, remove skin from haddock and flake coarsely. Dissolve $1\frac{1}{2}$ oz. butter in a small pan, stir in $1\frac{1}{2}$ oz. flour to make a thick *roux* and add the haddock-flavoured milk gradually, beating well between each addition until you have achieved a smooth creamy sauce. Taste and correct the seasoning with pepper, add a (optional) level teaspoonful of anchovy *purée*, stir well, fold in the fish and at the last, stir in 1 small teacupful of finely grated cheese. Keep warm in a double pan over hot water.

Turn your attention once again to the rice mixture. Put all the ingredients we gave you for the filling into a large bowl. Oil a border or savarin mould or failing this a large ornamental jelly mould. Turn the strained rice into the bowl and mix well until the butter is melted and the filling is evenly distributed throughout. Press into the prepared mould **very firmly indeed.** Invert on a large dish, give a jolly good shake and lo and behold the mould will come away cleanly leaving a highly decorative border or shape! Either pour the haddock mixture into the centre or around the rim if using a solid shape. Now hang on to that savoury border in your mind because if you think for a moment, you will realise that it represents a savoury mixture which can be served with (and used to make go further) left-overs of any cold cooked fish, meat, game, poultry or indeed just eggs and vegetables.

Now here comes one strictly for garlic addicts called **Aioli** which to our knowledge is the most pungent garlic sauce ever invented. Just remember that the flavour remains. To begin with, you steam cod—1 good steak per person. Remove the skins from the steaks after cooking. Arrange the fish very wide apart on a very large dish indeed and then warm the fish under a loose tenting of kitchen foil in the oven at gas $\frac{1}{4}$ (240°F) while you assemble all the other items you have cooked—1 large old potato per head steamed and skinned, 1 hard-boiled egg apiece, a dish of French beans steamed with a *bouquet garni* of thyme, bay, sage and wild thyme (*oregano*) and 1 small steamed globe artichoke apiece. Put the beans in the middle of the dish, the other vegetables

145

around the outside of the cod steaks and serve with **Aioli,** bearing in mind that the highest quality wine you may drink with this dish is a humble rough white or *rosé*.

For the **Aioli** peel a dozen garlic cloves, put them in a mortar and pound them to pulp with a pestle. If you want to drive yourself absolutely hairless, work in 4 egg yolks with the pestle and pound the whole lot up to the consistency of mayonnaise by whipping in small quantities of the **right olive oil.** This is obviously *la veritable huile de Provence* (page 369) for a Provençal speciality. You can indeed make the whole thing even more difficult by making **Aioli sans Oeufs** which even expert Provençal chefs agree requires a special *tour de main*.

What we do with the egg version is much easier if it is not quite correct. Having pounded the garlic cloves and scraped them into the bowl of an electric mixer, add the egg yolks and go on whipping for about 4 minutes until the mixture is thick and then whip in your oil gradually and easily.

Incidentally the **Aioli** tastes exactly the same made this way; but you are all so eagle eyed and apparently so well informed that we try to avoid letters signed "Angry, Adml., retd., Billericay", pointing out that we have not given you The Lot. There is also **Le Grand Aioli,** an extension of this family one with which is eaten all the meat and vegetables of a *pot-au-feu* (page 100) and the cod platter is garnished with baby octopus, snails and *limace*—you can turn it up in the French dictionary if you like but it reads so nastily that we prefer not to print it!

If we turned from fresh to dried cod (page 367) we can plunder the *cuisine Portugaise* of **Bacalhau à la Braz.** This is one of thousands of versions of **Bacalhau** chosen because we think it the most suitable for the national palate, being served without great sloshings from the sauceboat of hot olive oil!

Take 1 lb. dried cod and soak it overnight in cold water; then dry it and shred it into matchsticks. Mix these with $\frac{1}{2}$ lb. of raw, old potatoes shredded the same way. Put $2\frac{1}{2}$ oz. butter with 2 oz. oil into a thick frying pan and while these are heating, grate a large onion, being careful to conserve all juice as well as pulp. When the oil and butter are heated, tip in cod, potatoes and onion and fry, turning very gently so as not to squash the whole up into a mushy dog's dinner. In between turnings and shakings, beat up 6 eggs in a bowl and when the potato tastes tender turn in the eggs and stir over a moderate heat until mixture is thick and creamy.

Pike, perch, tench and eel are not staple foodstuffs in Britain, but keen fishermen's wives will be thankful to obtain a really good recipe for **Pauchouse** which calls for 1 lb. each of all four of these special fish. First they must be cleaned, topped, tailed, cut into small neat pieces and poached in fish *court bouillon** to cover. While this is going on

*bacalhau à la Braz*

*pauchouse*

gather up all the heads and tails, put them in a pan with a quart of cold water, a sprig of thyme, a bay leaf, 2 large coarsely cut onions, 4 or 5 parsley stalks (with a bit of root if possible) and 2 peeled, split cloves of garlic.

There are two ways of treating this *court bouillon*. First you simmer it (40 minutes), then you either emulsify and rub vigorously through a sieve or put it into a Moulinex grinder and turn the handle until the residue is dry. Throw residue away.

Lift out the fish pieces from the *court bouillon* and set them on a warm dish. Strain fish stock and simmer to half its own bulk. Soften 3 oz. white *roux** in a thick pan. Add the sieved or emulsified fish stock gradually. Add a further ¼ pint white wine (white Burgundy ideally), simmer again until creamy and finish with a ¼ pint thick cream. Sink the fish pieces into this in a deep container and hand separately small rounds sliced from a *flute* of French bread, spread with garlic butter and browned in the oven at gas 4 (355°F).

crabe
pilau

By extending our travels in France to Provence we can add **Crabe Pilau** to our repertoire. First put 7 fluid oz. olive oil into a large thick frying pan and heat through. Chop up 2 large onions finely, put them into the oil over a very moderate heat with 8 oz. raw, unwashed rice, simmer and stir for 5 minutes. Then add ¼ pint of fish stock (page 95) from a batch of 1 quart and stir gently from time to time until the rice absorbs the first addition, repeat and stir again,

148

adding after the second lot of fish stock a sprig each of fennel, thyme and sage, 2 parsley stalks and a bay leaf all tied together. Go on adding stock and stirring until the rice is almost cooked. Then add a level coffee-spoonful of saffron powder, 6 medium, peeled, de-pipped tomatoes and 2 quarts of mussels which have been scrubbed, bearded and steamed until they open (approximately 1 minute). If the rice has absorbed all fish stock by this time and is still not completely cooked, add dry white wine sparingly. With a little care you will achieve a total absorption of your fluid additives by the time the rice is soft to the teeth but not a flabby goo. Now mix in 1 lb. of mixed crabmeat, correct the seasoning to taste and pile on to a large heated dish. Thereafter you can if liked sprinkle liberally with finely chopped chives and finely milled parsley, place finely chopped hard-boiled egg yolk and white in alternate quarter sections around the edge of the dish and hand cut lemon separately.

If we nip across from Provence to Bordeaux, we can regale ourselves with **Rougets à la Bordelaise,** one of the nicest ways of enjoying this temperamental fish which can be very disagreeable if ill-treated. Take 6 red mullet weighing between 7 and 8 oz. Soften 3 oz. of butter in a thick pan. Fry the fish on both sides for just long enough to "stiffen" them, approximately 1 minute each side over a moderate heat. Add 4 finely chopped small shallots (or onions). Swill with 10 fl. oz.

dry Graves, cover and poach for 12 minutes. Drain off the fish, set them on a heated dish and make the sauce.

Soften 3 oz. white *roux*\* and add the strained poaching liquors gradually, stirring in 1 teaspoonful of concentrated tomato *purée* with the second addition. The sauce should now be slightly too thick so you can thin it down to a creamy consistency with (a) water, (b) fish stock or (c) dry Graves, adding 1 level teaspoonful of finely chopped tarragon and correcting the seasoning thereafter. Pour sauce over fish and hand plenty of crusty new bread to mop up the juices.

If you move off from here to Margaux (and who wouldn't if they had the chance to drink Margaux *in situ*) you will sooner or later be regaled with THE dish made from eels fished in the river Gironde. It is called **Anguilles Pouyfauçon**. Begin by putting eight 3 inch pieces of cleaned, skinned, raw eel in ½ pint strained fish stock (page 95). Simmer gently for 11-13 minutes depending upon the thickness of the eel pieces. Lift them out in exchange as you immerse 8 very young slim, neatly-trimmed leeks and 1 gill claret. Poach these until leeks are tender and arrange on the same plate as the eel to keep warm.

Take a suitable-sized casserole for serving these two items in their sauce and in it dissolve 2½ oz. butter over a low heat, add a teaspoonful of lemon juice and ¼ lb. of small, whole button mushrooms, cover and simmer for 5 minutes.

anguilles
pouyfauçon

In a separate, small frying pan pour in just enough oil to skin the base. Add a crushed garlic clove and 8 small slices from a *flute* of bread. Fry these briskly on both sides, lift out, moisten with a few drops of cognac or Armagnac and keep hot with leeks and eels. Dissolve 1 heaped teaspoonful of arrowroot or *fécule de pomme* in a liqueur glassful of either cognac or Armagnac and pour on to the heated wine and stock liquor (transferred from casserole to a separate pan).

Put half the eels into the casserole, then half the mushrooms, then the remaining eels, then the remaining mushrooms, put the leeks round the edge, put the sauce on top, stand the 8 little *croûtons* over all and serve.

Now we are off to Alsace, where in the main we find the cooking is a shade on the heavy side due to having brushed shoulders with the Germanic influence of stodgery. Yet this certainly cannot be said of **Filets de Sole à l'Alsacienne** which is not beyond any quite inexperienced cook who has learned how to boil *pastas*\* and to make an easy *Hollandaise* (page 136), though perhaps we should confess it is not the least expensive dish we have given you so far in this book!

filets de
sole à
l'Alsacienne

First there can be no compromise between plaice and sole. You must have six large sole fillets and a modest Alsatian wine, preferably Reisling. Use 17½ fl. oz. with 3 finely chopped shallots. Put these ingredients together into a thick pan and poach (a shivering simmer) for 3 minutes. Then throw in $3\frac{1}{2}$ oz. of the smallest possible button mushrooms and simmer (slightly stronger heat) for long enough to cook the soles without letting them go past "cooked" to "leathery". We reckon a maximum 5 minutes. Strain the liquor into a small pan, add $3\frac{1}{2}$ fl. oz. double cream and simmer until mixture is creamy. Now add the *coup de foudre* —$3\frac{1}{2}$ fl. oz. *sauce Hollandaise* (page 136) and taste so as to correct the seasoning with salt and pepper. Run in a small nut of butter to impart a final sheen to the sauce.

Arrange the sole fillets on a neat bed of cooked (see spaghetti*) ribbon noodles (page 369), mask with the sauce, slip under a fierce grill for about 1 minute and serve.

It is small wonder really that every chef creates specialities of his own with sole. Take a dish like **Sole au Beurre Blanc**—superb! It is easy enough for the tyro and it is as delicate as a gardenia. You simply need a shallow copper *sauteuse*, the best butter that money can buy, prime fillets of Dover sole, French *gros sel*, black peppercorns, a mill and *sauce Hollandaise* (page 136) without the egg yolks. Heat enough butter to cover the base of a pan to about $\frac{1}{8}$ inch thickness. Slide in the fillets, cook them for $2\frac{1}{2}$ minutes, turn them over, repeat, add 1-2 tablespoonsful brandy, step up to fiercest heat, ignite, shake for 30 seconds to burn out grease in butter, turn off the heat and arrange the fillets on a warmed dish. Decorate with fine sprigs of dill or fennel. Turn back to the recipe for *sauce Hollandaise*

sole au
beurre
blanc

(page 136) and study it carefully. You will see that after simmering the tarragon, shallot and vinegar down and straining it, you leave it to descend to blood heat. **Ignore the rest.** From this point onwards the *Hollandaise* information becomes irrelevant. All you do is to achieve your *beurre blanc* is add the 8 oz. of *beurre fondu* or softened butter, in flakes, whipping furiously all the time. Then you flavour to taste with strained lemon juice and serve. This is how sole is served in and around Niort.

salmon
pie

At this point we shall leave France and return home to US. We recently created a **Salmon Pie** which we serve with *sauce à l'estragon** and it is always a howling success. To begin with we used English Raised Pie Paste (page 83), then we found that it was far nicer made with our cold yeast dough*—the one we use for croissants. Nor is it necessary to use *darne* or middle cut of prime Scottish salmon. The far less expensive Pacific salmon does well enough but the whole thing begins with rice.

You boil and strain 6 oz.* While this is cooking you line a 10 inch by 7 inch by 3 inch pie dish with thinly rolled croissant dough. Skin 2 lb. of raw, middle cut salmon. Cut the four collops of flesh from the bone and cut these into fingers like very fat chips. Chop the yolks of 6 hard-boiled eggs. Slice 4 oz. unskinned mushrooms thinly and as soon as the rice is cool enough, you start your assembly. Put half the salmon into the pie dish, cover with half the mushroom slices, half the chopped egg yolks, half the rice, sprinkle lightly with salt and pepper, pour in 2 oz. of melted butter and repeat using up remaining ingredients. Add a further 2 oz. of melted butter and when this has seeped into the mixture, moisten with 1½ gills of single cream.

Press in the pastry edges over the filling all round the pie dish, brush them with cold water and press a paste "lid" on top. Decorate with trimmings as required, brushing each with cold water to hold it securely, wash the top with raw beaten egg, to which you have added 1 level teaspoonful of coarse salt, and bake middle shelf of the oven at gas 6 (400°F) till the pastry is a rich golden brown. Serve hot or cold.

filets de sole en croûte

We also use our croissant or yeast dough for **Filets de Sole en Croûte** which is another sort of "pie". Roll out the dough thinly and cut into a 13 inch by 15 inch rectangle. Lay just over half this on a lightly floured baking sheet with about 6 inch of the 15 inch sides lying over the baking sheet on to the table. Now coil 12 large fillets of sole round your fingers and set them in two rows of six down the length of the dough on the baking sheet, leaving enough border all the way round to bring the uncovered part over the top so as to pinch the edges together when you have finished—**but don't do so yet!** Fill the central cavities of the coiled sole fillets with shelled shrimps. Slide a dessertspoonful of white wine over each. Season well with salt and pepper. Spoon sufficient thick *sauce béchamel** over the top to cover the coils completely. Dot all over with tiny flakes of butter. Wet the edges all round with cold water, bring over the pastry flap and pinch the edges very securely together. Brush all over with raw, salted, beaten egg and finish the top of the pastry by nicking 2 lines of "vees" all the way down the length with the tips of a small pair of scissors. Bake at gas 6 (400°F) until pastry is just coloured a very pale golden. Mix ¼ pint double cream with ½ gill of dry white wine and a tablespoonful of brandy and gently spoon this into the little holes made by those nicks you did with scissors. Return to the oven, finish baking to a rich brown and serve this with *sauce à l'estragon**.

Many years ago now we featured fine pancakes and the storage thereof in a stage cookery performance which we gave under the aegis of the DAILY TELEGRAPH and this was when **Crêpes Bon Viveur** were born. You need to allow 8 pre-made pancakes* per person and we stress here and now that if they are not thin enough to be semi-transparent, DO NOT USE THEM.

crêpes
Bon
Viveur

Prepare their filling in a small bowl by mixing together 4-5 oz. of shelled shrimps, a level teaspoonful of anchovy *purée*, the strained juice of ½ a lemon, 2 heaped tablespoonsful mayonnaise*, 2 heaped tablespoonsful of whipped double cream, 1 heaped teaspoonful of finely milled parsley and when possible the same of finely chopped chives. Mix well together.

Spread this filling into the pancakes, roll them up into cylinders and arrange in line astern down a shallow heat-resistant dish, which you have previously buttered liberally. Sprinkle the tops thickly with grated Parmesan, swill generously with cream, sprinkle again with Parmesan, giving a final smaller swirl of cream, dot with tiny flakes of butter, cover with kitchen foil and bake at gas 4 (355°F) middle shelf for 20 minutes.

# Chapter 9

# *All tied up*

Onion and Garlic Tresses
Herb Garlands and Swags
Knots and Plaits
Bread Plait
Barding
Larding
Trussing
Ballottines

Poulet à la Ficelle
Crown Roast
Selle d'Agneau Bridée
Pot-au-feu
Paupiettes de Boeuf
Vegetable marrows
Melons

*Question: I never know how to tie things, from strings of onions and garlic to Crown Roast, or a chicken which I've undone to get the stuffing in. Do these jobs need specialised knowledge?*

*Answer:*

Anyone can do any of the culinary tying given in this chapter. So next time a Breton onion seller calls at your door and tries to separate you from a great deal of money for a décor-conscious tress of onions, tell him, "No thank you, I make my own."

It takes a bare 10 minutes to make a 1½ yd. **tress of onions** and another 3 or 4 minutes to make one in garlic. Do remember, however, that it can only be done successfully **if** you either grow your own onions or can buy them freshly harvested and before the dry stalks have been pulled off— these are essential.

onion and
garlic
tresses

Take three heads—of either onion or garlic—
with about 5 inch of stalk left on. Plait them
for half this length, doing an ordinary three-
strand plait. Take in a fourth onion and plait
**once** with its stem used double with one of
the original ones. Take in a fifth, repeat and
continue in this way until you have plaited
in enough for your required length.

If they are to be stored in a shed, just tie off
the final tuft of stems with twine. If they are
to be used decoratively in your kitchen, tie at
each end with a suitably coloured ribbon bow,
attach a strong base or string loop behind
and hang pendant or draped, using one or
as many as you please.

herb
garlands
and swags

One of the prettiest garnishes we know for
using with savoury items is made with herbs.
Provided the herb is attractive to look at,
there is no limit to the kinds which may be
used. You will need very fine florists' wire
(stockists, page 368) for **garlands** and **swags**
and "stems" of firm florists' wire for special
shapes. Just pause to reflect before you
embark on your first that the size of each
sprig or bunch of herbs that you use will
determine whether you have a very fine and
delicate strand (such as you would obtain by
using tight little sprig-heads of parsley or
tight little spray heads of thyme or tarragon);
or a fat, lush one such as you might want to
use for garlanding the fronts and swagging
the corners of buffet tables; in which case
sage tufts or borage sprigs would be ideal.
Wind one end of a strand of fine wire around

160

a little bunch of herbs, overlap a second bunch so that the heads are touching the first, wind again, lay in a third, wind again and continue to the required length.

The beauty of this type of decoration is that it can be coiled into a bowl of cold water (or bath-tub) and kept for a couple of days without deterioration.

Four tiny strands of parsley make a fine finish to a square savoury item. A bigger swag of sage or lemon balm is charming round the rim of a circular dish of salad. Two swags curved along the sides of a long, flat, oval dish set off a cold salmon or salmon trout (use dill or fennel) or fillet of beef (use chervil or parsley).

You can elaborate on the theme the moment you use the "stem" wire, which is sold in 10 inch lengths (page 368). Bind small herb heads or sprigs to any number of stems with fine wire and then bend them in "vees" or crescents for bordering large dishes or the edges of buffet tables. You can even bend them into circles and use them to frame individual portions of cold savoury food-stuffs.

Ribbon plays its part too in culinary Tying Up. Without it even the best *Charlotte Russe* would be in danger of bulging out and eventually subsiding in a very warm room. Use the narrowest possible baby ribbon and as soon as you have unmoulded your *Charlotte* on to its dish, tie it very neatly around the midriff and finish with a tiny bow.

**Bread dough** ties up most impressively too—

at the stage after proving, when it is scaled off for large or small items, and **before** the last proving, which precedes egg-washing and baking.

bread
knots and
plaits

For individual bread rolls there are two exceptionally attractive easy ones— **knots** and **plaits.** For the **knots,** roll out pieces of dough into long thin sausages, about the thickness of chipolatas. Cut into 8-9 inch lengths. Tie each into a single knot so that the knot is central and the two ends are as nearly equal as possible. Prove, egg-wash and bake.

bread
plait

For the **plaits** just roll out three chipolata-thick sausage strips. Nip them together at one end—or get someone to hang on—while you plait the three together, pulling a little as you do so to ensure the plait does not get too thick. Lop this plait off into suitable lengths ($2\frac{1}{2}$ inch to $3\frac{1}{2}$ inch), prove, egg-wash and bake.

For **big plaits,** unless you are to go quite hairless with frustration, you must follow the diagram, p. 390.

Roll out a $\frac{1}{4}$ inch to $\frac{1}{2}$ inch thick rectangle of dough about 6 inch wide and 14 inch long. Divide it lengthwise into 5 equal strips, making sure you leave one end—the one furthest away from you on the table—**still in one uncut piece.** Then study the diagram, and sail ahead serenely, according to the following directions.

Space your cut panel out so that it is the same as

the diagram. Now put 2 over 3, then 5 over 2 and 1 over 3. Repeat this until the end is reached, remembering that after the very first move the strips do not retain their initial numbers, but are numbered left to right as they appear at the time of making each move. Be patient with it the first time you try because it is the most effective of all the plaits, three-sided, triangular and absolutely symmetrical. By the way, this plait, used with $\frac{1}{4}$ inch strips of pastry on top of pastry "lids", is wildly effective and makes a large home-baked item look extremely clever and professional.

larding and barding

In its widest culinary sense you also "tie" with raw, unsalted pork fat cut into panels or strips, although in some cases you use fine, strong string as well to secure it. The two most classical uses are for **larding** and **barding,** but before we explain these operations, let us examine the purpose of these exercises. By either larding or barding, dry flesh is lubricated with pork fat during cooking. For both, the pork fat is cut from the rind in $\frac{1}{8}$-$\frac{1}{4}$ inch thick slices and then either cut into pieces which are wrapped over or around the meat, game or poultry—this is barding; or else the slices are cut into $\frac{1}{4}$ inch strips which are pressed into the groove of a larding needle (stockists, page 368) and darned through the flesh—this, as you may guess, is larding.

Dry birds should be barded. After stuffing (if desired) and trussing the bird cover the

whole of the upper part of the bird with a
thin, neatly trimmed strip of unsalted pork fat
and tie this on very securely with fine
string. Birds which cry out for this treatment include grouse, pheasant, guinea fowl,
partridge, capercailzie, peahen and ptarm-
igan. If you think about it for a moment, you
will accept that no one in their senses would
add fat to such fatty subjects as duck or goose;
and a fatty chicken does not qualify either
because if you wanted to cover it with any
kind of fat, you would use its own, pulled from
its innards.

Larding is more complicated—in one sense
only—you **must** have a larding needle to do
the job. Once you have one, the whole thing
becomes perfectly simple. Press a strip of
prepared pork fat into the needle's groove,
drive it through the meat, hang on to the bit
which protrudes at the point of the needle
and then withdraw the needle. This leaves
the fat threaded through with the ends protruding at either side. Snip these off neatly to
within $\frac{1}{4}$ inch of the flesh—and do not waste
the bits. Snip them up finely and fry them in
a dry pan—frizzle them in fact, and when
they are crisp, stir them into a handful or
two of hair-thin garlic crusts and add the lot
to a green salad.

Alternatively, you can put the snippets into a
dry baking tin, let them ooze out their fat in
a very slow oven, gas 1 (290°F) and use this
fat as a basis for *roux* instead of using butter;
OR as the covering to a *pâté*. Indeed in short
lengths the strips can be layered with pre-

pared *pâté* mixture in a *terrine* as well as dissolved and poured over the top after cooking and before chilling.

On page 379 you will see a diagram of how to bard poultry or game with strips of raw, unsalted, pork fat, and the position of string for tying securely into place. Also on page 379 is a diagram showing how to bard and tie-up slices of batted beef for *paupiettes de veau*. Barding is used for a whole fillet of beef which is marinaded and baked in paste to serve as *filet de boeuf feuil.lété*.

trussing   **Trussing** can be a headache too, so we have added a diagram for that showing how the job can be done with one simple tie from a single length of string and one wooden or metal skewer. Incidentally we find that it is much easier and neater to use a pointed wooden skewer than the blunt ended ones beloved by poulterers. To obtain our desired sharp points we thrust the ends into a pencil sharpener, churn away and drive in easily.

Next time you put up an assortment of *bouquets garnis** or faggots of herbs, make sure you tie the little muslin bags up properly. By this we mean with a long loop on each secured bag so that this can be looped over the handle of a saucepan or stock-pot and thus save all that fishing about to find the wretched thing.

ballottines   **Ballottines** present problems too, for even if these are inner-wrapped with butter papers (as they must be) and then outer-wrapped with kitchen foil (which is the modern,

165

simplified method) they should still be tied—
every 4 inch along the roll. Wrap the prepared **ballottine** in its papers, enclose it in
foil and roll it up. Fold in the ends like a
parcel, corners to centre triangle-wise, point
brought upwards and then pass thin, strong
string around the length, top and bottom,
and tie off securely. Then you can interlock
your banding strings and after poaching or
steaming, snip one end and slide the lot off
easily.

At this point we will only give you the definition of a modest **ballottine** such as a
Sociable Cook would embark upon for an
exceptional meal when she is able to obtain
a boned bird of any kind from her poulterer.
In simple terms the boneless carcass of a bird
is stuffed, while raw, with fillings ranging
from the simplest *pâté maison* to *pâté de foie
gras truffé* which latter is interspersed with
lambs' tongues, kidneys, breast pieces of fowl
and innumerable other varieties of extravagant tit-bits. When filled the embryo **ballottine** is rolled into the shape of a whole slender
*mortadella* such as you can see in any good
*charcuterie* shop and then tied as already
explained.

Nowhere is there more crying need for
expertise among the public than in the field
of domestic butchery. The standard of the
average meat cutting in butchers' shops
throughout Great Britain is deplorably low.
Here and there you can winkle out some
elderly man who is a master at his trade but

in the main they do not know a *tournedos* from a toadstool, have never heard of a *noisette*, are quite incapable of cutting an *escalope* of veal, while the porcupined objects they falsely call Crown Roasts are a crying disgrace.

crown roast

So let us go over a few of these things together so that we are independent of their mal-practices, beginning with a **Crown Roast.** For it you will need to select 2 best-end necks of lamb. You must go to the shop, you must see them and you must insist on the main bone that holds the eyes of the cutlets together being chopped into neatly, at intervals, so that you can take each piece and curve it round into a half circle. Understand first that this bone holds the piece rigid. When you have checked this, check that the bone tips at the opposite ends to the eyes of meat are even. If they are not, insist that all are chopped level with the shortest; other-wise you will have a cockeyed crown with tips that lurch up and down tipsily.

When you get home, find some strong, fine string and a small, sharp knife. Stand each piece upright with the eye-end on the table and pare down between the bones cutting away all skin and scraps of flesh to within 1 inch of where the actual eyes of meat begin. This makes each bone stand clear of its neighbour, diagrams pages 380 and 381.

Then snip off the tips so that each one forms a small "vee" because if they are broad and blunt, you will not be able to get the cutlet frills on, or the stuffed olives or anything else!

167

Now put both pieces down on the table with the fatty sides uppermost and the lean, convex sides underneath. You will see that the fatty upper surface wears an overcoat of skin on each one. Pare this away thinly at whichever corner you like of each piece and when you have pared back enough to get a good purchase, pull slowly and steadily towards you and the skin will come cleanly away. If what lies underneath has too great a depth of fat, trim some of it off. This is a matter which is governed purely by personal preference.

At this point it is a help if you can have someone with you but it can be done alone. Stand the two pieces upright and back to back with the fatty sides inside. Curve them both out until they form the crown. Then thread a large trussing needle (page 370) with fine string and drive it through the inner side of the first bone just above the eye of the cutlet. Continue through the opposite piece in the same way and then draw the two ends together and tie them in a double strong knot, thus securing the two best end necks together. Cut off the string ends.

Now do exactly the same on the opposite side with a long piece of string about a yard and a half because this time you will need the long ends. When the string is threaded through the two cutlet bones as described for the other side, draw the two ends of string level, make strong knots and pass the string right round what is now the waist of the crown. It is now completed, awaiting whatever kind of stuffing you choose to push down into the centre to hold the crown in shape during baking time and to make the meat go further.

Stand the crown in a baking tin. Cover the top of the bones with a small circle of kitchen foil to prevent them blackening in the oven. Bake at gas 6 (400°F) middle shelf, for 1 hour, if you like lamb slightly underdone, and 1 hour 15 minutes, if you prefer it well done.

When removed from the oven and set on a dish, stab the cutlet bone tips alternately with one maraschino cherry (page 368), or one stuffed olive, or you can just use cutlet frills.

If you study the diagram on page 381, you will see two dots showing where the needle goes through for tying the two halves of the crown together and how the string ties round the waist of the crown thereafter. Please note the little ledged cuts at the base of each bone tip showing how this separates each one from its neighbour and leaves them standing free.

selle
d'agneau
bridée

Some extraordinary things are done to a saddle of lamb, **Selle d'Agneau Bridée,** but none of them includes what is always done by a good French butcher—what we refer to as the "holding in" process. The sides of the saddle should be brought in and drawn tightly underneath the simple caging of fine trussing string. Otherwise it tends to be sprawling for the carver and disorderly on the plate.

Study the diagram on page 380. Make the numbered figure 1 to 7 ties first. These are the ones that bring in the saddle rim to base centre. For the actual tying make a small loop in each length of string, bring this round the meat as in diagram, thread the string end through the loop end, draw it together tightly and thread under the string and through to form a second reverse loop, the one which holds it securely.

Continue doing this looping, tightening and tying in each of the diagram's 1 to 7 positions. Then follow the same process from position A straight down the length of the beast as drawn and exactly the same round the other side until you bring the string back to   A where you tie it off in a knot as shown. Repeat at B all the way round too and the job is done.

Then put the saddle in a baking tin and bake at gas 5 (380°F) uncovered so that the outer skin becomes crisp.

pot-au-feu  The beef for a **Pot-au-Feu** (page 100) should not loll about in the pot like an exhausted schoolgirl. You are going to cut it up eventually so it too must be neatly tied. Turn to the diagram on page 379 and tie exactly   as shown, starting with the string marked A which goes round the meat centrally and is tied up tightly when it has encircled the piece completely. Then tie the B string next, looping and pulling exactly as explained for *Selle d'Agneau* above. Do C next and finish with D remembering that after having tied A, you loop and tighten B, C and D at all string intersections.

If for some extraordinary reason we need *paupiettes* of beef or any other meat that we have not time to do ourselves, we have to do without or go to London to obtain them, for there is no butcher in our village who does them properly, yet they are easy enough! Cut thin, 4 inch by 6 inch rectangular slices of heavily batted, raw beef. Lay these over matching rectangles of thin, raw, unsalted pork fat. Spread the raw beef with stuffing and then roll each one up and tie it with string as shown in the diagram for

paupiettes de boeuf

**Paupiettes de Boeuf** (page 379).

To cook 6, fry a teacupful of diced pork fat trimmings in a copper *cocotte* or earthenware casserole. While this is melting, roll the *paupiettes* in seasoned flour. When the fat is melted and angry-hot, sear the *paupiettes* therein, turning them round with a pair of metal lifting tongs. Toss in a teacupful of chopped carrots, the same of onions and a *bouquet garni*\*. Moisten with 1 breakfastcupful of stock or Beaujolais and cook at gas 4 (355°F) for approximately 1 hour 25 minutes under a lid.

When tender lift out the *paupiettes*, sever the strings, arrange on a dish and border with the strained vegetables. Thicken the pot liquor with a nut or two of butter worked into flour and reduce slightly by simmering. Taste, correct the seasoning and pour over the contents of the dish.

vegetable marrows

**Vegetable marrows** should be tied into cages of string made on the already explained, loop-knot principle as used for *Selle d'Agneau Bridée*, with an additional large loop at one end of each, so that they can be hung in a slightly draughty place. This way they keep marvellously. It is a good idea to seal the cut ends with a bit of sealing wax.

melons

Just in case some of you may be keen gardeners with glasshouses may we pass on a tip about **melons.** We have caged all ours extremely successfully this year by putting them in hairnets and looping these on the cross-bars of their supports. Admittedly these little inverted balloon shapes of pink and blue mesh-net look a bit odd in the hothouse but the melons are very happy. Which—*en passant* we must add, for the benefit of anyone who found a recent shopping list of Fanny's— explains the surprising entry—"hairnets for melons and me."

If you should be as foolish as we have been for years, you will go to endless trouble and frequently make a drippy mess all over the place tying straining bags to hooks or cross bars and putting basins underneath to stop the drips. We put up an infinite variety of jellies, and make a great many cheeses, so with reckless abandon we have bought a real jelly bag (cone-shaped and with 4 loops). With this goes a slim metal stand. You merely hook the loops over the four tips of the stand, slip the basin underneath and forget the whole thing until the next morning. We never cease to bless this gadget (page 368).

172

A RADIATION PRODUCT

# The New World 51 gas cooker adds spice to your cooking!

Good cooks use good cookers—and the New World 51 is an outstandingly good cooker—to put it mildly. The 51 gives you automatic ignition throughout, the unique Sola grill, optional glass door panel and oven timer. See it at your Gas Showrooms.

RADIATION NEW WORLD LIMITED · RADIATION HOUSE · NORTH CIRCULAR ROAD · LONDON NW10

# Plucked, hung, drawn and quartered

| | |
|---|---|
| Sausage and Bacon Casserole | Spaghetti Pie |
| Alabama Gammon | Country Parson |
| Brisket and Bean Pot | Poulet Marengo |
| Duck, Pigeon, Partridge, Grouse or Pheasant Pies | Poussin Florida |
| Terrine | Poussin Coronet |
| Meat, Poultry or Game Mayonnaise Slices | Faisan Souvaroff |
| Chicken-in-a-Mountain | Croûte Lucullus |
| Poulet Fondue | Filet de Boeuf |
| Poulet aux Oranges | Pork Spare Ribs |
| Ossi Bucchi | La Fondue Bourguignonne |
| | Mustard Sauce |
| | English Cumberland Sauce |

*Question: Like so many Englishwomen, I am far better at making cakes and puddings than I am at main course dishes. These tend by comparison to be rather dull. I need inspiration. Can you please help?*

*Answer:*

If a lot more home cooks took stock, they would find that your very honest self-analysis would apply to them too. Indeed, though we are dotty about all kinds of cookery, Fanny (who never eats them) adores making puddings and cakes and Johnnie (who eats too much of what he bakes) is a baking and pastrywork addict!

Main course dishes are a headache to the busy Sociable Cook. The plain fact is that only the professional, cooking professionally, can surmount the home cook's main difficulty—being at the table when the main course is served.

Twice-cooked meat (with few exceptions) is an abomination. Accurate timing is one of the three keys to professionalism (the others are buying and the making of a proper menu). And it is not all that easy for the average, untrained cook to arrive at the right dishes and the right ways of cooking them so as to eliminate dashings-about, dishings-up and finishings-off if not actual watching and doing, in the period covering the service of a previous course, or as the family sits waiting expectantly, hands poised over knives and forks.

basic
approach
to casseroles

To understand the position, whether dealing with plucked, hung, drawn or quartered items, we must first eliminate the dishes which **do** re-heat successfully, and, as we said in the Cook's Book, those which actually improve with re-heating. There are the two closely-related oven cooking methods—*en salmi* and *en casserole*—which we consider to be practically twin. But let us profit by a poor reader's recent question as to whether or not she should use her "flour and water paste" for "coating the meat to be fried for a casserole", either before or after frying! The succinct reply to that one (softened off a bit in the delivery!) was NEVER. There is NO room for flour and water paste inclusion in any casserole or salmi, or we shall find ourselves right back with those nauseous ponds— stews which are an abomination. Let us go over it once more so that we all understand fully what we are talking about.

For either salmis or casseroles (there are no "stews" in our repertoire) the flesh of what-ever-it-is, is first turned in flour, or seasoned flour*, and then "stiffened", by brisk frying in a shallow pan containing dice of raw un-salted pork fat, or carefully cleaned fresh (not vintage) dripping (we once found a bluebottle in the ninth layer down of a friend's "dripping jar" of extremely uncertain age!) or poultry or game fat, or just butter and oil used together, rather than butter alone. This tends to blacken during quick frying. The oil stops the "blackening". This must be done as a matter of pure routine.

If the flesh is not "stiffened" by frying, the juices will all purge themselves out into the liquids in the casserole or salmi pot.

If seasoned flour or just flour is used beforehand, this automatically adds the very necessary thickening agent and no one will need recourse to using any of those disagreeable packaged substitutes because the liquor is too thin after cooking.

Of course you must also know what to do if, for some reason or other, you have used too much fluid or a too thin flour coating. Just dissolve a teaspoonful or two of *fécule de pomme* in cold water, stock or wine and stir it briskly into the bubbling mixture. This thickens, clears and leaves no trace of itself behind in floury flavour. The hallmark of a fifth-rate *roux*-based sauce is that naughty back-taste of flour which has been insufficiently cooked out at the *roux* stage. We mention *roux* here because you can fry your chosen flesh without a flour overcoat, make a *roux*-based sauce* from the liquids given in a casserole or salmi recipe and pour **this** over the contents in your pot **before** cooking if you prefer. We offer you both to choose from, though with us, the seasoned flour method wins every time.

It is equally easy for the home-cook nowadays to know the precise moment to stop cooking her meat whether by roasting or boiling. Thanks to a splendid and very reliable modern meat thermometer (page 367) which you just prod into the cooking meat, you can read what the dial registers and settle for rare, medium or well-done according to your tastes.

Boiling is beastly, in terms of stews, vegetables and fruits; but there are certain things . . . For example, nothing becomes an English table better than a really good, rolled, boned **Salted Silverside,** provided this is not purged in the cooking. The water containing the onions, carrots (turnips are mere make-weights and have such a poor taste, the tops are much better!) parsley stalks and (when possible) a wisp or two of fresh fragrant hay, must be brought to the boil before the meat is immersed, "sealed". This sealing method ensures that **all** the meat's flavour is not in the liquor. Then you merely simmer away gently under a lid until your meat thermometer registers "boiled beef cooked."

There is no need to fuss about the dumplings either—we will give you two kinds (page 182 and 183). If you calculate wrongly and they and the meat are cooked before you want to dish up and serve, they will not become bullets by being kept at the gentle "shiver." This is just one stage below "simmer."

Do not achieve this admirable dish to perfection and then ruin the whole thing in the service. Lift out the meat. Drain the vegetables, put them in a covered container and keep them hot with the **soup,** not flat meat plates. Pour off a big family jugful of the liquor, holding back enough to cover a large meat baking tin to a depth of $\frac{1}{2}$ inch. Carve the meat and put each slice as it is carved into the hot liquor, standing the pan over a mere thread of heat or in the oven at gas $\frac{1}{4}$ (240°F). Only thus do you ensure everyone in a large gathering gets a piping hot serving. And do not forget the mustard, English mustard. French mustard is all very well for some French dishes but it is totally unsuited to British boiled or roast beef.

If you think we have spent rather a long time on such a simple dish, let us remind you that any really experienced chef will nod away like a mandarin if he hears you utter the greatest culinary truism, "It is far harder to cook a simple dish to perfection than an elaborate one." Indeed we say that if a cook can serve the following plain meal, he or she will undoubtedly be very good indeed: *Consommé double en Tasse* (this must be piping hot and sticky on the lips if you smack them together vulgarly), grilled lamb cutlets which are pink in the middle, neat in the "eye" and slim and trim down the bone, baby Brussels sprouts without a trace of toughness or horrid bath sponge texture, and a transparently thin suite of unblistered, pale golden pancakes with properly cut lemon and a bowl of soft brown, not white, sugar.

Let us go back to our boilings for a moment.

As yet we have said nothing of another boiled item **Boiled Mutton,** which saves us from having to talk about Mint Sauce, the malt concoction which successfully slays all the delicate flavour of a fine roast of prime English Southdown lamb.

Treat the mutton exactly as the beef adding a dessertspoonful of salt to strained lamb stock instead of water and cooking with small shallots added **50 minutes** before serving, with as many baby carrots as you can get into the liquor **30 minutes** before cooking time is over.

As soon as the lamb is a-boiling start the **Onion Sauce.** Rough cut 1½-2 lb. onions and **boil them too** with a level teaspoonful of salt in the water and only a sufficiency of water, not a miniature lake. When tender, strain and chop up while you re-simmer the liquor to a mere ¼ pint.

Add ½ pint milk and keep hot while you dissolve 1½ oz. of butter in a sauce saucepan, stir in 1½ oz. flour to make the *roux*, remembering to cook and stir for at least 2 minutes to cook out the flour taste. Add the milk mixture gradually, beating well between each addition, finally add ¼ pint top-of-the-milk or single cream, stir in the chopped-up onions, correct the seasoning to taste with milled black peppercorns and if you want to charm your guests and make them curious, stir in one *demi sel* until dissolved and merged, or two *petit Suisse* cheeses.

Pour sauce over the lamb on a heated dish

and surround with the carrots and shallots, or, as we prefer to do, carve the lamb in the kitchen on to a heated dish, then pour sauce over all, border with vegetables and send to table for easy service.

boiled fowl with onion sauce

Now be daring and give an old **Boiling Fowl** the same onion sauce and vegetable treatment; but **please** rip off and discard that alpine-combinations-textured old skin before dishing up! Only young roasted poultry or game skins should be allowed access to the dining room.

semolina dumplings

Whichever you decide to serve, give them dumplings, which are such a great help in making main course dishes go further. Ham loves them and so of course does gammon. Boiled beef is desolate without them and they can be relied upon to do a lot for oxtail. When reduced to a quarter of their normal size they will transform bowls of family soup into filling supper items. In Norfolk they are made with yeast. Unless you are Norfolk born and bred to them, they can be tricky to do. But the **Austrian** ones with semolina are easy.

Heat 1 pint of milk. Shake on 3 oz. fine semolina as the milk boils and stir over moderate heat until very thick and smooth. Remove from the heat and beat in 2 egg yolks. Season to taste with salt and pepper. Allow to cool. If using for soup, put the mixture into an icing bag with a plain ¼ inch diameter writing pipe and with the aid of a knife dipped in cold water, pipe out and lop

off little "corks" into the simmering soup.
As the last one rises to the top of the soup,
turn off the heat and leave for 1 minute before
serving.

If using as a side dish drop larger blobs with
a dessertspoon into simmering liquid—either
stock (which is better) or water (which
will do)—and let them simmer and rise up.

breadcrumb dumplings Excellent too are **Breadcrumb Dumplings**
made by creaming 1 oz. of butter and then
adding $\frac{3}{4}$ oz. flour and 1 egg with a level
eggspoonful of salt and a generous grate of
nutmeg. Then work these up to a paste by
hand-beating in 4 oz. of fine soft brown or
white breadcrumbs. Cover and leave for 1
hour. Shape into medium-sized dumplings
and slide them into either boiling salted
water or stock. These need only between 8
and 11 minutes depending on how you
interpret "medium-sized."

We offer you the breadcrumb and not the
standard suet dumplings, because these can
be found in almost every British cook book.
But do remember there are some very accept-
able variants on the two we have given.
Semolina dumplings welcome a tablespoonful
of freshly milled parsley in their depths: or
they will make no complaint at being
offered sage when intended for serving with
pork or duck. They can, too, be given tara-
gon when accompanying a boiled chicken.

Breadcrumb dumplings take very kindly to
a couple of finely diced rashers of streaky
bacon — fried before blending into the

mixture—and they too respond to the herb treatments suggested above. Alternatively you can add raw, grated onion to the semolina ones: indeed you can go further and fold in the very finely scraped-to-pulp liver of a fowl and the onions as well—but not to the breadcrumb dumplings, as this variety does not poach for long enough to cook the onion properly. Even so, taken all round, these recipes are reasonably versatile!

Now for one of the best ways in the world of
boiling ham or gammon **Boiling a Ham or Gammon.** For baked Gammon see page 201.

Give your chosen piece a thorough soaking. Use pork-bone stock this time and to one gallon add either 1 pint of cider or light ale. Add 2 dozen well-soaked dried prunes and 2 dozen well soaked dried apricots, a wisp of hay (when possible), a few parsley stalks, plus a dozen peppercorns and a couple of outside celery stalks.

When the ham (or gammon) is done—the meat thermometer will tell you—skin it, keep it warm and reduce the liquor by simmering down to 1 quart. Of course it stands to reason you will have to by-pass this part if your liquor is salty due to the fact that you have under-soaked the ham.

Assuming all is well, add the strained juice of 2 large oranges and the grated rind of one, thicken the liquor with *fécule de pomme* (page 367) as explained on page 178, and "finish" with a tablespoonful of cooking-standard brandy. Pour enough of this sauce over the ham to "glaze" it. Serve the rest in a big bowl with ladle. Surround the meat with the apricots and prunes (now stoned) and serve with a big dish of Creamed Swedes (steamed swedes, sieved or emulsified to a *purée* then ridged up with a fork into a jelly mould shape and topped with peppery cream).

Before we leave Good Boiling (really simmering) as opposed to Bad Boiling, we will answer a whole raft of requests with a recipe for **Tête de Veau Vinaigrette.** This is, of course, a classic and as such must be treated with the care and respect it deserves.

tête de
veau
vinaigrette

Remove tongue and brains from a calf's head and set aside the brains. Wash the head and tongue thoroughly under running water, place in a *blanc\** and keep just simmering for long enough to make the flesh and tongue tender. Wash and plunge into cold water. Keep the liquor. Cut away the meat carefully and slice up neatly keeping hot while you do so. Skin and slice the tongue separately.

Meanwhile you will have soaked the brains in cold water until they are quite white after removing the membranes. Drain, wipe and place in a pan with stock or *court bouillon\** to cover well. Bring to the boil, skim and simmer for 30 minutes. Please bear in mind that **longer** cooking merely hardens them.

Arrange the calf's head pieces in the centre of a large dish. Surround with alternate slices of tongue and collops of brains, interspersed with small neat sprigs of parsley. Having got thus far you should serve in a three panelled dish (or three small ones) capers, finely chopped raw onion and finely milled parsley.

sauce à
l'huile

Finally, in a sauceboat you put a **Sauce à l'Huile** which is achieved by working up 3 fl. oz. wine vinegar with 6 fl. oz. olive oil and 2 fl. oz. of the calf's head cooking liquor, or *blanc* well seasoned with salt and pepper. With this dish you hand plain, steamed, skinned potatoes and plenty of French bread.

oxtail

Now let us have a look at the casserole situation. Johnnie would (almost) leave home for a good potful of **Oxtail.** We always order two—which even the most ornery butcher will joint for you. Anyway, the job is easy enough to do at home provided you possess a proper chopping block and a proper chopper. We went to Switzerland for our chopper and a charming acquaintance gave us a very grand housewarming present when we moved here, a chopping block made from a three-hundred-year-old tree which he had sawn down for our treasure. Should you encounter such a character tell him you want oak, ash, beech, walnut, birch, elm or maple. It is not much use expecting a soft wood like larch, spruce or deal to stand up to consistent bashing.

Having jointed the oxtail one way or the other, follow the method explained on page 177 using 2 tails, 1½ lb. diced, raw carrots,

2 lb. diced raw onions, ½ pint of coarse red wine, a *bouquet garni** and a few drops of Worcestershire sauce. We also slip in a couple of crushed garlic cloves but this is not classic and can of course be omitted.

When the meat is fried, and packed into a roomy earthenware pot in alternate layers with the vegetables, cover (meanly) with beef stock or stock and Beaujolais and cook under a lid and at gas 2 (310°F) for hours and hours—until the meat is sufficiently tender to collapse from the bone. Now let the whole thing chill because oxtails throw a great deal of fat and the dish is enormously improved if you first skim away the surplus and then re-heat at gas 2 (310°F). again.

Flemish
beef
casserole

As easy, and as much a take-care-of-itself recipe is ours for **Flemish Beef Casserole.** Use 3 lb. stewing steak cut into 2 inch by 3 inch rectangles; 1¼ lb. large onions cut into 8 pieces, 1½ lb. tight, white cabbage cut into 12 hunky pieces, 3-4 peeled crushed garlic cloves, a *bouquet garni** or faggot of herbs, a largish thin strip of lemon peel, ½ pint of beer bulked up with sufficient beef stock to cover the contents of the pot scantly, and 6 oz. diced, raw, unsalted pork fat. The only deviation from the standard method here is that you dissolve the pork fat over a low heat until it crisps and shrivels. Discard the shrivels. Then follow standard casserole procedures (page 177) with the given ingredients. Cover and cook for 30 minutes at gas 6 (400°F). Reduce to gas 2 (310°F), and continue until meat and vegetables are completely tender.

Of course if you happen to possess one of those hefty iron pots beloved by the French, you can have a fling in the casserole field with **Boeuf Beaujolais.** This is not a cheap dish, for you really should use a middle cut of fillet weighing about 3 lb.

boeuf
beaujolais

What you then do is simple enough. You put the pot over a lowish heat and leave it there—bone dry until it is almost white with fury at such treatment. Then you put in the fillet which provokes a nice spate of rude hissing and swearing. This searing must be done all round the meat which you handle in the pot with a pair of those sensible spade and claw metal lifting tongs. Turn and turn again.

When a nice crust has been seared around all the beef's outsides, pour in a bottle of Beaujolais. You can then add 2 dozen very small shallots alone or give them ½ lb. of small button mushrooms to keep them company (unstalked and of course unskinned!) and certainly at least one crushed garlic clove, and a seasoning of salt and black pepper, with a sprig each of marjoram and thyme or a *bouquet garni\**. Clap on the heavy lid, put in the oven at gas 4 (355°F) and cook for ¾ hour—for the people who like their food like lions—or 1 hour for the more temperate, pink-centred beef-devotees.

Drain off the pot liquor, fish out all the bits and pieces and stir the liquor in a thick pan until it bubbles. Stir in little balls of butter thickly rolled in flour—until the sauce is the consistency **you** like. Add a small wineglassful of port, another of brandy, boil up once more and swill over the beef.

Serve this sitting inside a border of onions or onions and mushrooms with, ideally, *Pommes Dauphine*.

Now let us turn our attention to what an old help of ours always referred to as "Hoffal" which is the source of some of the most agreeable main courses in the world.

You can indulge in a little *empressment* in the dining room with beef kidneys if you turn

rognons de boeuf Bercy

them into **Rognons de Boeuf Bercy.** Skin 1-2 kidneys per head, slice them and dissolve enough butter in a thick shallow pan to cover the base. When butter bubbles, slide in the sliced kidneys. Add 2 very finely chopped shallots for every six kidneys and let them stiffen together in the pan over a fairly strong heat. Pour in 5 fl. oz. of dry-ish white wine, and leave them to simmer while you collect the dish of pre-made round or square *croûtons**, which you have left in the oven in a light kitchen foil wrapping. Stir your pan mixture, add 2 scant fl. oz. of beef stock reduced by simmering down 1 pint of it and simmer for a moment or two longer. Lift out the kidney slices and heap them on to the *croûtons*. Add a dessertspoonful of chopped parsley to the sauce in the pan. Bubble up fiercely, pour in 3 fl. oz. double cream, stir fast and pour over the kidney *croûtons*.

If you **are** going to make this in the dining room, comb the recipe beforehand and then assemble everything you will need on a small tray, covering items like raw shallots with a scrap of kitchen foil and set all ready beside your chosen heater.

rognons
feuilleté

This merely leads us on to recollections of a particularly delightful way of cooking whole lamb's kidneys—**Rognons Feuilleté.** Skin them without dividing, wrap each in one piece of No. 3 cut back bacon, roll out home made or bought (page 369) puff paste very thinly, and cut into squares large enough to enclose a prepared kidney apiece. Place one on each square, spoon 1 teaspoonful brandy and the same of double cream, over the top, and add a sprinkling of salt and pepper. Wet the pastry edges, fold up corner over corner, (like old-fashioned apple turnovers), set them on a baking sheet with the folds underneath and brush the tops with salted, raw, beaten egg. Bake, two shelves above centre, in pre-heated over at gas $7\frac{1}{2}$ (435°F) until the pastry is a strong, rich brown.

Done this way the kidney juice seeps into the inner wall of pastry while the outer remains very puffy and crisp. Please remember to put both French and English mustard on the table with these.

escalopes de
ris de veau
Maréchal

There is a dreamy dish with sweetbreads called **Escalopes de Ris de Veau Maréchal** which can safely be made just before a meal. Get everything ready—this assembly is called the *mise en place*—then get dressed and come back to the kitchen in a wrapper if you are scared of your frock, and do the actual cooking. Then slip the dish into the oven at gas $\frac{1}{4}$ (240°F) until 5 minutes before eating. Nip back to do the butter and breadcrumb part and brown them swiftly under the grill. Return them to the oven until required.

You must have the large "double breads" for this dish. **Blanch** them, refresh them in icy water, and flatten them viciously under extremely heavy weights. Then cut them up into neat, small *escalope* of veal shapes, season with salt and pepper, turn them in sifted flour and leave for frying later.

tomato
sauce

Make a good **Tomato Sauce** by putting 1 oz. butter and 1 fl. oz. oil in a thick pan. Let these heat through together, then toss in 1 lb. of skinned, rough-cut tomatoes. Add 1 teaspoonful of juice obtained by grating a bit of raw onion coarsely. Simmer together until the tomatoes are tender. Pour in a wineglassful of sherry and the same of very strongly-reduced stock. Simmer, while tossing in two or three tiny balls of butter thickly worked up to a paste with flour. Stir and simmer until mixture is creamy, rub through a sieve and put into the top of a small double pan over hot water to re-heat when required.

Remember that circle of wetted greaseproof to fit over the top, thus avoiding any crust on top.

Rub a scant teacupful of fine breadcrumbs through a sieve and chop $\frac{1}{4}$ lb. mushrooms finely. When cooking time arrives, put $1\frac{1}{2}$ oz. butter and the same of olive oil into a frying pan. When it bubbles well, slide in the *escalopes* and cook over a moderate heat for 6 minutes on each side (8 minutes if they are thick ones). Lift them out and keep them warm while you fry the mushrooms in butter and oil. When they are cooked (about 3-4 minutes) stir in half the fine crumbs. Taste and correct seasoning with salt and pepper. Heap this on top of the sweetbread *escalopes*, sprinkle with the remaining crumbs, moisten with a little extra melted butter and allow to brown in the oven gas 4 (355°F) or just keep warm at gas $\frac{1}{4}$ (240°F) and brown under a strong grill immediately prior to serving. Hand **Tomato Sauce** separately.

foie de veau à la Piémontaise

The ways of using calves' liver are almost endless. One of the best easy ones is **Foie de Veau à la Piémontaise** and this again is a dish which can be kept warm without deterioration. Cook $\frac{1}{2}$ lb. rice, strain, and arrange in a ring on a heat-resistant dish. Slip into the oven, gas $\frac{1}{4}$ (240°F) under a light covering of kitchen foil. Heat $1\frac{1}{2}$ oz. of butter and $1\frac{1}{2}$ oz. oil in a thick frying pan. Turn 9 oz. very thinly sliced strips of calves' liver in seasoned flour* and fry briskly lifting and turning for ease with a pair of metal tongs. After 3 minutes swill with a liqueur glass of Madeira, or a port glass of white port and add, while stirring, 3-4 fl. oz.

strongly reduced veal or chicken stock. Stir in a coffee cupful of thick cream, taste, re-season if desired and scrape into the hollow centre of the prepared rice border. Replace the foil and return to the cool oven until required.

If you wish to elaborate on this a little, fry the liver pieces until they are cooked. Lift them out into the centre of the rice border. Pour in pan a liqueur glass brandy, step up heat to fullest, allow brandy to ignite and shake violently to keep flames burning for at least 30 seconds. Stop shaking and they will subside. Put them out with a liqueur glassful of Madeira. Add the stock as before, simmer for 4 minutes and stir in 4 tablespoonsful of thick cream. Re-simmer to creamy consistency, stir in a rounded dessertspoonful of chopped, fresh parsley, taste, correct seasoning and pour over liver.

les
allumettes
de boeuf à
la crème

timbale de
rognons à la
crème

escalopes de
veau natur

You can do exactly the same with matchsticks of beef fillet for **Les Allumettes de Boeuf à la Crème** or with veal kidneys for **Timbale de Rognons a la Crème.** But to achieve the simplest and probably the most internationally popular veal dish, **Escalopes de Veau Natur,** you merely require *escalopes* of prime veal, oil and butter. Heat enough butter and olive oil—in equal darts—to cover the bottom of a shallow frying pan. Slide in the thin, well-batted veal *escalopes* as soon as the oil/butter mixture is hot enough to **seal** the natural juices in as the meat impacts. Give about 1 minute, turn over and repeat for 1 minute. Then reduce the heat so that it cooks through more gently. To sustain the strong heat would toughen the meat as it cooks!

When tender, lift out, drain (for the average English taste); cover with the oil/butter mixture (for Latin tastes); sprinkle lightly with salt and pepper and moisten with a few drops of lemon juice, or serve wedges of lemon on the sides.

To make and serve one of these really well, with an accompanying dish of well-cooked *haricots verts*—neither too flabby nor too crisp, but tossed after steaming, in butter, crushed garlic (only a *soupçon*), and with some sliced new potatoes sautéed to a rich crisp brown *à la Lyonnais* with finely chopped onion, is as good a test of a good, careful cook as any more elaborate fal de lal. When all these things are impeccable the result is not easily forgotten.

Once this simple dish has been mastered you can retrace your steps to the point where the meat was "stiffened" on both sides and thereafter pursue a different culinary route ending up with a dish of irresistibly delicious

escalopes de veau à la crème

## Escalopes de Veau à la Crème.

Having completed the "stiffening", step up the heat to immediate full strength, slide in a little cooking-type brandy from the bottle using 2 or more tablespoonsful according to the size of the pan and the number of *escalopes*. Tip pan sideways to ignite brandy and shake away like a mad thing, in an aura of flames. Douse these flames after about half a minute with a good libation of dry white wine—3 fl. oz. dry white to every 2 *escalopes*—simmer up, reduce heat to gentle, stir in the same quantity of thick cream and let the *escalopes* cook through.

Lift them out on to a heated dish and simmer the sauce fairly hard until it is thickly creamy. Then correct the seasoning to taste with salt and pepper, add a generous teaspoonful of freshly chopped parsley, stir, pour over the *escalopes* and, for the final touch, surround with little crescents cut from remainders from a batch of puff pastry work. Egg wash these of course, bake till golden brown, arrange alternately crescent up, crescent down around the dish rim and serve.

escalopes de veau forestière

At this point you can pursue the development theme yet another stage to achieve **Escalopes de Veau Forestière.** Carry on as for the preceding recipe until after the brandy has flamed out the grease and flamed in its flavour. Slide in about 4 oz. of very thinly sliced, unpeeled mushrooms and proceed exactly as before thereafter.

les côtelettes en surprise Erwin Schleyen

One of our splendid stand-bys for single-handed sociability is **Les Côtelettes en Surprise Erwin Schleyen,** named after the great flamboyant character who dreamed them up. They require careful cutting which we shall explain in detail. But if, for some reason or other, you want them done for you then go to Cobbs in Sloane Street— their butchery is impeccable.

Each cutlet should be cut with a double "eye" attached to a single bone which is tapered trimly at the tip to accommodate a speckless white cutlet frill after frying. A fat cut is made centrally on the bone-less side of each "eye". Dig your pointed knife cautiously right through to the bone side and gradually cut a big "mouth". Fill this up with *foie gras* (or substitute) mixed with a few drops each of cream, sherry and brandy. Pipe the filling through a plain $\frac{1}{4}$ inch writing pipe in a nylon icing bag into each "mouth". Seal the filled "mouths" by turning each stuffed cutlet in flour, and then dipping each in strained, beaten, raw egg, finally turning each one in soft breadcrumbs. Pat the crumbs in thoroughly. Rest in refrigeration.

When required use a pair of lifting tongs to place cutlets into slightly smoking hot olive oil in a deep fryer without splashing. Leave for 1 minute, then **turn off the heat** and allow cutlets to cook for an overall 6 minutes in the slowly diminishing oil-heat.

Lift out and arrange in an overlapping crown on a dish centrally filled with a forked-up mound of spinach *purée* with *pommes croquettes** in between the cutlets.

moussaka à
la Turque

Now what about a **Moussaka à la Turque?** So many people have asked for one that we felt we really should include it, more particularly since it uses up cold mutton which is regarded with total disfavour in many households, including our own.

Mince up a good 1¼ lb. of the horrid stuff, being careful to exclude its chill and pallid fat. Split 4 shiny black aubergines (egg plants) lengthwise. Soften 1 oz. butter and 1 oz. oil in a frying pan and fry the split aubergines, cut sides downwards, until the flesh is tender, always cooking over a low heat. Scoop out the flesh, and set aside the skins, Fry 6 very coarsely grated shallots in the same frying pan, adding a little more oil and butter as required. Add 3 medium skinned tomatoes, roughly chopped. When this mixture is tender, taste, correct seasoning with salt and pepper, add a rounded dessertspoonful of milled, fresh parsley, remove from the heat and **mix** with the aubergine pulp, the minced mutton and a little optional crushed garlic. Add 3 fairly well beaten raw eggs. Butter a *charlotte* or *soufflé* mould (approximately 6 inch diameter) liberally. Line out the base and sides with the aubergine skins cut into fairly thick strips, putting shiny sides to wall and base of mould. Fill in the prepared mixture, press down and smooth off. Cover with kitchen foil, stand in an outer pan of hot water and cook on top of the stove or in the oven, gas 4 (355°F) for 45 minutes. Allow to settle in the mould for 1 minute.

Unmould and serve with tomato *coulis*\*. This is a particularly *recherché* way of using up cold mutton left-overs.

Now let us develop the theme and see what we can do with a miscellany of odds and bits, hairy or feathery. Imagine you have a few scraps of cold chicken, some from a dish of *Tête de Veau Vinaigrette* (page 185), a tag end of that confounded mutton and maybe even a bit of calves' liver left from the *Foie de Veau à la Piémontaise* dish. Turn the lot into a

fritot **Fritot.**

Cut meat up into neat small collops, or slices. Jumble them together pell-mell in a basin. Add the strained juice of 1 large lemon, 1 level teaspoonful salt, $\frac{1}{2}$ level teaspoonful black pepper and 1 level tablespoonful chopped, fresh parsley for every 1 lb. of "scraps". Make up a batch of Vegetable Fritter Batter*. Heat your deepfryer, half filled with olive oil and with frying basket inserted. When the oil begins to smoke, dip the pieces of meat into the batter and fry them fast—just giving the batter time to puff up and turn golden but not long enough for anyone to claim you have inflicted that old twice-cooked routine on the meat, game or poultry!

Heap all on a dish, previously covered with a paper d'oyley. Fry several sprigs of parsley in the hot oil and use for garnish. Serve tomato sauce (page 191) or *sauce Béarnaise** or just a *vinaigrette** separately (the one with the herbs in) in a sauce boat.

This same odd collection, cut into cubes this time, can be threaded alternately on to skewers with cooked prawns and pieces of cooked onion in between. The trick is that you do not then grill the skewer loads, you literally tow them gently through slightly smoking hot oil after turning each load in seasoned flour. Serve these humble **Kebabs** on a bed of rice* cooked with a thread of saffron and 3 cloves of garlic in the water and hand tomato sauce page 191 or tomato *coulis** separately.

kebabs

We have given you two sorts of **Coquilles St. Jacques** in the fish chapter, so we thought you might enjoy trying **Coquilles Volaille Mornay.** Use old scallop shells for the job.

coquilles
de volaille
mornay

Make a batch of *pommes duchesse**. Place in a nylon icing bag with a $\frac{1}{4}$ inch crown pipe and pipe thick, decorative borders around each shell to make the tiny "walls" which hold the mixture in. Then just chop up any amount you like of cold cooked chicken, fold this into a thick *sauce Mornay** and fill into the prepared scallop or *coquille* shells. Put a dab of melted butter in the centre of each. Sprinkle with fine crumbs and bake at gas 4 (355°F) as high up as possible in the oven, for just 14 minutes so that the ridges of piped potato get really browned and the crumbed and butter centres bubble and darken properly.

Think about this very simple thing and realise that you can, in fact, have *coquilles* of any cooked meat, game or poultry because this recipe abides by the rules which outlaws twice-cooked flesh. It is only heated through.

Come to that it is one of the best (easy) ways of using up the really mingy ends of that Christmas turkey. It is also a good solution to the problem of unexpected arrivals and not enough family cold-cooked chicken to go round.

Now let us talk about some more really modest, everyday main course dishes. In the main the cheaper the meat the slower the cookery; which is exactly suited to the requirements of busy cooks, who can then get on with other chores while the cooking takes care of itself.

sausage
and bacon
casserole

There is little better, in the Filling Cheap and Good category, than a **Sausage and Bacon Casserole.** Assemble 12 pork sausages, 12 rashers of de-rinded streaky bacon, 12 blanched inner leaves from a tight, white cabbage, ¼ lb. rice, 1 bay leaf, 2 lb. chopped raw onions, salt and pepper to season, stock or milk to cover and 1 or 2 crumbled basil leaves. Wrap each sausage in a bacon rasher and then in a cabbage leaf. Sprinkle the base of a casserole or other heat-resistant pot with ⅓ of the onions, cover with ⅓ of the raw rice, and place 4 of the wrapped sausages on top. Season with salt and pepper, add a pinch of the basil and repeat with two more identical layers. Pour in stock or milk to cover. Put on lid and cook on a shelf well below oven centre at gas 3 (335°F) until the rice has drunk up all the liquids and is swollen and tender.

Gammon is always a good inexpensive buy and provided it is soaked for far longer than the six hours given by some experts (which leaves it very salty!) it is an excellent subject for the family main course dishes.

Alabama gammon

For one of our favourites, **Alabama Gammon** put a piece weighing about 3¾ lb. into a casserole. Pour on ¼ pint of hot cider and sufficient stock or water to cover the meat. Bring to the boil and simmer under a lid (20 minutes to the pound) and add 12 large, well-soaked prunes after the first 40 minutes' cooking time. Remove gammon and prunes after cooking is completed. Skin the gammon and set in a dry meat-baking tin. Then make a paste with 1 egg, 4 oz. soft brown sugar and two heaped tablespoonsful of Oxford Sauce (page 258). Spread this over the meat. Pour the remaining stock around it. Bake uncovered one shelf above centre at gas 6 (400°F) and baste every 15 minutes for 1 hour.

Stone the prunes, set them around the gammon on a heated dish. Reduce the liquor to 1 pint by simmering, hand this separately and serve young turnip tops and jacket potatoes as accompaniments.

We delight in omnibus recipes, ones which can be made to do duty for several different dishes and just such a one in the inexpensive range is **Brisket and Bean Pot.**

brisket and bean pot

For the basic recipe use one brisket with 2 lb. of chopped, raw onions, 1 lb. soaked, white haricot beans, 2 heaped tablespoonsful paprika powder, 1 *bouquet garni**, 1 heaped tablespoonful concentrated tomato *purée*, some

201

seasoned flour* and stock or stock and red wine. Trim up the brisket, (which is fatty) by cutting away some of the side and central pockets of fat. Put this in a thick frying pan and melt it down slowly. Dredge out the surplus shrivelled bits and make the liquefied fat very hot. Turn the brisket in the seasoned flour and fry it briskly all over.

Now lay it in a casserole over a bed of the onions and beans, leaving enough to make a top layer of them. Tuck in the *bouquet garni*\*. Mix your chosen fluid with the paprika and tomato *purée*, pour over all and bulk up with more stock or stock with red wine until contents are just submerged. Clap on the lid and cook at gas 2 (310°F) until meat is really tender. Drain off the liquid, simmer it down to half its original bulk, return to pot, cover top with layer of soft brown breadcrumbs and cook uncovered on a high oven shelf until crumbs are crisped and brown.

Of course if preferred the brisket can be cut up raw, and then used as explained. But then so can pie veal, stewing steak or rabbit pieces which is what we mean by an omnibus recipe!

In a sense all cut-and-come-again dishes are omnibus. At least we think you will agree when we have explained ourselves a little. Fanny's Mum used to make superb Beefsteak, Kidney and Oyster Pie* and game pies. In hot weather she disapproved of pastry so with the contents cooked "*en salmi*" or casseroled for the Beefsteak Pie, using a

gelatinous stock (pigs' trotters) so that it jelled well, she would turn the cooked mixture into a mould, chill it, unmould and serve in its own jelly with a great bowlful of salads.

duck,
pigeon,
partridge,
grouse or
pheasant
pies

We can develop this theme a little by producing a recipe for **Duck Pie, (Pâté de Canard en Croute)** which can also be employed for **Pigeon, Partridge, Grouse or Pheasant Pies.** It can then join the omnibus ranks, because steamed (without paste) in the oven in an outer pan of hot water, gas 4 (355°F) for $1\frac{1}{4}$-$1\frac{1}{2}$ hours, it turns out as a *terrine!*

This is a family one which used to be taken as a matter of solemn routine on shooting parties in our youth. The only difference is that we have moderated the quantities somewhat ruthlessly.

terrine

Take a plump duck, rip off the skin and cut away any surplus fat. Place skin and fat into a heat-resistant container and melt in the oven at gas 1 (290°F). Strain and discard skin and residue. Cut all the flesh from the duck. Keep the leg meat separate and mix it with 6 oz. lean ham or gammon, 6 oz. lean veal and 9 oz. pork fat. Mince with the liver of the bird. Dice all the remaining flesh and mix with 4 oz. diced lean ham or gammon, the same of pork fat. Place in an earthenware container. Add a rounded teaspoonful of mixed spice and a generous seasoning of salt and pepper. Stir in 4 tablespoonsful of brandy. Leave to marinade for 4 hours. Mix together minced and diced mixtures.

Line a pie dish with thinly rolled French or English Raised Pie Paste (page 83). Press in the prepared duck mixture. Moisten with the melted duck fat. Cover with a pastry "lid" and bake at gas 3 (355°F) for at least 2 hours one shelf below centre or until paste is crisp and a dark biscuit colour.

This pie should be served cold. If we are to give you the traditional garnish, you must stamp out dozens of 1 inch diameter fluted circles with a miniature pastry cutter. Overlap them over the entire surface of the pie "lid"—but you and we will accept that this is optional!—and then bake.

You can also turn good old Russian Salad into a main course dish for hot weather and still omnibus madly because, if you fold in diced meats, game or poultry, you can transform this accompaniment to main dishes into **Meat, Poultry or Game Mayonnaise Slices.**

meat, poultry or game mayonnaise slices

Here is how it is done. Oil a sandwich loaf tin liberally with olive oil. Assemble 2 large cupfuls each of diced cooked potatoes, French or runner beans, carrots and peas. Add 1 large cupful well-drained cooked young turnips, and fold in 1 pint of real mayonnaise*. Stir in at least 1½ cupfuls of your chosen cooked, diced meat, game or poultry and 1 teacupful of top-of-the-milk or single cream. Finally beat in 1 oz. of powdered gelatine dissolved in 4-5 tablespoonsful of wine or water. Stir fast and scrape instantly into the prepared mould. Level off and if it is ridgy because it has begun to set, smooth the top with a knife dipped into boiling water. Refrigerate until needed.

Turn out and cut in slices for eating with green salads and plenty of hot fresh home-made bread (page 335) and butter.

When we were in Italy last year, exploring and as usual not minding our own (culinary) business, we came up with a fascinating, new-to-us way of cooking a chicken. What followed when we reached home was standard practice . . . dump luggage in hall, tear down to kitchen, grab chicken (ordered by postcard) and test immediately. We find anything new irresistible and can never wait a split second to try it! This turned out a winner but before we explain it we emphasise that we have never done it with any other kind of salt than *gros sel*, the real, coarse French kitchen salt, or Maldon Salt (page 368).

Spread out two huge rectangles of turkey-width kitchen foil so that they overlap centrally by about 4 inch. Make a central flat bed of salt about 1 inch deep (about 3 cupfuls). Put the perfectly dry, stuffed or unstuffed chicken on this salt bed. Pull up the foil sides and nip in the corners to make a high wall all the way round and embrace this with arms outstretched—it is an inelegant position but necessary—while someone else

205

pours in cupfuls of salt until the chicken is completely buried in it. Wrap up tightly like a bundle. Put on a flat baking sheet in a pre-heated oven at gas 9 (470°F) and leave for 1½ hours for a 3½ lb. bird. Thus **Chicken-in-a-Mountain.**

chicken-in-a-mountain

When you unwrap that bundle, you will find the salt has crusted which enables you to break it away easily. Lift out the bird and go over it with a pastry brush to flick off any little clinging grains. Think what this kind of cooking means; that every single scrap of flavour and fragrance has been locked in by the salt and as a result the chicken tastes superb. As a vicar's wife remarked with a happy sigh when we told her, "Just right for me to do from the time the church bells start ringing. Then I can nip in to Matins and be back by the time it is ready to dish up."

Incidentally you leave the salt to cool, crumble it down again, store it in a lidded tin and use over and over again, even when it has begun to turn brown!

poulet fondue

Cooked this way a chicken can be turned into a very distinguished item if you just divide it into neat portions, and serve under a sauce as **Poulet Fondue.** The *fondue* sauce is simply made by dissolving 4 oz. of leaf thin Gruyère or Emmenthal in 1½ pints of strong chicken stock. Meanwhile mix 1 rounded teaspoonful of arrowroot or *fécule de pomme* (page 367) with 2 tablespoonsful of inexpensive cooking kirsch, beat in 2 egg yolks and stir carefully into the dissolved cheese and stock. We do this part over an asbestos mat to avoid the mixture coming to the boil and then curdling. When the sauce is thick, season with salt and pepper, and, if liked, stir in 1 or 2 crushed garlic cloves. Pour on to the chicken and provide some crusty bread for mopping up the sauce on each plate.

poulet
aux oranges

Cooked in precisely the same "mountain" style you can swiftly turn a neatly divided fowl into **Poulet aux Oranges.** Boil 1 orange for every two people, simmering away merrily until the oranges are really soft. Meanwhile make $1\frac{1}{2}$ pints of thick basic *sauce velouté** and after seasoning, add grated rind and strained juice of 1 extra orange simmered together until strongly reduced. Pour over chicken portions, set out on a shallow dish and keep warm at gas $\frac{1}{4}$ (240°F) under a loose covering of kitchen foil. Halve the oranges centrally. Flip out the pips. Spread each thickly with French mustard. Cover by patting on a layer of soft brown sugar. Moisten with a few drops of Madeira and brown under a fairly strong grill until the tops have bubbled and browned.
Arrange around the sauced chicken. Here you have something very unusual, for you eat the orange, peel and all!

ossi
bucchi

One of the best family dishes that ever came out of Italy is **Ossi Bucchi,** for which you will need about 3 lb. of knuckle of veal cut into neat 3 inch long pieces by you or your butcher. Turn them in seasoned flour* and fry them briskly in a shallow pan containing 2 oz. butter and 2 oz. of oil, heated together. When they are browned all over, fish them out and pop them in a casserole while you brown 3 large carrots, 1 large onion and 1 small head of celery (all diced small) in the same pan. Tip the vegetables on top of the knuckles. Add ½ pint of fresh tomato *purée*, ¼ pint chianti and a large ladleful of stock. Cook until tender under a lid for 1½ to 2 hours at gas 4 (355°F). After the first hour add a leaf of lemon peel, a crushed garlic clove and a level teaspoonful of chopped basil and parsley. Serve in soup plates.

spaghetti pie

Then there is a vastly filling **Spaghetti Pie,** which we can best describe as a sort of poor man's *lasagne verde*. Rare for us, it used two tins: a small one of concentrated tomato soup and a small one of spinach *purée*.

First cook and strain ¾ lb. of spaghetti. When it is cool, assemble all the remaining ingredients in a bowl:— 1½ lb. raw minced beef mixed with 1 level dessertspoonful powdered sage, 1 rounded teaspoonful salt, 1 level teaspoonful milled black pepper, 1 breakfastcupful stock and 1 tin tomato soup. Also assemble (separately) some butter and 4½ oz. grated cheese. Butter a large pie dish. Put in ⅓ of the spaghetti, cover with ⅓ of the meat mixture, dot with ⅓ of the spinach, sprinkle with ⅓ of the cheese and repeat twice more until all ingredients are absorbed, finishing

with the third $1\frac{1}{2}$ oz. of grated cheese. Dot
with flakes of butter. Bake at gas 6 (400°F)
for 30 minutes on the middle shelf of the oven.
If desired this pie can be re-heated under a
light covering of foil at gas 1 (290°F). We
have yet to find an occasion when any is left
to re-heat but you may be more fortunate.
Fill any left-overs into pre-made pancakes*,
roll up, lay into a buttered heat-resistant
dish, swill with tomato sauce (page 191) and
heat through under foil at gas 3 (335°F).

country
parson

Even simpler than this family filler is
**Country Parson,** a very old recipe indeed
for using up left-overs of cold game or
poultry. It is really nothing more than a hot
sauce in which the flesh, cut into neat slices,
is warmed through. Begin by dissolving 2 oz.
of goose, duck or other bird fat, then fry
until tender 1 large onion, chopped finely.
Add 2 oz. of flour, stir until the paste is
smooth and thick and then work in 1 teaspoonful of masala paste (page 369) and 1
raw, grated cooking apple. Now begin to
dilute, first with a gill of stock or cider, then
with $\frac{1}{2}$ pint of strong stock, beating until
smooth between each addition. Then work
in $\frac{1}{4}$ pint of sieved, cooked tomatoes or
tomato sauce (page 191). Now go back to
the cider bottle or stock-pot and add more
liquor until a thick sauce consistency is
obtained. Slip in the cooked, left-over flesh
slices, turn them carefully until they are hot,
spread all on a heated dish and border the
edges with triangular *croûtons*\*.

poulet
marengo

This sort of culinary remembering always starts up a chain reaction with us. Thinking how good left over chicken is as **Country Parson,** reminds us of how little used **Poulet Marengo** is today. There have been some odd things said about it and some even odder things done to it in the name of Napoleon's chef Dunand—its creator. It was not really so much a creation as a *force majeure*. Dunand sent out a scavenging party after the Battle of Marengo. They came back with an odd miscellany:— eggs, tomatoes, crayfish and a small chicken—so with these Dunand went to work, making in fact a dish already well known in Paris—*Poulet à la Provençale*—with the crayfish instead of mushrooms.

He divided the fowl, fried it in hot oil in a shallow pan, and as soon as the fowl pieces were browned, he threw in a large chopped onion and ½ pint of white wine and let the panful simmer. Meanwhile he used the tomatoes to make a *coulis**, added this after the wine had reduced to half by simmering, popped in salt and pepper to season, more than one crushed garlic clove (one is enough today), a *bouquet garni** and simmered all under a lid for 20 minutes. This was the moment he added the crayfish (fresh water variety) instead of the small-stalked button mushrooms of the Provençal recipe, having first poached them in a fish *court-bouillon**.

After eating it, Napoleon ordered it to be served to him after every battle. Subsequently Dunand, realising there was no valid reason for the crayfish, withdrew them and put in

the mushrooms instead. Explosion followed
from Napoleon who declared, "This I will
not have, you have ousted the crayfish which
has brought me bad luck; whether you like
it or not they must be returned." You merely
choose which **you** prefer crying "a fig for
Napoleon."

You have no such problems with another
favourite dish of ours, made with *poussins*. The
most straightforward way of explaining this

poussin
Florida

dish—**Poussin Florida**—is to give you the
way for one and leave you to multiply at will.
Fill a spring chicken with *foie gras* or substitute
*pâté*. Dissolve 1 oz. of butter in a thick pan
and when it is hot, fry the *poussin* on both
sides. Pour on 1 gill of veal stock, the strained
juice of 2 crushed tangerine segments (taken
with such care from their skins that these
remain intact with just the "lids" cut off)
and 2 tablespoonsful of Madeira. Cover and
simmer until the *Poussin* is cooked.
Meanwhile boil 2 oz. of rice with a pinch of
saffron, in plenty of fast-bubbling salted
water for 11½ minutes. Drain and stuff into
the empty tangerine skins. Set the cooked
*poussin* on a small dish with a rice-filled
tangerine at one side. Reduce the liquor in
the pan until it is syrupy and pour over the
*poussin* **without scraping the pan.** Lay a
split-lengthwise, peeled banana in the coated
pan, simmer and turn (3 minutes in all).
Arrange these 2 pieces on the empty side of
the bird and heap *pommes pailles* (page 212)
at each end. If you make this dish with a

large *poussin* it is sufficient for two if preceded by a fish course. In which case use 2 rice-filled tangerines, 2 bananas and twice as many *pommes pailles* hair-thin *juliennes* of potato.

poussin
coronet

**Poussin Coronet** is a one portion recipe too if made with one fairly precocious baby bird. Split down the middle from vent to neck to make two equal halves. Heat 2 oz. of butter in a *sauté* pan, brown the two sections. Reduce the heat to a thread, put on the lid and allow to cook until just faintly pink at the bone. Lift on to a lightly buttered dish and keep warm under a light covering of foil. Fry in the pan juices 1 medium onion or 2 small shallots finely chopped. Cook them slowly until they are soft but not browned. Then put in 4 oz. finely sliced mushrooms and 2 whole ones (for garnish). Lay 2 small slices of lean ham on this mixture, press down a little and let the slices warm through before slipping them under the *poussin* halves on their dish. Place a whole cooked mushroom on the top of each half, centrally.

Now finish the sauce. Swill the pan contents with 1 gill strongly reduced stock and stir well. Pour in a sherry-glassful of white Burgundy. Add a heaped teaspoonful of chopped parsley. Correct seasoning with salt and pepper. Simmer for about 1½ more minutes and pour over the top of the *poussin* halves. Sprinkle 1 tablespoonful of grated Gruyère cheese on top, place in the oven gas 2 (310°F) and leave for 8-10 minutes—

this will ensure a nice glazed look on each section. Serve immediately. This is enough for two at a meal of several courses.

Now let us go back to omnibus recipes—an aristocratic one this time generally known as not just **Souvaroff** (that is the professional kitchen designation) but as **Faisan Souvaroff** although it can just as well be made with chicken! This is a very good show-off subject when you are entertaining because there is all the ceremony of cutting away the crust and loosening and lifting the lid to let out the gorgeous aroma. Ideally this should be served in an oval copper casserole but we often use a *pâté terrine* in earthenware with a bird lid.

faisan souvaroff

Classically you must use whole truffles and real *foie gras* but acceptably you may substitute *pâté de foie* type (page 369) and truffle peelings, which are a fraction of the price of whole ones (page 370).

Begin by putting 5 fl. oz. Madeira and 5 fl. oz. strongly reduced white stock into a small pan with 4 rounded tablespoonsful of truffle trimmings or 4-6 whole truffles (!) Simmer for about 3 minutes, strain and strew the truffle item (whichever) into a lidded casserole, copper or not. Cut up 7 oz. *foie gras*, or substitute, into neat dice. Simmer for 1 minute in the Madeira liquor. Drain and add a quarter of the dice to the truffles in the pot. Slip the remainder into a plump pheasant. Wrap up completely in 6-8 rashers of best back bacon and cook gently in the pan under a lid on top of the stove in the liquor used for the truffles.

When the bird has been simmering for 25 minutes, lift it out and set in a *terrine*. Swill with the reserve of liquor, a port-glassful of Madeira and the same of very strong stock or game liquor. Add two tablespoonsful of either brandy or Armagnac and put on the lid. Make a fat sausage of stiff-ish flour and water paste rolled out on floured surface. Place this around the rim of the pot midway between rim and lid so that the edge of join is hermetically sealed. Put immediately into the oven at gas 7 (425°F) and cook for 20-30 minutes depending upon the size of the bird. Remember to back-time the oven process so that you can start it before going in to dinner—allowing time for previous courses.

As you will doubtless have observed by now, this is not exactly the thing for feeding a hungry family. Nor will the next recipe be either, because we did say in our opening chapter that everyone comes down heavily for a touch of grandeur once or twice in a lifetime.

croûte
Lucullus

Have you ever met **Croute Lucullus?** You will need a capon to make it. If you cannot bone the bird yourself **you must get the job done by your poulterer,** but just in case you would like to have a go, here is how to do it.

You **must** have a really sharp, small French kitchen knife, with a very fine point. Begin by loosening the neck skin and starting to roll it back like the top of a stocking, until you meet resistance, which means flesh adhering to bone. Roll back to this and then scrape the knife inwards, **always** pressing downwards against the bone and **always** pulling back the flesh to keep it taut. This way you pare and pare away, rolling back as you advance into the bird. When you reach the wings, chop off their tips or *ailerons*, and then push these inwards as if you were trying to turn them inside out like the thumb of a glove. As you do this pare and pare again. Then go right on rolling back and paring until you reach the legs. Give them the wing treatment, pushing them inside out. Finally pare down to the Parson's Nose. This produces the most sinister final effect of a roll of skin and flesh in what looks a perfect hodge-podge from which you can now detach the whole skeleton, legs, and wing bones attached to carcass. Keep this treasure for the stock-pot.

Unroll the bone-free flesh and push out the legs and wings. Having got them out, tuck in the tips (like a turned-in glove-thumb) until the outer part is level with the main part of the flesh. Fill the inside with a wall of *pâté de foie gras* which you have studded with whole, skinned pistachio nuts. Insert 4 lambs' tongues which have been poached in $\frac{1}{2}$ pint Madeira and $\frac{1}{2}$ pint strong white stock for 10 minutes and then skinned. Fill the cavities with more *foie gras*.

Now line a casserole with puff pastry (page

369) (bought or home made) rolled out fairly thinly. Press in the boned, stuffed capon. Fill in any little gaps with more *pâté* and moisten well with the Madeira and stock liquor simmered down to $\frac{1}{4}$ pint. Add 3 tablespoonsful brandy, and a liberal sprinkling of salt and pepper. Brush the casserole's rim with cold water. Lay on a lid of puff paste. Brush this with *Anglaise\**. Decorate with pastry leaves, brush these too with the *Anglaise* and bake at gas 6 (400°F) until pastry is a good rich brown (minimum $\frac{3}{4}$ hour) one shelf above centre.

Send to table with great pride even if it does mean bread and cheese for a week afterwards!

filet de boeuf

Far, far simpler to make but good enough for the most critical guest is a **Filet de Boeuf** which has been marinaded for 24 hours in a bottle of very dry white wine with 1 very small clove of garlic, 2 medium sliced shallots or 1 large onion, 1 gill oil, a large sprig of thyme and of marjoram, 3 or 4 parsley stalks, a stick of celery and 3 or 4 peppercorns. Turn this at least 4 times during the marinading period, then drain the meat and lay it on a bed made by overlapping rindless No. 3 cut back bacon rashers. Roll it up in these and tie exactly as shown for Saddle of Lamb (page 380).

Scrape the marinade into a saucepan and let it simmer gently. Soften 4 oz. butter in a large oval copper or earthenware casserole. Seal the whole fillet by turning it over in the butter. Put on the lid, put it in the oven and cook at gas 6 (400°F) for 30 minutes. Take out, strain about 2 tablespoonsful of the marinade over the beef, re-cover, return to oven and during the next half hour pour the remaining marinade over at three intervals of $7\frac{1}{2}$ minutes.

Lift out the fillet, cut off the string, remove the bacon and set the meat on a long dish. Keep this warm while you *sauté* 24-36 very small button mushrooms in $2\frac{1}{2}$ oz. cream and $2\frac{1}{2}$ fl. oz. dry white wine for 4 minutes. Then strain this liquid into the remaining marinade in the pan and arrange the mushrooms round the beef. Dissolve $1\frac{1}{2}$ oz. butter in the empty mushroom pan, add $1\frac{1}{2}$ oz. flour and stir to a smooth paste. Add the contents of the marinade pan gradually beating well between each addition. Stir in 3 fl. oz. Madeira and 2 fl. oz. brandy. Correct the seasoning and strain over the meat.

We always like to choose something rather special with which to end a chapter and for this one we have chosen two very sociable and informal dishes—first **Pork Spare Ribs.** Whether you are serving them at a buffet or round the family table, you will need at least a communal finger bowl because **Pork Spare Ribs** must be gnawed in the fingers! Order about 5 lb. of pork spare ribs and either get the butcher to chop them up for you or do the job yourself. Put these in a pan with $1\frac{1}{2}$ pints cold water and 8 tablespoonsful soy sauce (page 370). Add 2 level teaspoonsful

pork
spare ribs

salt. Bring to the boil, cover, reduce to a
steady simmer and maintain for 1 hour
stirring occasionally. Now take off the lid
and slide in 4 heaped teaspoonsful of brown
sugar, raising the heat so that the mixture
bubbles well. Then add 8 tablespoonsful of
sherry, ½ a small can of pineapple pulp, and
6 tablespoonsful of wine vinegar and continue
turning and bubbling for a 2-3 minutes
longer. Reduce the heat to a gentle simmer
and prepare the thickening.

This is made with 3 scant rounded tablespoonsful of arrowroot or *fécule de pomme* into
which you stir ½ pint cold water. Pour quickly
into pan, stir vigorously and continue until
the mixture is thick and clear.

If you want to make this an hour or so in
advance, then just scoop into a casserole,
cover with a lid and place in the oven at
gas ¼ (240°F).

la fondue
Bourgui-
gnonne

Our second special is **La Fondue Bourguignonne,** for which as you will doubtless
know, special fondue pots are sold with little
spirit stoves to heat them from beneath.
You can equally well use one of the heat-
resistant china pans which can be put over
direct heat (page 368).

Into chosen pot or pan put enough heated
oil to half-fill. Assemble a dishful of raw
steak cubes cut to about the size of very
large lumps of sugar allowing about 4 oz. of
raw steak per person. If you have not got the
special fondue forks use metal skewers, they
do very well, but be careful to wrap the ends

in several thicknesses of kitchen foil lest they become too hot for you to hold. You will also need a number of small bowls to contain (i) very finely chopped gherkins, (ii) very finely chopped raw mushrooms, (iii) very finely grated onions, (iv) mayonnaise, (v) mustard sauce, (vi) tomato sauce (page 191) and (vii) *sauce tartare* (page 73).

The routine thereafter is for everyone to grab a fork or skewer, impale a piece of beef, plunge it into the fondue pot, fry it in the hot oil until it is rare, medium or ruined, (overdone) according to their choice and then swirl it round in any one of the mixtures we have suggested, eat and start all over again!

mustard
sauce

You may also like to know how to make the **Mustard Sauce.** Put 3 tablespoonsful of Dijon mustard into a small bowl with 6 tablespoonsful of lightly whipped double cream. Beat well, then cut in the strained juice of $\frac{1}{2}$ a lemon, 1 eggspoonful salt and $\frac{1}{2}$ an eggspoonful pepper. Beat again to make it light and foamy. Now dunking can begin.

English
Cumberland
sauce

But if you want to be a little different you can also serve with very great success a bowl of good old **English Cumberland Sauce** with this dish. This keeps. It is immensely popular with what the children call "cold cuts" and the French "*charcuterie.*" All the prepared ingredients are slung into a pan pell mell, heated through slowly until the jelly is dissolved and the mixture boils.

There is just a bit of preparation which must be done carefully. You need 1 rounded teaspoonful of very finely chopped shallots. Put them in a cup, pour boiling water on top, stir for about 30 seconds and press out the moisture in a tiny sieve. Toss the pulp into the pan. Then cut sufficient rind, **very thinly** from an orange and a lemon to yield 1 table-spoonful of *julienne* from each. *Julienne* is simply the classic name for **hair-thin strips** —no matchsticks please. When cut the strips must be pre-cooked in boiling water for 1 minute. Then strain and toss into the pan with the onions. Add 4 heaped tablespoonsful of redcurrant jelly (your own whenever possible rather than that bought stuff) $\frac{1}{2}$ pint inexpensive cooking port, the strained juice of 1 orange and $\frac{1}{2}$ lemon and a very generous pinch of cayenne and powdered ginger. Thereafter we put our sauce into a lidded bowl suitable for the dining table and, in between meals, keep it in refrigeration.

The English are a shy race. Some of the most fascinating human beings are introverts rather than extroverts. Serving either **Pork Spare Ribs** or **Fondue Bourguignonne** with or without **Cumberland Sauce** is one of the best ice-breakers or culinary relaxers of sensitive nerve-ends that we know.

# Baco Foil
## *makes good cooks better!*

### *— and good food tastier!*

**SAVES FLAVOUR** ★ juicier roasts with no basting—and no extra fat ★ cooks fish without odours in the kitchen ★ makes perfect pudding covers—no cloths, no string

**SAVES FOOD**
★ keeps 'leftovers' moist and tasty ★ stops cheese from going dry ★ packed meals stay fresh overnight

**SAVES CLEANING**
★ stops meat-juices splashing your oven ★ catches oven drips from casseroles and pies ★ a Baco Foil lining avoids messy grill-pans and baking tins

**NEW! Super Baco Foil**
*The pure aluminium foil with the built-in cutter*

NEW **AF50** PROCESS **FOR EXTRA STRENGTH!**

**For more information** *and recipes, write to the Baco Foil Advisory Bureau, Dept. D.T.C., Thorn House, Upper St. Martin's Lane, London W.C.2.*

# *Spice of life*

*Question: You always preach "waste not, want not" and offer us suggestions for using up left-overs of many kinds; but even so there are things which get thrown away! Can you use up left-overs of things like tea, empty halves of oranges and lemons after squeezing or am I being unreasonable?*

*Answer:*

If any item is basically edible, a really experienced cook should know how it can be lifted out of its own context and used in some other way to produce something agreeable to eat. This is one of the most practical and fascinating ways of obtaining variety in cookery—the Spice of a Good Cook's Life in fact. The cry "don't throw that away" rings round our kitchen as we salvage items which students have not yet realised will "come in for something."

Mark you there are pitfalls in this. One youngster who worked with us also worked himself out again on an ineradicable economy-cult which resulted in appalling wastage. It is very easy to do and only discipline in the pursuance of one basic Rule For Cooks can keep it under control. **Inspect everything in your refrigerator every day,** lest the lurking menace of overlooked corners defies economy with verdigris.

It is no mortal use wrapping up hollow citrus fruit cups in foil and tucking them into the refrigerator **to mildew**— or covering bowls of strained, cold tea until they accumulate **moss!** When bowls of stored confectioners' custard\*, *béchamel\**, *velouté\**, fruit and vegetable *purées, et al*, are also overlooked, the situation becomes untenable. If there is a practical use for the item under consideration, and you are not just making something extra to offset wastage, please keep whatever-it-is. But **do not make work** by using ingredients unnecessarily to absorb something else, and then find the results are overmatter which in turn is left to stale or sour!

Provided we understand these things quite clearly, there is a fascinating culinary game to be played on ringing the changes and indeed—also spice of life to enthusiastic cooks —vast opportunities for making something you already know with an entirely unexpected ingredient, which changes its character completely.

A typical example of this is pancakes*. You know how to make them with milk, milk and water or milk and cream. You know that they must be paper-thin and you know how to store them. But do you know that there is a very simple way indeed of producing **Orange Pancakes** with a little tinned or fresh orange juice and, if possible, the grated rind of an orange (which in turn can be used up elsewhere)?

orange
pancakes

Measure off 4 heaped tablespoonsful of flour into a bowl. Break in 1 whole egg and 1 extra egg yolk. Add the grated orange rind and then thin the mixture down to the consistency of single or coffee cream by gradually working in equal quantities of orange juice and water.

You can serve **Orange Pancakes** just flipped over into half circles and laid over-lapping down a long, narrow dish with nothing more exotic than a dusting of sifted icing sugar; but you can do a great many other things with them besides.

stuffed
curd
pancakes

Try **Stuffed Curd Pancakes.** Spread them with orange or lemon curd before rolling them up in cylinders, setting them on a heat-resistant dish and slipping them into the oven at gas $\frac{1}{4}$ (240°F) under a light covering of foil while you make the sauce. You just put a tablespoonful of orange or lemon curd (to every 4 pancakes) into a small saucepan and dilute while stirring over a low heat, with sufficient orange juice to produce a thin pouring consistency. Pour over and serve immediately. (The sauce can be kept waiting before it covers the pancakes of course but not afterwards).

crêpes à l'orange flambées

A third variant **Crêpes à l'Orange Flambées** is a little more elaborate. You allow the thinly peeled skinless segments of 1 medium orange to every 3 portions. Put these in a tiny pan with all the orange juice which accumulates while you are first cutting and then squeezing the "wheel" of inner skin. Heat through, over a bead of light. Stir in a level dessertspoonful of castor sugar to each orange. When melted stir in 1 tablespoonful of orange Curaçao to every 3 portions. Fill the mixture into pancakes. Roll them up, pour a little warmed brandy over the top, set alight and carry flaming to table.

The story of how we invented our chocolate pancakes is the reason why Alison Leach always edits our cookery books. She is the non-cooking, theoretical expert in this household and is always coming up with remarks like, "Why can't you make *choux* paste with coffee for *éclairs* and cream buns?" or "Isn't there a chocolate sauce that you can make and keep for re-heating?" Of course such questions are challenges to us and if we do not know the answers, we set about finding them.

On one such occasion she complained, "Why can't we have chocolate pancakes?" and Fanny replied rather tartly, "Because, dear, the chocolate in the mixture would make the pancakes stick on the pan," and then with a gleam in her eye, "But what about chocolate powder?"

crêpes au chocolat

Within 10 minutes we were eating our first **Crêpes au Chocolat.** All we had done was to extract 1 heaped tablespoonful of flour from the standard 4 and replace it with the same amount of sweetened drinking chocolate. Then we added the standard 1 egg and 1 extra yolk and beat the mixture down with milk to the consistency of thin cream. The resultant chocolate *crêpes* were delicious but you do not want to play any elaborate tricks with them. Either serve them plain with a thick dusting of sifted icing sugar and pour a little cream over each portion or hand

chocolate sauce

**Chocolate Sauce** separately.

Here is how we made the one when Alison challenged us. You put 5 oz. cooking chocolate (*couverture*) or chocolate chips into a small pan. Add 2 level tablespoonsful brown sugar and the same of water. Stir together over gentle heat until all is smoothly blended. Then beat in 2 oz. butter in small flakes. Add 1 teaspoonful of rum and you will be able to reheat any surplus over hot water if you have any left-overs.

Then there is the *choux* paste story which we began by proving not only that *éclairs* and cream buns were easy to make but that there was never any shameful goo in the middle if cook used the right recipe and the right method.* Having established a standard recipe with water, butter, flour and eggs, we

227

began to explore—again egged on by Alison —in order to discover to what extent other fluids could be employed to produce exciting results. It was not long before we saw the enormous potentials in what we have named

pâte à choux au café

**Pâte à Choux au Café.**

Put 1 oz. butter in a small pan with ⅞ths gill of strong black coffee (surplus?) and allow butter to dissolve by the time coffee comes to the boil. Toss in 2½ oz. sifted flour, turn off heat and beat until smooth adding about half-way 1 level eggspoonful of salt. Now beat in 2 whole, raw eggs, singly, beating very thoroughly between each addition. Cover with saucer or plate and leave out of refrigeration until stone cold. Spread a little, neatly into carefully-oiled, individual tartlet cases until the mixture is nearly level with the tins. Brush the tops thickly with raw beaten egg. Sprinkle with flaked almonds and bake at gas 7½ (425°F) for approximately 30 minutes until risen and a good golden brown.

petites tartelettes au café

Now you can split them and fill them with coffee-flavoured *crème Chantilly** which turns them into **Petites Tartelettes au Café,** or with *Crème Chiboust* which makes them

choux de Lyon

**Choux de Lyon,** or you can fill them with coffee-flavoured confectioners' custard* and keep this name.

crème chiboust

For **Crème Chiboust** you only need to understand that it is basically confectioners' custard* **which must be boiling hot** when you whip in 3 stiffly whipped egg whites bit by bit. Just a word of warning here—whip

228

and add very fast indeed, otherwise you may find that the mixture collapses.

Straightforward coffee-iced *éclairs* or cream buns are far better made with this **Pâte à Choux au Café** than with the ordinary water version.

You can also use this mixture to make **Tartelettes à la Cévenole.** Follow the instructions for **Choux de Lyon** as far as filling the tartlet cases but omit the flaked almonds. Split and fill with sweetened chestnut *purée*. Make squiggles of the same *purée* on top (with the mixture in an icing bag with a fine writing pipe affixed), top with squiggles of *crème Chantilly\** and decorate with scraps of *marrons glacés*.

Now let us have a look at what can be done with a savoury *choux* paste mixture—the one called **Pâte à choux aux gnocchi.** For the mixture itself you use the exact method given for **Pâte à Choux au Café** but the ingredients are very different. You heat $7\frac{1}{2}$ fl. oz. of milk with 3 oz. butter, then stir in 4 oz. flour with a pinch of nutmeg and a pinch of pepper, then beat in 3 eggs singly and finish with $1\frac{1}{2}$ oz. grated Parmesan cheese.

Like this, with no further additions, this mixture is transformed very easily into **Gnocchi à l'Italienne.** Fill the cooled mixture into an icing bag with a $\frac{1}{2}$ inch writing pipe affixed and lop off $\frac{1}{2}$ inch pieces with a knife dipped in cold water, holding the bag over a pan of hot oil which is **just below the stage when it begins to smoke.**

*tartelettes à la cévenole*

*pâte à choux aux gnocchi*

*gnocchi à l'Italienne*

Let them puff up and turn a good golden brown. Lift out, drain and put a double layer over a well-buttered heat-resistant container. Cover with *sauce béchamel\**, sprinkle thickly with grated Gruyère or Emmenthal and bake for 20 minutes at gas 5 (380°F) one shelf above centre.

Oddly enough the recipe which does need the addition of a further $1\frac{1}{2}$ oz. of grated Parmesan cheese is correctly titled **Les Gnocchi Simples.** This time you do not wait for the paste to cool but put it straightway into an icing bag with $\frac{1}{2}$ inch writing pipe and lop off $\frac{1}{2}$ inch stumpy "corks" into a roomy pan of salted water which is just heaving gently. The proportion of salt to water is $\frac{1}{3}$ oz. coarse salt to $2\frac{1}{4}$ pints water. Let the little "corks" poach. They confirm their readiness to be lifted out and drained by rising, considerably swollen, to the surface of the water. Then you lay them on a well-buttered shallow, heat-resistant dish, sprinkle them thickly with grated Parmesan cheese, moisten with a little extra melted butter on the top, brown under a strong grill and serve immediately.

les
gnocchi
simples

Which, if you think about it, is a long way from the standard water *choux* paste for *éclairs* and cream buns! As one of our children has said, "It is just the same only very different!"

We have already given you a recipe for Italian *zabaglione\** and explained how by using a sweet French table wine instead of the fortified Marsala of Italy this became a *sabayon\**, which seems unfairly to debar this very delicate pudding from teetotallers, so they, and indeed all lovers of coffee-flavoured food, will rejoice that a non-alcoholic *sabayon* can be made with coffee. It is called in French

sabayon
au café

**Sabayon au Café.**

Separate 6 eggs. Put the yolks in a basin with 6 slightly rounded teaspoonsful of castor sugar. Measure off 6 half eggs shells of strong black coffee into the top of a double saucepan over hot water. When the coffee begins to steam, pour in the batter made by whisking the yolks and sugar together. Begin whisking at once and go on until the mixture rises like thick beige foam up the sides of the pan. (As with all forms of *sabayon/zabaglione* there is a point of no return if you go on whisking for too long, when the mixture will subside into a little puddle of gritty sulks!)

Made properly and spooned liberally over portions of coffee ice cream this gives an extra culinary dimension to what would otherwise be a most unimaginative "afters."

Next time you bemoan a surplus of egg yolks —don't, because there is a most subtle and exciting **Omelette Crèmeuse** which can be made without any egg whites at all. Just do not be so emboldened by this statement that you rush at it with the slip-slop method any of us can use for making classic French omelettes in a hurry! **This needs care** but no skill.

omelette
crèmeuse

First you replace the egg whites in any given number of eggs by adding a tablespoonful of thick cream for each one. Then you beat the mixture together with a fork. Add any desired seasoning and run about 1 oz. softened butter for every 4 egg yolks through your fingers on to the mixture. All the while of course your omelette pan has been standing over a low heat, getting very hot. Toss in the usual nut of butter. Step up the heat to fullest till the butter melts and turns brown at the edge and then—this is the trick of it— turn the heat down a little as you pour in the mixture. Now work it very gently with a flat of a fork at least half the speed you use for a French omelette*. When the mixture begins to thicken, stop and let it settle on the pan. At this moment you can slip in any desired sweet or savoury filling, flip over and turn out.

While we are talking about egg yolks do you by any chance know that these will poach perfectly in little ramequins—one yolk to each—if you replace the absent egg white each time with about $\frac{1}{4}$ inch depth of double cream and then sink the egg yolk into this nest. We prefer to poach these in an outer pan of hot water on top of the stove rather than in the oven. Sometimes we stir a tea-spoonful or so of chives or parsley or a mixture of both into the cream first. On other occasions we use very finely chopped mush-rooms to stir into the cream, or minute dice of back bacon, or very small snippings of the fat and lean of thinly cut ham. With all or any of these the tops can be sprinkled with grated cheese, for which ideally you should use a mixture of Parmesan and Emmenthal or Gruyère. All variants of **Les Jaunes en Cocotte** are sheer luxury to the taste buds.

It is a very short step indeed from here to using up the egg whites for what must be the easiest *soufflé* in the world. We have given up using *soufflé* moulds which are costly and fragile, since we discovered how easy it is to make *soufflés* hold up in large water lilies made of aluminium kitchen foil (see diagram page 392). They do not even need buttering inside. You just pile the mixture in till it is well domed and then bake one shelf above centre at gas $7\frac{1}{2}$ ($435°F$) for 14 minutes. The water lily looks attractive on a dish for serving.

Nothing becomes this method more than a **Jam Soufflé,** for which you need 8 stiffly whipped egg whites and $\frac{1}{2}$ lb. of any jam which, if made with the large fruits such as plums, peaches or apricots, should be sieved first—not through a hair sieve, an ordinary one is adequate. Then all you have to do is whip up the egg whites very stiffly indeed. Whip in the jam. Add a teaspoonful of strained lemon juice to bring out the flavour and, if possible, a tablespoonful of a liqueur which flatters the fruit in the jam.

Here is a little table of **Happy Marriages:**
    apple and calvados
    apricot and apricot brandy
    blackberry and kirsch

blackcurrant and cassis
cherry plum and mirabelle
cherry and kirsch
grape and brandy
peach and peach brandy
plums and prunelle, quetsch or slivovitz
raspberry and framboise or kirsch
strawberry and kirsch

You can spice up your repertoire with pastry too. Let us suppose you have a bowlful of oven-cooked fruits and neither custard nor cream to serve with them, but you do have tucked into the refrigerator some puff paste trimmings or a pack of bought puff paste (page 369). Roll out a small amount very thinly indeed. Stamp it into $1\frac{1}{2}$ inch diameter rounds with a plain or fluted cutter. Throw these into slightly smoking hot fat, a few at a time. They puff like baby balloons and, thickly dredged with sifted icing sugar, the taste is irresistible.

fried
pastry
puffs

These **Fried Pastry Puffs** can be made in little triangles, or squares, or you can cut $\frac{1}{2}$ inch wide strips, twist them, knot them and throw them into the oil to fry into amusing puffy shapes.

This is just the start of frying with pastry. Try rolling out a panel very thinly to measure about 12 inch by 6 inch. Mix up a very stiff paste of grated hard cheese, butter, salt, pepper and paprika. Spread this within an inch of the edges all round. Wet the edges with water, roll up the paste panel into a very

tight sausage, lop off in $\frac{1}{2}$ inch lengths and
fry **Cheese Puffs,** which is enough to start
you thinking of many variations with sweet
and savoury spreads.

cheese
puffs

bacon
and cheese
rolls

Try **Bacon and Cheese Rolls.** Roll out
bought (page 369) or home-made puff
paste into 4 inch (instead of 5 inch) wide
long sausage-roll panels and then cut
fat fingers of Gruyère, Emmenthal or any
other melting cheese to equal the same lengths
as your paste strips. Brush the paste strips
with raw, beaten egg. Cover with de-rinded,
No. 3 cut bacon—to within $\frac{1}{2}$ inch of each
edge. Lay the cheese fingers on top, brush
lightly with made English mustard and roll
up as for sausage rolls. Brush the tops of the
completed rolls with raw beaten egg, prick
down the (top) length with a fork, lop off into
convenient lengths, sprinkle each top with (a)
poppyseeds, (b) finely milled nuts, (c) grated
hard cheese (like Parmesan) and bake, one
shelf above centre, at gas $7\frac{1}{2}$ (435°F) until
pastry is puffed and a good rich golden brown.

savoury
pastry
puffs

One of the most recent ways we have spiced
up the routine uses of puff pastry opens up a
huge area of economical experiment and we
have called the new discovery **Pastry Puffs.**
The day we tried them for the first time we
were looking for something quite different.
We had the shavings left on the bone of a leg
of pork; freshly made tomato *coulis** for
winter-storage, a few dregs in a cream bottle
and about 4 oz. of cold, cooked rice. We

minced the pork trimmings, blended them with the rice, stirred in the lees of cream and sufficient *coulis* to make a paste, and then rolled out bought (page 369) puff paste trimmings to an almost transparently thin panel. This we then stamped out into rounds with a 6 inch diameter flan ring.

We planned to turn this assembly into a **Savoury Pastry Gâteau** using the mixture as filling but this swiftly became **Pastry Puffs** when we saw what happened to the frying pastry. The transparently thin circle blew up like a golden-brown puff ball in the pan of hot oil. So we lifted it out and drained it, heated the pork and rice mixture, split the puff ball half way round the side with a pair of scissors, inserted some of the hot mixture, closed the gap (like filling *éclairs* or cream buns) dusted the puff with paprika powder **and tasted.** It **looked** extremely clever and impressive, it **tasted** gorgeous and it is now standard usage for using up both sweet or savoury left-overs at speed.

sweet
pastry
puffs

For our first **Sweet Pastry Puffs** experiment we filled some fried pastry puffs with a thin base of confectioners' custard* (our 3 oz. remainder was enough for four) then we spread jam on top of the custard, closed the puff and dusted the top liberally with sifted icing sugar. Both sweet and savoury variants can be made wildly economical or impressive enough for poppers-in and they are a triumphant new addition to our emergency range for busy Sociable Cooks.

236

Even so we still achieved the original intention—**Savoury Pastry Gâteau** by frying three 8 inch diameter rounds, cooling on a rack and halving. Then we spread savoury mixtures (sandwich spread types) between the layers and when the *gâteau* was assembled brushed the top lightly with a little whipped cream and sprinkled a mixture of grated cheese and parsley overall.

savoury pastry gâteau

fried mille feuille

This can, in turn, be made into a **Fried Mille Feuille** if the layers are spread with (a) confectioners' custard*, (b) jam, (c) cream, and a repeat for the six layers. Then just spread the top with simple *glacé* icing (page 293).

savoury torrijas

We have been using *Torrijas** for many years now as a family pudding. These mock spice doughnuts are always very popular but we scored much more heavily when we rang a change on this sweet item by turning it into **Savoury Torrijas.** Here is what you do. Stamp out 2½-3 inch plain rounds of new bread cut to about 1 inch thickness. Put about a teacupful of cold water into a soup plate and add half a gill of sherry. Beat up 2 eggs and strain them into a second soup plate. Pass the bread rounds through the sherry mixture first, then through the beaten egg. Fry them in very hot oil until they are browned and puffy. Then if you bury them in a third soup plateful of mixed stale grated cheese, milled parsley and powdered paprika and serve with *sauce Mornay**, you can be certain of no left-overs!

237

You may all know about soaking and cooking dried fruits in tea but perhaps not quite so many of you are familiar with other aspects of tea cookery. You can make an excellent batch of **Tea Scones** when there is not a drop of milk in the house, if you sift 8 oz. flour with 1 heaped teaspoonful of baking powder into a roomy bowl, rub in 2 oz. each of lard and butter, stir in 1½ oz. castor sugar and 3 oz. sultanas and bind to a firm dough with cold tea. Roll out to about ¾-1 inch thickness. Stamp into 1½ inch diameter rounds and bake at gas 5 (380°F) for about 16 minutes.

tea
scones

There is just the same scope for "Spice" in cookery with mincemeat which is generally cribbed, cabinned and confined to mince-pies at Christmas when it should be an all-the-year-rounder, used in a number of easy ways.

mincemeat
swiss
roll

Try a **Mincemeat Swiss Roll,** baking the fatless sponge* as usual, in a Swiss roll tin, and spreading with mincemeat **which has been pre-cooked** in the oven for 15 minutes at gas 6 (400°F) (in a pie dish). Roll up the spread roll, dust with sifted icing sugar as usual and watch the speed at which this variant is devoured.

apple
and
mincemeat
tart

We also use mincemeat for an **Apple and Mincemeat Tart,** by filling an oiled, paper lined Victoria sponge tin with (a) mincemeat, (b) a thick layer of thinly sliced cooking apples, (c) a moderate coating of soft brown (pieces) sugar and (d) a fairly thickly rolled out fitting circle of short sweet paste*. Bake at gas 5 (380°F) until the pastry turns a good biscuit colour, cool a little in the tin, turn out on to your chosen dish. Peel off the paper at the base and either dust thickly with sifted icing sugar or wait until it is quite cold and pipe the top with whipped cream and a final dusting of icing sugar. Of course we use our own home-made mincemeat!

our
mincemeat

**Our Mincemeat** excludes the minced beef which our grandparents used; but it can always be added (8 oz.) to the given quantities. Sling, pell mell, into a large mixing bowl—1 lb. each of currants and rough-chopped seeded raisins, 1½ lb. beef suet, 1 lb. darkest possible soft brown (pieces) sugar, 1 oz. of mixed spices, 1 lb. of peeled, cored, minced apples with their juices, the grated rind of 2 lemons and 3 oranges and 1 tea-cupful each of rum and brandy. Blend these together very thoroughly. Pot up, cover with inner jam covers passed through a little brandy in a saucer and tie down.

Always remember to make **well in advance of using.** Mincemeat, like Christmas puddings and cakes, matures with keeping. Unashamedly we flick the tops of this mixture with more brandy after putting into raw pastry and before affixing lids.

Even Christmas cake lays itself wide-open to a bit of spicing up with variation. Far more people than will ever admit to it, dislike black fruit cake. They merely eat it through tolerant affection for tradition. When you can offer both the accepted form and the unorthodox-but-so-agreeable **White Christmas Cake** you may well find as we do that the ratio of disappearance at the tea table comes down heavily in favour of the white one.

As usual with all these types of cake the preparation takes some time and the actual cake-making only a few minutes. Try this routine to save time and increase quality—**if you have an electric mixer.** Put 12 oz. of butter to beat at about half speed. Meanwhile line out (for the given quantities) one 7 inch diameter 3 inch deep sliding-based cake tin and one 9 inch diameter 3 inch deep sliding-based cake tin. Use greaseproof paper, treated exactly as for black Christmas cakes. Be fairly liberal with the oil with which you brush these papers. Let the butter alone; the more it whips the better, the cake will be.

Weigh out and sift together 7 oz. flour and 7 oz. cornflour plus an additional 1 oz. flour and 1 oz. cornflour also sifted together. Add 12 oz. castor sugar to the creamed butter and let it alone again. Throw the 1 oz. flour and 1 oz. cornflour quantities into a large bowl. Add to them 6 oz. chopped angelica, 6 oz. flaked almonds, 4 oz. chopped walnuts, 12 oz. chopped *glacé* cherries, 10 oz. chopped crystallised pineapple and 12 oz. sultanas. Measure off into a cup or beaker 1 tablespoonful of rum, 2 tablespoonsful of brandy and 1 tablespoonful of strained orange juice.

Grate up the rinds finely from 2 small lemons or 1 very large one. Toss the grated rinds into the butter cream and let it go on mixing. Take the rest of the sifted flours, 6 standard eggs and the brandy mixture over to the butter cream. Put 2 heaped table-spoonsful of flour mixture on to it, let it whip in—then add a whole egg and continue in this fashion until all eggs and flours are incorporated. Add the brandy mixture and whip again.

Now bring the lot back to the fruits and extra flour on the table. Mix these well together and hand beat into the cake mixture.

Fill into the two tins. The mixture will weigh 6 lb. 1 oz. if your measurements have been spot on. The 7 inch diameter tin will take 2 lb. 4 oz. and the 9 inch one 3 lb. 13 oz. Put each filled tin on to a baking sheet. Cover the tops right over the paper rims with double folds of foil and put in the oven two shelves from the bottom at gas 4 (355°F). Cook for 1 hr. 20 min. and reduce heat to gas 2 (310°F) for a further 25 min. Oddly enough we found the baking time the same for both cakes.

While the cakes are hot pour simple *glacé* icing (page 293) over the tops because the heat helps the icing to set and make an (agreeable) crust. Stab this all over with an assortment of crystallised fruits including a few *glacé* cherries and "twigs" of angelica. Then spoon more *glacé* icing between the fruits to enable you, layer by layer, to build them up into an impressive (and secure) pyramid.

Band the cake sides with a plain white frill held centrally with a 1 inch wide piece of satin ribbon. Avoid any busy bows which will draw the eye from the top-decoration.

Even biscuits are far too infrequently considered as a basic cooking ingredient, yet that is precisely what they can be—as exemplified on page 324 for *Gâteau l'Ambassadeur* and on page 281 as Caribbean Refrigerator Cake, so now we are going to give you a third variant, when you are in the mood for something different, which produces a **Chocolate Saucepan Cake.**

chocolate
saucepan
cake

It is made in a few moments; it keeps for months if, when set, it is tightly enclosed in kitchen foil. It is a Night Starvation Special as well as a face-saving standby for perennial tea-time poppers-in! It goes like this . . . You can choose between ½ lb. rough crushed *petit beurre* and rough crushed digestive biscuits. Either make a wildly exciting **Chocolate Saucepan Cake.** Oil a baking sheet and oil a 7 inch diameter flan ring. Place ring centrally on the baking sheet. Put together in a small saucepan 2 oz. butter, 2 tablespoonsful golden syrup and 4½ oz. chocolate chips or cooking chocolate (page 367). Soften slowly, stir well and gradually work in the crushed biscuits. Turn into the flan ring. Flatten the top surface by pressing with a cut lemon or orange and when cold remove flan ring.

Store in waxed papers and aluminium foil if wishing to keep in perfect condition for several weeks. Serve plain, or decorate with a top-coat of whipped cream. Sprinkle this with oven-browned flaked almonds.

acacia flower fritters

Finally may we jog your memory over garden produce—always assuming you have a garden—those sweetly scented **Acacia flowers** make delightful **Fritters** if you macerate them for 30 minutes in a spoonful or two of brandy with a sprinkling of castor sugar. Just drain them, turn them in fritter batter* and deep fry them as usual.

chrysan-themums and other flowers in salad

You can do the same with the otherwise useless male marrow flowers, using just the circle of petals for each one. When you have fat white **chrysanthemums**—preferably the incurved variety—you can bring a very glamorous and Chinese touch to an autumn salad if you just scald the pulled-apart petals for about 2 minutes in boiling water, refresh them in cold water, shake them in a salad basket and add them to any tossed type of salad.

substitute capers

You can do exactly the same with **nasturtium** and **borage** flowers and by treating the soft young **nasturtium seeds** exactly as pickling onions you can pickle your own capers instead of buying.

# *Set fair*

Fruit Jelly
Real Orange Jelly
Lemon Jelly
Tea Jelly
Sweet Milk Jelly
Savoury Milk Jelly
Jelly à la Zizi
Bavarois à la Zizi
Bavarois au Kirsch
Bavarois au Café
Mocha Bavarois
Bavarois au Chocolat
Gilbert Harding's Lemon
  Mousse

Charlotte Russe
Simple Aspic
Standard Classic Aspic
Crème de Caviar en Gelée
Foie Gras en Gelée
Les Crevettes en Gelée
Petits Tournedos à la
  Choron
Oxford Sauce
Basic Savoury Mousse
Mousse de Tomates
Mousse aux Epinards

*Question: How can I be sure things made with gelatine don't bounce like India rubber or fall apart when I unmould them?*

*Answer:*

It maddens us when home cooks are deceived into thinking gelatine cookery is difficult and nothing gives us more pleasure than debunking old wives' tales about cookery. Consider the case of gelatine. Time and time again we have sad letters from enthusiastic cooks, like the questioner, who write confessing ruefully that they "never seem to succeed with gelatine." The result is that simple, economical, quickly made dishes are by-passed because they have been given a false reputation for complexity!

Try a little experiment with us. Learn one simple table; it goes like this:—

1 oz. gelatine will stiffen 1 pint fluid or sweetened fruit juice

½ oz. gelatine will stiffen 1 pint mayonnaise or thick sauce

⅘ oz. gelatine will stiffen 1 pint thick (canned) fruit syrup

¼ oz. gelatine will stiffen ¾ pint stiffly whipped cream

fruit jelly     Now put 1 oz. gelatine in a small pan with 5-6 tablespoonsful of cold water. Stir the two together. Put the pan over a very low heat and stir continuously (it only takes a moment) until the mixture clears. Pour this on to 1 pt. cold, strained fruit juice from a jar of your own (sweetened) bottled fruits. Stir in quickly and thoroughly. Leave the mixture to set. Then you will have a **Fruit Jelly** worthy of the name, which can be tiddled up for parties with a spoonful or two of a matching fruit brandy (pages 233-4).

If you have followed us thus far you will now know why we stress that it is an absolute fallacy to say hot, dissolved gelatine cannot be added to a cold mixture without it going lumpy. Ours has never done so in all the years we have been cooking. Nor is it necessary to strain the gelatine mixture if you have dissolved it thoroughly!

When you want a **Real Orange Jelly** grate
the rind of 2 oranges very finely and thinly.
Then cut all the inner skin away with a very
sharp knife so that you can remove the flesh
in neat sections without any skin. Once the
orange is down to bare flesh, slide a knife tip
down between flesh and skin of one segment.
Turn the knife under and bring it up against
the opposite skin section. This will cut down
and jerk out a perfect skinless orange segment.
When all segments have been removed
squeeze the pithy skin over a bowl and
make up to $\frac{1}{2}$ pint with fresh (or tinned)
unsweetened orange juice. Dilute with $\frac{1}{2}$ pint
water or $\frac{1}{4}$ pint water and $\frac{1}{4}$ pint cider, mix well
and dissolve 1 oz. powdered gelatine in
5-6 tablespoonsful cold water in a small pan
over low heat. Stir in 3 oz. castor sugar and
when this is dissolved stir into the cider-
water-orange juice.

Pour into a wetted mould and when the jelly
has become syrupy slide in the orange segments so that they do not all sink to the
bottom. **This is the way to ensure the
even distribution of any fruits in jellies.**
Once the gelatine has done its work sufficiently for the density or syrupy texture to be
greater than the weight of the chosen small
fruits or fruit segments, you will be sure of
good overall distribution.

A moment ago we advised you to wet moulds
before pouring in jellies. This is what you do
for aspics too—but NOT for any creamy
mixtures, whether sweet or savoury. Their
moulds should be brushed thoroughly but

sparingly with olive oil. If you do this you will eliminate all that exhausting prodding and shaking. The set creams will slide from their moulds easily and swiftly and thus put an end to cooks turning themselves into human cocktails.

lemon
jelly

When making a **Lemon Jelly** use orange segments, strained lemon juice and water in the proportions of $\frac{1}{4}$ pint lemon juice to $\frac{3}{4}$ pint water and stir 4 oz. castor sugar into the $\frac{1}{2}$ gill of mixed fluids and 1 oz. of gelatine dissolved in 5-6 tablespoonsful cold water. This plain lemon jelly can be used with 1 teacupful of crushed pineapple (fresh or tinned) or with sliced peaches or apricots, 5-6 oz. to every pint.

tea
jelly

If you want a more unusual mixture you may like to try **Tea Jelly** for which the ingredients are 2 egg whites, the strained juice of 1 lemon and 1 orange, 1 oz. China tea, preferably Lapsang Souchong, 1 oz. powdered gelatine, 1 pint boiling water and sugar to taste. Pour the boiling water over the tea and strain immediately into a pan or bowl. Add fruit juices, gelatine and egg whites, place over a moderate heat and whisk unceasingly until mixture boils and accumulates a deep topping of foam. Strain through a jelly bag (or several folds of butter muslin) into a bowl, stir in sugar to taste and pour into a wetted mould.

sweet
milk
jelly

In very natural sequence we must now propose two very old recipes for **Milk Jelly.** The first is a sweet one. Put 1 pint of milk into a thick pan and bring to the boil very slowly with a vanilla pod. Turn off heat and leave to steep for 15 minutes while you stand your chosen mould full of cold water ready for tipping out at the last moment. This done, grate enough nutmeg finely over the milk to speckle the top surface all over. Set castor sugar to hand and break 1 egg into a 2 lb. pudding basin and whip it well. When the 15 minutes is up remove vanilla pod, pour milk over the whipped egg, whip again, add sugar to taste, dissolve 1 oz. gelatine in 4-5 tablespoonsful water over low heat, stir resultant syrup **slowly** into milk mix, and strain into a wetted mould.

savoury milk jelly

**Savoury Milk Jelly** much doted upon by Victorians, deletes the vanilla pod and sugar and replace these with salt and pepper to taste, 3 oz. finely grated Parmesan and about 1 tablespoonful of milled fresh parsley. The cheese is turned into the boiling milk, stirred steadily for about 2 minutes, then the gelatine mixture is poured on slowly and you must always stir it while you pour. Then season to taste and finally add the parsley and nutmeg after which the mixture is poured quickly into a wetted mould.

jelly à la zizi

For parties, small fry will take a very favourable view of a **Jelly à la Zizi.** This means "at the slant." The name was given by the great chef Soyer, who ruled the kitchens of the Reform club for many years. Soyer had a zizi complex which would have doubtless

made him a victim to modern psychiatry—
but he managed very happily without this in
his day—wearing diagonally striped "wes-
kits", ties, cravats, stocks and even coats;
tipping his hats at the slant and finally
working out how to make puddings with
slants to them.

To do this successfully, you will need jellies
of different colours—emphasise the colours
with **harmless** vegetable colouring so that
contrasting layers are clearly defined. Stand
a wetted, plain round or hexagonal mould
with one side tipped up by an inch wedge
underneath. Pour in the first layer of jelly
until it is $\frac{1}{2}$ inch up the tipped-up side and
thus $1\frac{1}{2}$ inch deep on the opposite side. Allow
this to set. Pour the next colour of jelly (at
the syrupy stage) into the mould which you
have now reversed, so that the tipped-up side
is down and vice versa. Continue in this
manner varying the colourings—light against
dark—until the mould is filled. Be careful not
to pour on the jelly until it is syrupy, or it will
still be warm and thus will melt the preceding
layer and spoil everything.

bavarois
à la
zizi

You can turn this treatment to good account
for grown-ups with **Bavarois à la Zizi**
without any further exhortations from us.
You merely need the classic recipe for
*bavarois* which is undoubtedly the most
useful and variable of cream pudding mixtures.

The basic ingredients are confectioners'
custard\*, cream, and softened gelatine.

Hundreds of variants can be made with this one mixture, for which the confectioners' custard can be advance prepared, the cream whipped and the gelatine dissolved very speedily. The completed *bavarois* in its mould can be stored safely in refrigeration for 2-3 days—and for longer when there are liqueurs in the flavouring—**but,** because the balance of gelatine with both cream and custard needs to be very carefully adjusted to suit this blending and allow for an incidence of liqueurs, fruit *purées* or other flavourings, with liquid content, we will give you the variations as we explain the recipes which do not fit into standard proportions.

*Bavarois* can be turned into fancy moulds, provided these are well brushed with oil. They should always be garnished with *crème Chantilly\** which is flavoured with a liqueur complementary to the flavour of the *bavarois* itself. For example, a **Bavarois au Kirsch** requires $\frac{1}{2}$ oz. gelatine dissolved in $\frac{1}{2}$ gill of water. This is stirred into $\frac{1}{2}$ pint confectioners' custard, to which is added quite quickly $\frac{1}{2}$ pint double cream, whipped till it hangs from a whisk. Then 2-3 dessertspoonsful of kirsch are stirred in, by which time the mixture has already begun to thicken, so hurry it into its oiled mould, and if making *à la zizi*, keep the balance **loose** by standing it over hot water until it is needed and colour each layer differently with harmless vegetable colouring before adding to the mould.

bavarois
au kirsch

| | |
|---|---|
| bavarois au café | For a **Bavarois au Café** use $\frac{1}{2}$ pint confectioners' custard, $\frac{1}{2}$ pint cream, 1 gill strong black coffee and $\frac{3}{4}$ oz. gelatine which you dissolve in the coffee. If you want to add a liqueur this time, you use from a teaspoonful to a dessertspoonful of Crème de Caçao. |
| mocha bavarois | Transforming this into a **Mocha Bavarois** is simply a matter of dissolving 3 oz. of cooking chocolate (page 365) or chocolate chips (page 367) in the gill of coffee given for **Bavarois au Café** and otherwise proceeding exactly as detailed in this recipe. |
| bavarois au chocolat | For **Bavarois au Chocolat** you merely substitute water for coffee where 1 gill of strong coffee is given in **Bavarois au Cafe.** Then you heat the water, dissolve the gelatine therein and fold in $4\frac{1}{2}$ oz. of already-softened chocolate chips or cooking chocolate. In both, or either, of these variants a tablespoonful or two of Crème de Cacao or Tia Maria is permissible and indeed strongly recommended, except when very small children are to be served with it. |
| Gilbert Harding's lemon moussé | If you were serving a very rich meal and you wanted a party pudding that would cut the richness, you could serve **Gilbert Harding's Lemon Mousse,** which we devised for him. It is extravagant but it is exceptional. You need 5 eggs and 5 extra egg yolks, the strained juice of 3 lemons, the grated rind of $1\frac{1}{2}$ lemons, 1 well-rounded tablespoonful of powdered gelatine, $\frac{1}{2}$ pint of double cream and 7 oz. icing sugar. Put the lemon juice, |

rind and gelatine in a small pan and let
gelatine dissolve slowly by the side of a
burner at lowest possible temperature. Put
the eggs and extra yolks into a bowl with the
icing sugar and whip relentlessly until the
mixture is almost white and very frothy.
Then whip in first the strained gelatine syrup
and then the cream until the mixture leaves
the sides of the bowl. Tip it into a small
*soufflé* mould with a 2 inch above-rim wall of
oiled greaseproof paper pinned around the
outside. Leave in refrigeration until the
moment of service, whip off the paper and
serve absolutely plain and ungarnished.

An old-fashioned pudding which should
always find a place on a large party buffet is
charlotte **Charlotte Russe.** The only difficult parts
Russe are the wall and the base, so we will tackle
these first. You begin by wetting a 7½ inch
diameter sliding-based cake tin. Then you
cut ½ inch tips from one end of 25 Savoy
fingers. You then make a pint of **Fruit Jelly**
(page 246) and when it has reached the
syrupy stage, you pour a ½ inch layer into
the cake tin, so that it is really setting as it
hits the tin. Arrange halved *glacé* cherries
(with the cut uppermost) and "stems" made
of strips of softened angelica in a decorative
pattern on the setting jelly. When they are
quite set in position, you lock them in with
a carefully spooned-on second layer of the
syrupy jelly.

It is at this stage that you stand the sponge
fingers all the way round the inside of the

tin, so that they make a wall with the rounded ends standing on the jelly. There will still be gaps. You take the cut-off tips of the sponge fingers and crumble them up with 8 more sponge fingers and make these crumbs into a firm paste with spoonsful of the syrupy jelly. Then, just as if you were using plaster on a wall, you take small quantities of the paste on the tip of a knife and press them in to the gaps between the sponge finger wall until you have filled in every single gap. Now the whole thing is easy.

The vanilla cream mixture which you now fill into the prepared *charlotte* is very simply made. Dissolve $\frac{1}{2}$ oz. gelatine with $\frac{1}{4}$ gill water. Whip 3 gills of cream until it hangs from the whisk. Stir in 6 level dessertspoonsful of vanilla-flavoured castor sugar and 1 gill cold milk. When this is done, whip up 2 egg whites as stiffly as possible. Now strain in the gelatine, stir quickly and whip in the egg whites. By the time this action is completed, the mixture will have reached the first stage of its setting point. Tip it into the *charlotte*, level it off and in about 5 minutes' time when it is set, pour any remaining jelly syrup over the top.

Leave in container in mild refrigeration until just before service, by which time you must have ready a piece of very narrow ribbon long enough to tie round the unmoulded *charlotte* and finish with a neat bow. This is necessary because no *charlotte* is worth eating if the mixture is set firmly. Therefore, the pressure of the very lightly set mixture might force the sponge fingers apart in a very warm room if they were not secured with the ribbon.

So much for a handful of puddings with which you can defeat any bogey about gelatine. These are, however, only the beginning of the gelatine story. Once you can make "classic" **aspic**—which very few people can do nowadays—you have hundreds of cold dishes at your disposal. Of course there is the substitute aspic which functions on two out of three levels.

simple aspic For the simplest (No. 1) use the strained juice of a lemon with a small sherry glass of dry sherry and enough water to bulk it up to ½ pint. Dissolve ½ oz. of gelatine in this mixture, which can then be used as a substitute aspic for masking fish or portions of bird and for locking in decorative bits of cooked vegetables and truffles as a base for savoury moulds; but you must never use much of it, for its taste is not sufficiently subtle!

Number 2 is achieved with very good veal or chicken stock which is strained and then cleared*. This tastes much better, so it can be used for making little vegetable moulds, meat moulds or moulds of shellfish.

The third level is classic aspic, for which there are several variants. We will give you standard a **Standard Classic Aspic** which, when it classic aspic is finished, is the colour of fine amber. You will need 1 lb. knuckle of veal, 1 lb. knuckle of beef, 1 lb. veal bones and 1 calf's foot. Put

255

these into a clean stock-pot, cover liberally
with cold water, bring to the boil, skim, add
1 rounded teaspoonful of salt and simmer for
3 hours. Leave till cold. Remove all the fat
from the top very carefully. Lift out the meat.
disturbing the stock as little as possible. Slip
in ½ lb. chopped carrots, 2 oz. chopped
onions, 2 oz. sliced leeks, a *bouquet garni*\* and
a stick of celery. Simmer for a further 1½
hours. Skim and then strain through a sieve
lined with muslin.

Add 1 lb. lean minced beef mixed to a paste
with a raw egg white, 1 teaspoonful of lemon
juice and ¼ oz. of gelatine for every pint of
fluid in the pot. Stir until the mixture boils,
simmer very gently for 30 minutes, strain it
again through double muslin and that is
**aspic.** This recipe will probably explain why
it is seldom made by home cooks in the
20th century!

crème de
caviar en
gelée
Nevertheless, if you want to make a perfect
**Crème de Caviar en Gelée,** this is the aspic
for perfect flavour . . . otherwise you will
have to use one of those substitutes. Whichever you decide to use, line a well-wetted
savarin mould with aspic, swirl it around at
the syrupy stage until it holds and sets, then
give it a second coating and let that set.
Meanwhile whip ¼ pint double cream until
it just hangs from the whisk (if you over-
whip the cream, the lemon juice might
curdle it). Fold in the contents of a small pot
of Danish or German type caviare, 2 teaspoonsful of strained lemon juice and a

generous flavouring of freshly milled black peppercorns.

Fill this *crème de caviar* into an icing bag with a 1 inch plain pipe affixed and pipe a thick band of this round the border mould on top of the aspic. Fill the mould up with aspic, unmould when set, pipe a peak of *crème de caviar* into the centre and border the outer rim with well washed cress.

If this fails to impress the chairman's or admiral's wife, we give up.

foie gras
en gelée

You can do exactly the same thing with *foie gras* instead of caviare for **Foie Gras en Gelée;** or you can make a more modest version with the central filling of diced cold bird folded into very thick mayonnaise*.

les crevettes
en gelée

Mayonnaise itself stiffened with aspic enables you to make incomparable small moulds for buffet parties. Let us suppose you want little dariole mould shapes of shrimp aspic—**Les Crevettes en Gelée.**

Wet the moulds and coat them with aspic (of your choice). When the aspic has set, fill up with shelled pink shrimps mixed with stiffened mayonnaise. Then cover to the rim with more aspic at the syrupy stage and turn out when set.

You can use diced lobster flesh in the same way. Of course, both can be made more elaborate by using equal quantities of mayonnaise and fairly stiffly whipped double cream and mixing these together before adding the standard ½ oz. of gelatine to 1 pint of mixture.

The Victorians were passionately addicted to individual portions of all descriptions for "ball suppers." There is one that still survives in our household called **Petits Tournedos à la Choron,** for which you need fillet steak, bread *croûtons*, tinned *fonds d'artichauts* (artichoke bottoms) cooked green peas and aspic. You cut 1¼ inch thick slices from raw beef fillet and you cut these into baby *tournedos* which will fit into the artichoke bottoms. You fry these on both sides in hot butter. When they are still pretty underdone, stand them by the side of the cooker in the warm on a heated dish and under a lid, and thus let them finish their cooking to a delicate pink. Leave them like this until they are quite cold. Stamp out and fry an equal number of round bread *croûtons\**. Stand an artichoke bottom on each *croûton*. Fit the baby *tournedos* into the artichoke bottoms. Dip the cooked peas in syrupy aspic (page 255) and set all the way round the base of the little *tournedos*. Mask with spoonsful of syrupy aspic. Serve these surrounded by well-picked watercress and serve with **Oxford Sauce.**

This keeps for ever and is splendid with all cold meats. Mix 4 oz. "pieces" sugar with 1½ oz. made English mustard, ½ oz. salt, ¼ oz. milled black peppercorns and 4½ fl. oz. oil which you add very gradually, a drip at a time, with alternated additions from 2 fl. oz. cider vinegar.

One of the most important stand-bys for the cold buffet addict is the savoury *mousse* family. If we think about it first as a generic recipe, we shall then be able to see quite clearly how we can vary the theme with fish, meat, game and poultry. It is wise to work with a double saucepan. You will also need a little saucepan for dissolving the gelatine.

basic savoury mousse

A **Basic Savoury Mousse** calls for 1 pint milk or ½ pint milk and ½ pint single or coffee cream, 3 separated eggs, seasoning, ½ oz. powdered gelatine, 3-4 tablespoonsful hot water and ½ lb. of any minced, cooked white meat of chicken, or salmon. We put either in a mortar with a spoonful or two of the cream or milk and we pound with a pestle until the mixture is broken down into a smooth pulp. Then we put the rest of the milk or cream in the top of a double saucepan over hot water. When it is hot, we pour it over the whipped egg yolks. Pour back and forth between pan and bowl two or three times and stir until the mixture forms a smooth custard. Then we strain in the gelatine which has been dissolved with the water and stir again. Remove from the heat and beat in the prepared fish or poultry flesh. Whip up the 3 egg whites very stiffly, beat them in, taste and correct the seasoning with salt and/or pepper.

This mixture is then poured into an oiled mould, unmoulded when set and garnished; or it can be poured, if preferred, into a small *soufflé* mould which has a 2 inch above rim wall of oiled greaseproof paper pinned securely around the outside, in which case

the paper is only whipped off at the moment
of service and the *mousse* is served in the
*soufflé* mould with savoury garnish on top.

You can, of course, pour the prepared *mousse*
mixture into individual oiled moulds. Or
you can wet these moulds and set them with a
lining of aspic before putting in the mousse
mixture. Or you can be very elaborate and
line the moulds with two layers of aspic,
setting little designs of cut cooked vegetables
(or truffles) on the first layer of aspic and
locking them in with the second.

Instead of using either salmon or chicken,
you can use lobster, crab, prawns, shrimps,
duck, goose or sweetbreads. With any of the
above you can withdraw $\frac{1}{2}$ gill of the cream
in the given basic recipe and replace with
wine, but be careful to do so by adding the
wine to the dissolved gelatine which you then
pour slowly into the custard, thus avoiding
any danger of curdling.

Suitable marriages include a spoonful or two
of brandy with lobster, sherry with crab,
Madeira with duck, vodka with goose, dry
white wine with salmon or poultry. As we
promised you, the variations are almost
endless.

The same may be said of vegetable *mousses*,
of which probably the most delicate of all is
mousse de tomates **Mousse de Tomates.** Skin enough tomatoes
to yield 1 lb. of cored, seedless pulp, soften
2 oz. butter in a small pan over a moderate
heat and cook pulp to a soft pap, stirring

occasionally. Soften ½ oz. gelatine in 4 table-spoonsful *sauce velouté**. Cook all together for 3 minutes and then sieve into a bowl. Add ½ pint of cream, whipped till it hangs from the whisk. Correct seasoning with salt, pepper and a few drops of strained lemon juice. Turn into oiled mould and unmould when set. You can make a **Mousse aux Epinards** in precisely the same way with 1 lb. of cooked spinach*.

mousse aux epinards

None of these recipes is beyond the scope of the nervous, not very experienced cook, but each and every one will be a disastrous mess if you skimp on the time taken in dissolving the gelatine. Always hang on to the knowledge that gelatine only fails to work successfully every time if it is inadequately "cleared". In simple parlance—dissolve it over a very low heat, stir it carefully and do not dream of tipping it on any prepared mixture until every solitary grain has vanished. Provided you do this, do not complicate matters with old-fashioned leaf gelatine or deviate from the scale of quantities set out by us at the beginning of this chapter, you will never again have any cause to be afraid of gelatine work in cookery.

# Chapter 13

# *Worth getting fat for*

Chufletes

Spanish Family Torrijas

Spanish Mountain in the Snow

Danish Apple Cake

Crêpes Caramelisées aux Pommes

Red Sea Apples

Les Pommes Rosées Meringuées

Apple Purée

Charlotte aux Pommes

Charlotte aux Groseilles, Abricots, Pêches, Prunes ou Poires

Marmelo

Tarte aux Cerises Noires

Gâteau de Cerises Renversé

Crêpes Suisses

Canadian Apple and Raisin Pie

Banana Upside-Down Cake

Pineapple Upside-Down Cake

Caribbean Star

Caribbean Baked Bananas

Rum and Mocha Refrigerator Cake

Grenadian Pineapple Ice Cream

Grenadian Pineapple Penuche

Coconut Pie

Coconut Meringue Pie

Coconut Sponge Gâteau

Hot Baked Oranges with Caramel Tops

Swedish Sand Cake

Madeira Sponge Cake

Jumballs

Steamed Chocolate Pudding

Austrian Nusspudding

Steamed Suet Puddings

Golden Sultana Steamed Pudding

Mum's Brown Betty

Lemon Meringue Pie

Lemon Curd

Walnut Crunch

Moist Gingerbread

Simple Glacé Icing

Ring Doughnuts

Plum Pudding de Rois Mages

Brandy Butter

Christmas Cake

| | |
|---|---|
| Gran's Pound Cake | Crème Caramel |
| Torta d'Amondoa | Baked Custard |
| Chocolate Soufflé Omelette | Macaroon Custard Pudding |
| French Bread and Butter | Apple Charlotte |
| Pudding | Beestings |
| Terre Goule | Mum's Fruit Salad |

*Question: I have always wanted to try my hand my hand at some of the things which make me drool outside Continental pastry-cooks' windows. I'm quite a reasonable cook but I've always had the feeling these should be left to professional pastrycooks. Am I right or wrong?*

*Answer:*

Wrong. Isn't it nice to know? With the possible exception of his famous foxhunting definition, "the pursuit of the uneatable by the unspeakable," nothing Oscar Wilde ever wrote appeals to us more than his "I can resist everything except temptation." Nor is there any quote more applicable to all the best things in a *pâtissier's* window than "all the best things in life are either illegal, immoral or fattening." It is an interesting fact, maintained by every doctor we have talked with about dieting, that less weight is put on by someone who has an occasional orgy than by someone who eats one little piece of rich, cream-stuffed sugar cake or a chocolate **every day.**

The Duchess of Windsor, whose figure is the envy of girls, let alone the middle aged and elderly, obviously accepts this dictum for she diets throughout the week, eats "everything I want on Sundays—when we entertain most," **and stays slim.** So this is a chapter for either the slender-whatever-they-eat, or else for those who subscribe to the occasional orgy.

Cake is an odd word, one of the few which have become common usage in French. Like week end, deep freeze and bacon, (even in the 13th century we read of "*le grand bacon*") there are no equivalent French words which is food for reflection anyway! The French use "cake" to describe a kind of Madeira mixture with *glacé* fruits in it, not *gâteaux* and not any of the delicate, subtle prides of the *pâtissier's* art. So this is not only a chapter about cakes but also one about family puddings and some of the *pâtisseries*, which can be used **in place of puddings** at luncheon, dinner, on buffets or for "*le five o'clock*", another English-French phrase, adopted by them to describe "afternoon tea."

Given patience, a meticulous attention to detail, an in-built refusal to use inferior materials (like granulated instead of castor sugar, vanilla essence instead of vanilla pods, any substitute for butter, almond essence instead of delicious *crème de noyaux* or any substitute for pure olive oil—and with the possible exception of the bought puff pastry which we have found to our gratitude and astonishment produces such really excellent results (page 369) anyone can make a wide range of real *pâtisseries* which are exact replicas of those sold by the best professionals all the world over—not just in France. Indeed we have always been in doubt as to whether the French have the edge on either the Danes or the Austrians when it comes to *pâtisseries*

Certainly, Danish *kransekage*—huge, costly almond paste fingers with their tips dipped in chocolate—are unique. You must go either to Aalborg and buy them at Kristine's or to Kolding where the Saxelhaus sells them; and accept that there are certain things which are not just copyable elsewhere!

Clearly these are fighting words from two people who have steadfastly maintained that the difficult can be done at once and the impossible merely takes a little longer; so before we resume making and baking here is a true traveller's tale to prove there is an exception to every rule.

On **one** island—Majorca—in **one** town—Palma—in **one**

shop **one** family has made *ensaimadas* for generations. These featherweight fruity, sugary, breakfast-buns are sold for home consumption and for the better grade of hotels to serve at breakfast. They are also produced in sizes from a single bun shape to a giant cartwheel for tourists to buy and take home in special wheel-shaped boxes. Their fame became so great that some years ago it was decided to establish a branch on the mainland of Spain, although to date no one had succeeded in producing the identical article elsewhere.

To beat this jinx, replica conditions were set up in the most minute detail which even included flying tanks of the Palma water over the strip of dividing Mediterranean Sea—even so, a wide gulf separated the mainland *ensaimadas* from the original Palma ones. Which only goes to show . . .

chufletes    There is, however, one excellent Spanish pudding called **Chufletes** which we **can** all reproduce without any fear of failure. For these you will need 1 lb. of soft breadcrumbs, 1 tablespoonful of castor sugar, 1 gill of inexpensive white wine (preferably a Spanish one) and 2 separated eggs. Place the breadcrumbs in a bowl, mix with the sugar, blend the wine and egg yolks together, pour on to the crumb mixture and leave for 30 minutes. Then mix up well and fold in the stiffly beaten egg whites. Drop spoonsful into slightly smoking hot oil, fry until golden brown and serve piled on to a dish with a top dusting of vanilla-flavoured icing sugar. Alternatively they can be served with a hot jam or jelly sauce or with **home-made lemon curd** (page 291) diluted to a sauce consistency with equal quantities of white wine and water.

Another which you can add to your Spanish list is a slightly more elaborate version of *torrijas**. This kind is baked instead of deep-fried and their name is **Torrijas de la Casa** or **Family Torrijas.** Cut de-crusted stale bread into plain or fancy ½ inch thick shapes. Dip each lightly into melted butter, arrange on a heat-resistant dish, spread the tops with jam or marmalade and cover with meringue made with egg white and sugar exactly as explained for **Coconut Meringue Pie** (page 284). Bake at gas 1 (290°F) until the meringue is a pale biscuit colour. Thus you have an admirable way of using up stale bread and surplus egg whites. Even so these are still good enough for guests, especially when you can offer a little thick rich cream for pouring over each serving.

Spanish
family
torrijas

There is a third, amusing, distant Spanish cousin to a *soufflé* called **Monte Nevade** or **Mountain in the Snow** which is a good way of using up stale sponge cakes. First you butter a *soufflé* mould then cover the base with a ½ inch layer of stale sponge cake which you moisten with flicks from a gill of wine, 2 fl. oz. of water and rum to taste. Then you whip 6 egg yolks with 3 oz. sifted icing sugar and spread a layer of this mixture over the moistened sponge. Repeat, layer by layer, until you have used up the egg yolk mixture. Then whip the 6 egg whites very stiffly indeed, add 2 table-spoonsful of stock sugar syrup*, whisk again, pour on the top of the sponge layers and

Spanish
mountain
in the
snow

267

bake at gas 4 (355°F) until the meringue is nicely browned.

Having told you how exclusive Danish *kransekage* are to themselves, let us see what we can pilfer from Denmark which we can make successfully. There is a very good **Aeblekage** or **Danish Apple Cake** which helps you use up some of an unexpectedly heavy crop of apple windfalls. Peel, core, quarter and weigh off a generous 2 lb. Place them in the oven in a casserole with a squeeze of lemon juice, a vanilla pod, and the very smallest possible amount of cold water. Cook them covered at gas 2 (310°F) until they are soft enough to sieve. Remove the vanilla pod, dry, wipe and store. Sieve the fruit and then sweeten to taste with soft brown sugar. Butter a *soufflé* mould or sliding based cake tin. Place a thick layer of soft breadcrumbs on the base. Cover with a matching layer of apple *pureé*. Repeat until container is filled, finishing with breadcrumbs and then very slowly pour on a teacupful of melted butter, allowing it to seep right through. Bake at gas 7 (425°F) for about 30 minutes. Leave in container until cool so that the edges contract a little and you can turn it out easily. Cover the top with crab apple or redcurrant jelly and decorate with whipped cream. Or you may prefer to use the Swedish version *Applekaka med Vaniljsas*—Apple Cake with Vanilla Sauce*.

There was a restaurant in Niort some years

ago which featured another good apple "speciality" made with pancakes and called

crêpes caramelisées aux pommes **Crêpes Caramelisées aux Pommes.** The way in which chef set out his daily *mise en place* is sufficiently valid for the busy home cook to merit recording.

A stack of heat-resistant pudding plates were set in the *bainmarie* cupboard (or warming drawer of oven) with a pile of advance-made *crêpes\**. A bowl of very thinly sliced apple rings cut from peeled, cored apples (swilled with lemon juice to stop them blackening); a bowl of very fine castor sugar; a sieve and a salamander were set beside the cooker and thus the *crêpes* orders could be executed at great speed.

Chef's salamander was a long, flat strip of metal $1\frac{1}{2}$ inch wide, $\frac{1}{2}$ inch thick and 20 inches long, which was made hot in a fire or over the gas.

You can of course pre-light and heat a grill for browning the sugar instead, but a salamander is so much easier for the job that it is well worth consulting the house-hold male, or the local blacksmith, regarding the making of a home version as these are rarely obtainable in English shops. Remember that the chosen metal must withstand fierce heat **without bending.** Then you simply make it red-hot and pass it over sugar-dusted items so that its radiated heat causes the sugar to burn and turn to caramel. It should be near enough the item to cause real flames for a moment or two as it passes slowly across. It should never smoke and

269

smoulder. So be bold and fierce with it; but pray remember to wrap one end tightly in thick cloth so that you can grasp it without leaving the palm of your hand behind!

To make these apple pancakes just lay a large pancake over a heat-resistant plate, cover it completely with fine apple rings, dust the surface very thickly with castor sugar, either salamander or brown under the grill until the sugar forms a crisp caramel over coat. Incidentally, this is an ideal way of obtaining a good brown skating rink over a *Crème Brulée* and over a number of Austrian, Danish, Swiss and French *gâteaux*.

Apples are also the keynote to an Escoffier recipe which we found a few years ago when a friend dredged up a giant ledger of the Master's which had lain for over forty years in the vaults of the Bank of England. Escoffier called them **Red Sea Apples.** One of the best apples to use for this is small to medium Bramleys.

Red Sea
apples

Take a large shallow saucepan. Pack in as many peeled, cored, whole apples as can be laid comfortably in the base and pour over 1 lb. of redcurrant jelly dissolved in $\frac{3}{4}$ pint of water. Add a vanilla pod and set the pan over the merest murmur of heat, thus allowing the apples to poach without any fear of bubbling, because this would cause the apples to start crumbling and flaking as they became tender. As they begin to tenderise, turn them over until they are completely soft through but still whole. Lift them out with a perforated spoon or slice, drain each one over the pan and arrange them on a flat dish. Remove the vanilla pod and simmer the liquor down till it is syrupy. It is best to do this by pouring the liquor into a small, deep pan.

Then spoon the final small amount of red syrup over the fruits so that their transpatent redness is masked with a deeper red cap. Place a *glacé* cherry in the centre of each. Stab a fairly large "leaf" or diamond shape of angelica into the side of each cherry and serve cold but do not put into refrigeration or it will spoil the syrup tops.

les pommes rosées meringuées

There is a variant of this—**Les Pommes Rosées Meringuées,** for which the poached apples are drained, set on a heat-resistant dish and then covered completely with the meringue mixture given for Coconut Meringue Pie (page 284). These are then browned in the oven at gas 1 (290°F) top decorated with cherry and angelica as before and the slightly less thickly reduced syrup residue is handed separately in a sauceboat.

apple purée

Escoffier also provided us with what we think is the nicest of all apple *charlotte* recipes. To do this easily you need to have apple *purée* on hand. Therefore, as it is so popular in our household, we bottle and store unsweetened **Apple Purée** to give us a good supply throughout the winter months. Whenever possible use windfalls. Cut out any

271

rotten bits, and cut up very roughly—skin, core and all. Place in earthenware or heat-resistant glass containers, add the least possible amount of water, cover with lids and cook at gas 2 (310°F) until the apples collapse. Rub them through a sieve. Pack the *purée* into warm bottling jars with rubber rings affixed, add metal tops, clip securely and sterilise at 190° for 1½ hours. Set aside for 48 hours, slide off clips and lift up each jar by its lid to check for certain that all are airtight. If any lid comes off you must re-sterilise.

charlotte
aux
pommes

Then you are ready to make Escoffier's **Charlotte aux Pommes** whenever you like. Begin by assembling the base of a large cottage loaf, 1 egg beaten up with ¼ pint of milk, a deep fryer with hot oil, about 1½ lb. of bottled or freshly made apple *purée*, soft brown ("pieces") sugar, butter, ½ lemon, a rounded eggspoonful of powdered cinnamon and 1 heaped tablespoonful of sieved apricot jam. Butter a 7 inch *charlotte* or *soufflé* mould. Cut the crusts from the cottage loaf neatly and cut off two approximately ¼ inch thick rounds from the now crustless bread. Cut each of these rounds into small irregular shapes, keeping both sets separately. Pass one lot through the egg and milk very quickly. Toss into slightly smoking hot oil. Fry briskly to a good golden brown. Drain and set aside. Repeat with the second lot and also with enough small "fingers" of bread to make a wall around the inside of the mould to the exact depth of the sides.

Now heat the apple *purée* with the apricot jam, cinnamon, 1 oz. butter, a generous squeeze of lemon juice and stir over a moderate heat with a wooden spoon until the mixture becomes thick and sticky. Taste and sweeten to your own judgement with soft brown sugar and melt small amounts of butter at a time in a separate small pan. Pass the fried bread pieces of one base circle through this butter and re-assemble them like a jigsaw on the base of the mould. Do the same with the finger pieces and fit them all round the inside of the mould. Tip in the *purée* and press it down well with the back of a spoon to within $\frac{1}{4}$ inch of the top. Now pass the pieces of bread from the second circle through a little melted butter and fit them over the top as a lid. This should bring your mould's contents flush with the rim. Trim off, with a pair of scissors, any protruding scraps of side fingers.

Bake at gas 4 (355°F) for 35-40 minutes. Leave in the mould until cold and then chill well in refrigeration and unmould. Tie the sides with a very narrow strip of ribbon if it is going to wait for some time, dust the top thickly with sifted icing sugar and serve with custard or whipped cream.

After this the procedure becomes constant and you merely change the fruit and flavourings for any **Charlotte aux Fruits** of your choice. Let us run over a few that are very

273

rewarding to make. For **Charlotte aux Groseilles** (gooseberries) omit the lemon juice, keep the apricot jam and soft brown sugar, cook the gooseberries with 1 inch stick of cinnamon to every 3 lb. of fruit and otherwise proceed as instructed for **Charlotte aux Pommes.** For **Charlotte aux Abricots, Pêches** or **Prunes** (apricots, peaches, plums) use the lemon juice, sugar and apricot jam but omit the cinnamon. For **Charlotte aux Poires** (pears) add a small piece of bruised root ginger tied in a muslin bag to every 3 lb. of pears.

Before we leave apples, apple *purée* and its uses let us hop into Portugal for a moment and at the same time explode a tiny, little old wives' tale. Time and again we have seen the statement concerning marmalade that this derived from the French phrase, "*Marie est malade*" and was coined by the French nurse to Mary Queen of Scots. It is said that this nurse accompanied the Queen to Scotland, where she fell ill, that the timely arrival of a case of Seville oranges inspired this nurse to put up a conserve which she was found stirring and when asked what she was making, she replied, "*Marie est malade*", infering that this was to be a cure for her malady.

Nothing in fact could be further from the truth. The word derives from **Marmelo** which is today a Portugese sweetmeat primarily made with quinces but which can also be

274

made with apples and oranges. Sundry experiments in this household have shown us that—for occasions when quinces are scarce—an excellent variant can be made with 70 per cent. cooking apples or windfalls and 30 per cent. quinces.

The choice of fruits is therefore yours. The method is as follows. Cook and sieve the chosen fruits as for bottled apple *purée* (page 271). Weigh the sieved mixture. Add pound for pound, soft brown "pieces" sugar or granulated sugar. Place this mixture in a very thick pan large enough for the combined *purée* and sugar to fill only one-third of the depth—you will see why in a moment.

At this point take a long-handled wooden spoon and put a thick glove on the hand that will do the stirring. You see, to achieve **Marmelo** you have to stir and stir (like *pommes duchesse*\* or potato *purée*) until sufficient of the moisture is steamed out to allow the wooden spoon to stand erect for an instant before toppling over. In short it must be a very thick paste indeed. This is fine for potato but dangerous with a sugary substance which, when it bubbles and blows, can explode little burning hot sugary blobs which you will know all about if they land on the back of your hand!

When you have achieved the correct texture, fill the mixture into oiled wooden candy frames or oiled square or rectangular flan rings set on an oiled marble or laminated plastic surface and leave to get completely cold. Then cut into neat squares or rectangles, wrap in waxed papers and store in an air-tight glass jar to serve as a sweetmeat or *petits fours* delicacy.

Additionally, you will find, as we do, that when the children find out about **Marmelo,** they weedle for it and eat it from the waxed papers, as many years ago we used to eat packet jellies under the bedclothes at school!

There are so many countries which have contributed so many fruit puddings, pastries and cakes to our repertoire that we are giving you a selection in this book of ones that we think are suited to the Sociable Cook's family-entertaining pattern.

tarte aux
cerises
noires

Take Switzerland. They do a black cherry tart called **Tarte aux Cerises Noires** in French Switzerland but given entirely different names in the Italian, German and Romansch speaking Swiss cantons. For it you fill the base of a raw sweet short paste flan case* with confectioners' custard* and then cover it to within $\frac{1}{4}$ inch of the paste rim with stoned black cherries. These are then dusted thickly with fine castor sugar and the whole is baked at gas 5 (380°F) until the pastry edge is a rich biscuit colour, by which time you have ready about 6 oz. of Swiss cherry jam warmed in a small pan with the strained juice of half a lemon and, if liked, a teaspoonful of kirsch. When the *tarte* is removed from the oven, this mixture is **strained** over the cherries. Because of the moisture-insulating layer of thick confectioners' custard which covers the base, the pastry does not get soggy.

gâteau de cerises renversé

There is also an excellent upside-down sponge version of French *tarte tatin* called **Gâteau de Cerises Renversé.** Cream 2 oz. butter, add 4 oz. sifted icing sugar and cream again. Add 3 oz. cornflour and 3 oz. flour sifted together and the yolks of 3 eggs. Put a little flour on to the butter cream first, then add the first egg yolk; whip and continue working with alternate additions of egg yolk and flour, adding just enough milk to make a dough which flops lazily off a spoon or spatula.

Line the bottom of a 8-9 inch diameter Victoria sponge tin with a fitted circle of oiled greaseproof paper. Drain in a sieve for several minutes 2 generously filled teacupsful stoned black cherries. When these are fully drained, cover the greaseproof paper with $\frac{1}{8}$ inch thickness of firmly patted-down soft brown "pieces" sugar. Press the cherries into a thick pad on top. Put the sponge mixture overall. Spread evenly over the top surface and bake at gas 4 (355°F) until the mixture is risen and springy to the touch. Leave in the container until cold, turn out on to a dish, peel off the paper carefully and cover the top with rosettes of thickly whipped cream.

crêpes Suisses

This reminds us that Swiss cherry jam makes an ideal filling for cold, advance-made pancakes*. You put a spoonful of jam into each pancake, roll them up like cigars and place them on a shallow, buttered, heat-resistant container. Moisten them with a few flicks of kirsch (optional). Dust them thickly with sifted icing sugar and bake them for 15 minutes one shelf below centre at gas 2 (310°F). The proper title for these is **Crêpes Suisses.**

Although the New World features very little in our records, we have to hand the palm to Canada for making the best Raisin Pie* in the world. Their **Apple and Raisin Pie** is equally good. For it you simply proceed exactly as instructed for Raisin Pie, except that you use half the amount of the raisin mixture and make up to the given quantity with sweetened-to-taste apple *purée* (page 271).

*Canadian apple and raisin pie*

When it comes to bananas, we have learned more in the Caribbean than anywhere else in the world. They make two very good upside-down sponges in precisely the same manner as we have explained for Swiss *Gâteau de Cerises Renversé*, merely slicing ripe bananas thinly, packing them over the sugar base on the oiled greaseproof paper and then moistening them liberally with lemon juice before turning the sponge mixture on top. This gives you **Banana Upside-Down Cake.**

*banana upside-down cake*

**Pineapple Upside-Down Cake** is made in the same way using small pieces of peeled, sliced, fresh pineapple for the fruit base.

*pineapple upside-down cake*

278

Of course, you can substitute well drained, tinned pineapple slices cut small.

From that most beautiful of Caribbean islands, Grenada, called "Spice Island" by the West Indians, we have one of the prettiest of simply made puddings for either a children's party or a grown-up's one. This is **Caribbean Star** which brings together pineapple and banana. For it you will need 1 small fresh pineapple, a minimum of 8 bananas, some cocktail sticks, a very sharp knife, about ¼ pint of stiffly whipped cream, soft brown sugar to taste, half a lemon and 2 tablespoonsful of the real Barbados rum.

Begin by grasping the pineapple tuft firmly in one hand and with the other cut from top to bottom, getting at least 8 slices from the fruit; but there is more to it than this. Cut each slice in such a way that the central core of the pineapple is left untouched and attached to the top tuft. Drive a quarter of a wooden cocktail stick into the centre of the inner flesh of each of the 8 sections and push the other end back into the core, so that the slices stand away from each other.

Bake the unskinned bananas at gas 4 (355°F) middle shelf, for 20 minutes or until they are pitch black. Split the blackened skin cases lengthwise. Mush up the now soft banana flesh from each. Mix it with the lemon juice, brown sugar and rum. Fill back into banana skin cases, cutting enough away from each side of the lengthwise split for the mounded

279

filling to show about a $\frac{1}{2}$ inch gap. Pipe this gap with little rosettes of whipped cream.

Set the bananas like the points of a star on a round flat dish with the pineapple in the centre. If you want to follow the original recipe of Mr. Heinz Fedovitch of the Grenada Beach Hotel, you will prepare a whole small coconut exactly as instructed for **Cocktail Coconut Strips** (page 90) and put piles of these in between each banana, moistening them with a few extra drops of rum and sprinkling with castor sugar instead of soaking them in brine as described.

It is such a pity that there are still people who think cooking is a limited and lowly job. On to the obsessive and/or dedicated cook there must brush off, by the very nature of the work, the pollen of additional information and experience which make the whole thing endlessly stimulating and exciting. As we recall many of these rather homely recipes, so each one evokes fascinating little gleanings on our travels.

Typical examples are discovering in Greece that a man called Socrates watered his lettuces with wine, and hearing in a mountain village 25 kilometres from Rome how the Romans grew rose-flavoured melons by planting the seeds in tubs of decomposed rose petals.

Again having used mace and nutmegs so very often at home, we drove through groves of nutmeg trees on Grenada in the Caribbean and picked their pale yellow fruits. When you break them open, you find that each black nutmeg is enclosed in a blood red filigree which reminds you of the delicate work in precious stones done by Fabergé. Peeled off and dried in the sun, this filigree becomes mace.

We kept playing with them at a dinner table the night we ate our first dish of **Caribbean Baked Bananas.** Peel and halve 4 bananas across their length. Place in a small, deep, well-buttered pie dish. Cover with the strained juice of 1 lemon. Sprinkle thickly with thick brown Barbados sugar. Add enough coarsely grated fresh coconut to cover. Moisten with 2 fl. oz. stock sugar syrup*, strongly flavoured with Barbados rum. Bake at gas 4 (355°F) for 20 minutes. Serve hot with slices of Coconut Sponge *Gâteau* (page 284) on the side.

Barbados has contributed to our recipe collection with a **Rum and Mocha Refrigerator Cake,** which can be transferred to deep freeze for long keeping . . . the trouble in this household is that it is never left long enough to keep. Besides tasting good, it looks very expert and decorative when it is unmoulded from an ordinary bun tin. Use one which measures 5 inch by 9 inch by 3 inch.
Line the base and sides with Savoy fingers and layer in the filling to about ½ inch depths, alternating these with layers of whole or broken Savoy fingers. The mixture should rise to within about ¾ inch of the top. Cut off the protruding tips of the side Savoy fingers and use these up for the top covering.

*Caribbean baked bananas*

*rum and mocha refrigerator cake*

281

Press the surface down well and when you unmould it after setting, decorate the top and sides with piped strips of whipped cream. The ingredients and quantities are 11 oz. Savoy fingers, 3 oz. chopped walnuts, pecan nuts or grated Brazil nuts, 11 oz. sifted icing sugar, 2½ oz. softened cooking chocolate, 4 oz. butter (preferably unsalted), 2 raw egg yolks, 2 tablespoonsful strongly reduced coffee, 1 tablespoonful Barbados rum, 1 tablespoonful strained orange juice, and 1 dessertspoonful Tia Maria.

Cream the butter very thoroughly indeed and then cream in the sugar gradually with the egg yolks. Finally whip in the softened chocolate, coffee syrup, orange juice, rum and Tia Maria and fold in the nuts. Use as explained.

Grenadian pineapple ice cream

**Pineapple Ice Cream** is a Grenadian favourite. For this you will need 1 lb. granulated sugar dissolved in a pint of cold water over a moderate heat. When the syrup is absolutely clear, bring to a slow rolling boil and maintain for 4 minutes. Stir in the strained juice of 1 large lime or lemon and 2 breakfastcupsful of finely shredded fresh or tinned pineapple. Pour into refrigerator ice trays and freeze in the ice compartment. Serve as a water ice plain, or scoop out half the set mixture into a bowl, fold in 2 stiffly whipped egg whites and re-freeze until required. Slip into glasses for service and flick each one with a few drops of Barbados rum.

The Grenadians also make a delicious sweet-meat which they call **Pineapple Penuche.**
Put 5½ oz. soft brown ("pieces") sugar, 5 oz. castor sugar, 3 fl. oz. of double cream and 5 oz. of pineapple into a thick pan. Allow the sugars to dissolve and the cream to heat without boiling until every grain of sugar has vanished. Bring to a slow rolling boil and stir carefully until a drop of the mixture in a cup of iced water forms a soft ball you can roll between finger and thumb. Stir in a teaspoonful of strained lemon juice and 2 oz. chopped pecan nuts or walnuts. Allow to cool down to blood heat. Then beat until the mixture becomes thick and creamy. Pour it into an oiled frame or oiled square or rectangular flan ring on an oiled surface. Spread out evenly and leave to set. Cut into squares and store in a tin.

As you would expect Barbados is bristling with recipes using coconut. Indeed coconuts are so profuse that we used to gather armsful of them as we walked over the sands with the shaggy heads of wind-bent palm trees drooping over the coral reefs. They make a gorgeous **Coconut Pie.**
First a flan ring or Victoria sponge tin is lined out with fairly thinly rolled sweet short paste*. Then freshly grated coconut, or dessi-cated coconut, is fried gently in melted butter. Start with 4 oz. butter and when this is melted in a shallow frying pan, sprinkle in 3½ oz. of chosen coconut. Step up the heat and turn the mixture over and over until it

*Grenadian pineapple penuche*

*coconut pie*

turns pale golden and swells. Put in enough stale crumbled Madeira cake crumbs to make the mixture into a loose paste. Scrape it into a bowl. Add soft brown Barbados sugar to taste; the exact quantity will depend on which coconut you are using. Beat in 1 egg yolk and about 4 tablespoonsful of stiffly whipped cream. Turn it into the raw paste-lined container, level it off, cover with a fairly thinly rolled paste "lid" and bake at gas 5 (380°F) until the paste is a pale biscuit colour. While still very hot, dust thickly with sifted icing sugar. Serve hot or cold.

coconut
meringue
pie

Alternatively transform this into **Coconut Meringue Pie** by omitting the icing sugar and treating exactly as for the topping of Lemon Meringue Pie (page 291).

coconut
sponge
gâteau

There is also an outstandingly good **Coconut Sponge Gâteau** for which 3 or 4 layers of the sponge are baked in Victoria sponge tins and then clapped together over thin spreadings of both guava jelly and the same of whipped cream. When the cake is assembled, it is completely masked with royal icing, sprinkled thickly (and immediately) with raw grated coconut or dessicated coconut and served before the icing has had time to set. The sponge layers are made with our Swiss Roll Mixture* to which 2 heaped tablespoonsful of dessicated coconut are added to the given quantity. This makes two layers so you make a double batch for a four layer *gâteau*.

All these, of course, are West Indian recipes from private houses and ones which chefs make for very special occasions and small numbers.

In South Africa, where we had some of the worst food we have ever eaten in our lives, we still found a very good recipe for **Hot Baked Oranges with Caramel Tops.** You can use ordinary thick-skinned oranges of course but far and away the best, we find, are the thin-skinned blood oranges.

hot baked oranges with caramel tops

Halve your chosen oranges centrally. Remove the pips and loosen the segments of flesh with a grapefruit knife. Sprinkle them lightly with rum. Put them on a baking sheet and bake them at gas 4 (355°F) middle shelf, for 15 minutes. Take them out and sift a thick layer of castor sugar on the top of each one. Place them close under a fierce grill, allow the sugar to caramelise and serve them piping hot, or caramelise with a salamander (page 269).

When we were children, no afternoon tea was complete without a **Sand Cake,** a real **Madeira Sponge** and **Jumballs,** either plain or stuffed with *crème Chantilly*\*. Our best **Sand Cake** comes from Sweden. Nowadays we serve it with a good *compôte* of fruits as a pudding course.

Swedish sand cake

Soften ½ lb. butter and beat until it is creamy. Beat in 7 oz. castor sugar until mixture is white and fluffy, then a very scant 3½ oz. potato flour sifted with a scant 3½ oz.

285

flour. Then beat in 3 eggs singly. Stir in 2 tablespoonsful of brandy and pour into a sliding-based 6 inch diameter cake tin which has been very thoroughly buttered and floured. Bake at gas 3 (335°F) centre shelf for 1 hour to 1 hour 5 minutes. Cool in the tin on a rack, turn out when cold and dust the top thickly with sifted icing sugar.

Madeira<br/>sponge cake

We are indebted to Mrs. Graham Blandy of Madeira for her family recipe for **Madeira Sponge Cake,** a recipe which has never been surpassed in our experience. It will keep for up to 7 days wrapped in kitchen foil.

Separate 7 eggs and place the yolks in a large bowl. Whip them until they are stiff, light and creamy. Tip in $10\frac{1}{2}$ oz. castor sugar and whip again equally thoroughly. Stir in 7 oz. flour gradually and when it is all blended, beat the mixture for a third time. Whip the 7 egg whites very stiffly indeed. Scoop them on top of the mixture and cut them in with a plastic spatula, blending them lightly but very thoroughly.

Butter standard bread tins liberally. Turn in the mixture, making sure it does not come more than two-thirds up the sides of each tin. Bake in a pre-heated oven at gas 4 (355°F) for 16 minutes, at the end of which time you must slip carefully domed pieces of kitchen foil over the top of each tin so that the tops of the cakes do not get too brown. Continue baking until the sponges are firm and lightly springy to the touch. The overall cooking should take about 1 hour.

Immediately turn them out on to cooling racks and sift the tops thickly with icing sugar.

jumballs

The **Jumballs** recipe is our own. Before you do anything else, you must have a small saucer of olive oil and a pastry brush beside you. You must brush a cleaned bit of broom handle (or any other short length of smooth rounded stick which is about $\frac{3}{4}$ inch in diameter) liberally with oil.

Heat the oven at gas 4 (355°F) and assemble 3 oz. of golden syrup, $3\frac{1}{2}$ oz. flour, $3\frac{1}{2}$ oz. castor sugar, 3 oz. butter, 1 level teaspoonful ground ginger and the grated rind of 1 lemon. Put butter, syrup, sugar and lemon rind into a small thick saucepan and stand over a low heat until it is all dissolved. Remove from heat add flour and ginger and beat until smooth. Let the mixture cool until it becomes thick enough to drop in small spoonsful **very wide apart** on oiled, greaseproof-paper-lined baking trays—please do not try to bake more than four to a tin at a time, staggering the second and third tins so that you allow about 4 minutes between each lot. They cook for exactly 12 minutes.

Remove the first tray from the oven and allow the spread, fat circles to firm until you can just peel them off the oiled papers. As you do each one, coil it around the stick. Slide it along the oiled surface and do the next. By the time you have finished the fourth, the first one will be set and can be slid off and put on a cooling rack.

Then either serve them plain or with rosettes of cream at each end.

If you intend storing them in a tin, you must obtain a pack of Silicagel (page 369). Put this on the bottom of the tin to combat the otherwise inevitable humidity troubles which will cause them to collapse into a sticky goo. Even with this precautionary measure, we do not counsel keeping them more than 2 days.

steamed
chocolate
pudding

Some years ago when the late Somerset Maugham was having a special luncheon with us, we made him a perfectly plain, featherweight **Steamed Chocolate Pudding,** because he had said to us rather wistfully, while sitting in his villa at Cap Ferrat, that this was the one pudding he could not get in France. It was an extraordinary item for a formal occasion but he enjoyed it so much (three helpings, aged then 84) that we were justified.

To make it, cream 4 oz. butter until loose and fluffy, add 4 oz. castor sugar and cream equally thoroughly. Sift $4\frac{1}{2}$ oz. flour and $1\frac{1}{2}$ oz. sweetened chocolate powder together. Beat this mixture into the butter-cream gradually, adding 3 eggs as you do so. Finally beat in 4 tablespoonsful milk, pour into a well-buttered basin, cover with kitchen foil and steam for $2\frac{1}{4}$ hours. So much for the pudding.

We serve it with a Hot Chocolate Sauce (page 227), a jug of fresh cream and a bowl of sifted icing sugar . . . and there is never any left!

But then if we go across to Austria and plunder them of their **Nusspudding,** we can make the same claims for it—one of the most subtle of all steamed puddings.

Take 7 oz. of fine soft white breadcrumbs, cover them with cold water and wring them out very firmly in a clean dry cloth. Set them aside on a plate. Cream 4 oz. butter until light and fluffy. Add 4 oz. castor sugar and cream again very thoroughly. Add yolks of 5 eggs and beat them in, working in the soaked crumbs gradually at the same time. Add 8 oz. milled hazelnuts or walnuts, and 5 stiffly whipped egg whites. Turn into a buttered *soufflé* mould or pie dish. Cover with kitchen foil and steam for at least 3 hours.

Serve with Hot Chocolate Sauce (page 227), a jug of cream and a bowl of sifted icing sugar. This is a piece of one-upmanship for cooks in terms of steamed puddings so we need some more modest ones as well for more mundane occasions.

**Steamed Suet Puddings** are the most obliging, good-tempered items. Left-overs can be re-steamed with complete success and double batches can be made and divided between two separate bowls: one to be steamed after making and one to be left raw for 2-3 days in mild refrigeration and then steamed, still with perfect success. In order to do this successfully you must get the quantities right. To 10 oz. flour sifted with a level dessertspoonful of baking powder, you need 5 oz. shredded suet for plain suet crust. Bind this to a stiff dough with cold water, working with a knife **not** with a spoon.

golden
sultana
steamed
pudding

For a **Golden Sultana Steamed Pudding** add at least 4 oz. sultanas to the flour, suet and baking powder before adding liquid. This quantity is exactly right for filling into a liberally buttered 2 lb. pudding basin, after giving this a $\frac{3}{4}$ inch deep base of golden syrup. Steam for $2\frac{1}{2}$ hours and this will emerge as light as air.

Alternatively you can use the plain crust for

mum's
brown
Betty

a very good family version of **Mum's Brown Betty;** there are many. Turn back to the **Apple Purée** recipe (page 271). Put at least 1 pint of unsweetened apple *purée* into a saucepan. Add a handful of sultanas, plenty of soft brown sugar (at least 4 oz.) and the strained juice and grated rind of half an orange. Cook until the mixture becomes thick and rather sticky. Allow it to cool. Meantime line the base and sides of a buttered 2 lb. pudding basin with plain suet paste, setting aside sufficient to make a "lid". Put the cold apple mixture in 3 layers moistening the top of each addition with 1 tablespoonful of melted butter. Wet the top edges of the paste, roll out and press on the "lid" and just cover with a loose cap of kitchen foil instead of that dreary business with cloths and string. Then steam for 2 hours.

For years now we have bracketed certain recipes "very suitable for a home-made food shop" and if ever we have the opportunity of selling home-made food to the public one of our specialities will be our **Lemon Meringue Pie,** to which we made a passing reference only in "The Cook's Book". Use sweet short paste* rolled out fairly thinly and lined into the usual Victoria sponge tin or flan ring. Fill with home-made lemon curd and top with meringue mixture*.

*lemon meringue pie*

The all important thing for the flavour is using **Lemon Curd** and not a cornflour and lemon paste! Peel the rind thinly from 2 good sized lemons and put with $\frac{1}{2}$ lb. butter and 1 lb. castor sugar on top, into a thick pan. Add the strained juice from 3 lemons. Allow this to liquefy **very slowly** over a low heat. Whip up 3 eggs until smooth and creamy. Stir into the mixture until it all becomes thick and creamy. Just remember that if this boils, it will curdle and **if** you hurry it, it **will** boil; so watch it and stir it continuously until it flops idly off a wooden spoon.

*lemon curd*

Pot it up in heated jars and when cold, tie down and store in a very dry place. When you have tasted one of these pies, you will not regret the time spent over making the lemon curd filling.

Another item we have marked SS (suitable for sale) is **Walnut Crunch,** a great, tea-time, family favourite. When cooled and cut

*walnut crunch*

up into squares, it does **not** however look very attractive, so remember to dust liberally with sifted icing sugar before serving.

Cream $3\frac{3}{4}$ oz. butter and work in $3\frac{3}{4}$ oz. castor sugar. Now beat in as much of 11 oz. of flour as you can, with 2 separated egg yolks but no fluid. When you **have** beaten in as much flour as possible, turn mixture on to a cold surface and knead well. Roll it out gently and press evenly into a 12 inch by $4\frac{1}{2}$ inch by $1\frac{1}{2}$ inch flan frame or tin, on a baking sheet covered with oiled greaseproof paper.

Work up 2 stiffly whipped egg whites with $3\frac{3}{4}$ oz. chopped walnuts and $7\frac{1}{2}$ oz. soft brown "pieces" sugar. Pile evenly on top of the dough and bake one shelf above centre at gas 1 (290°F) for 1 hour. Remove frame, leave until cold and divide into squares or fingers with a hot wet knife.

Yet a third SS recipe has the somewhat homely nickname of Night Starvation in this house because people will come downstairs and raid the tin. It is a **Moist Gingerbread** mixture baked in a Swiss roll tin, which you must first line out with oiled greaseproof paper. Once again we must warn you that this does not look very beautiful when it comes out of the oven. While it is still hot, take a long knife and ease the edges back on to the hot soft gingerbread as these almost invariably rise a little over the rims. When cold you should cover the whole tin in kitchen foil. It will then keep for up to a fortnight.

moist gingerbread

For special occasions clap two layers together spreading one with **Simple Glacé Icing** made with water and lemon juice. Spread the top with the same icing and decorate with "petals" cut from *glacé* ginger to form a "flower", then add a "stem" of softened angelica. To make the icing, sift icing sugar into a bowl and add a few drops at a time of any of these liquids—(a) water at blood heat, (b) lemon or orange juice and warm water in equal parts or (c) any desired liqueur and warm water in equal parts. First stir to a thick, smooth paste and then beat relentlessly to expel all air bubbles and thus avoid prodding iced surfaces with darning needles to get rid of bubble-blemishes.

Whichever presentation you decide to use make the gingerbread by melting 5 oz. lard and 1 generous tablespoonful of black treacle over a very low flame. As soon as this has melted enough for you to beat it, remove it from the heat and beat vigorously. Pour on to 7 oz. flour and 2 rounded teaspoonsful ground ginger sifted into a bowl. As you do so, add 1 rounded saltspoonful of bicarbonate of soda dissolved in 2 tablespoonsful of milk. Fold in $2\frac{1}{2}$ oz. soft brown ("pieces") sugar beaten to a smooth paste with a whole standard egg. Bake for 20-25 minutes, centre shelf, at gas 4 (355°F).

We also think that if we had a shop, we should sell freshly fried **Ring Doughnuts,** very probably having the mixture made up and the doughnuts fried to order. This is not a bad idea anyway if you are doing them for a children's party.

Sift ½ lb. flour into a basin with 2 rounded teaspoonsful of baking powder and ½ a level teaspoonful mixed spice. Rub in 1½ oz. butter; stir in 3 oz. castor sugar, add 1 well beaten egg and work up with milk to a fairly firm rolling dough. Roll it out to a ¼ inch thickness, cut into 1½ inch diameter rounds and stamp out centres with a 1 inch round cutter.

The small centre pieces can be fried separately. Strictly speaking these doughnuts should be fried in lard which must only be heated to just below slightly smoking point, as if the lard (or oil) is allowed to get too hot, the doughnuts will be too deeply coloured outside before their insides are cooked through.

Fry a few at a time and turn over carefully with a pair of lifting tongs to ensure even brownness all over. Then drain them and roll them in either ¼ lb. sifted icing sugar or castor sugar mixed with 1 oz. cinnamon until they are very thoroughly coated.

We should also sell Christmas cakes and Christmas puddings in our imaginary shop; but "our" Christmas pudding recipe **is not our own.** It is Escoffier's who named it **Plum Pudding de Rois Mages.** His were plum pudding de rois mages steamed in a special, hinged log-shaped mould, but they can also be made in pudding basins. The prime virtue of the recipe lies in the fact that although it is classic and rich, it has far less of the qualities of those English puddings which lie on over-strained stomachs like hearth bricks!

Here are the ingredients as we have used them for years now:— 1 lb. fine breadcrumbs, $\frac{1}{2}$ lb. suet, 4 oz. chopped cooking apple, $\frac{1}{2}$ lb. sultanas, $\frac{1}{2}$ lb. seedless raisins, $\frac{1}{2}$ lb. currants, 2 oz. mixed chopped peel, 4 oz. soft brown sugar, strained juice of $\frac{1}{2}$ an orange, strained juice of $\frac{1}{2}$ a lemon, 1 oz. finely chopped ginger, $\frac{1}{4}$ oz. allspice, 1 oz. flaked almonds, 2 small eggs, $\frac{1}{2}$ gill brandy and old ale. The amount of old ale must be sufficient to make a fairly moist mixture because the trick is that you make it up and then leave it under a cloth for 24 hours, during which time the bread content expands and absorbs the surplus moisture. Only then do you put it up into ordinary, oiled pudding basins, Victorian jelly moulds, Escoffier's log-shaped moulds, or border moulds before steaming for a minimum 10 hours.

These last look very pretty if when turned out they are encircled by pre-made garlands of holly berries and leaves. There is no fear these will catch fire when the brandy is lit if you use the old "*à la Vésuve*" method and pour equal parts of heated brandy and vodka into the central well of each one, set fire to it, and have an inner pyramid of flames separated from the garland by the protective wall of pudding.

brandy
butter

These puddings would be lost without their twin—**Brandy Butter.** Fanny's mother always maintained that she acquired the family recipe from an ex-Windsor Castle parlourmaid while in her employ and the parlourmaid always claimed that she stole it from a Windsor Castle chef. Whether this was luck or legend is not important. It is an excellent mixture.

Cream 8 oz. butter until very light and foamy, cream in 1 lb. soft brown ("pieces") sugar, 1 raw egg yolk, and as much brandy as the mixture will hold without becoming too flabby to pipe.

Serve it piped into a pyramid on a glass pedestal dish. "Jewel" the pyramid with little bits of *glacé* fruits and tiny leaves of angelica stuck all over. Firm it up in refrigeration and finally "tent"the whole thing with a large square of red cellophane which should be gathered together and drawn up lightly at the top of the dish's stem. Wire it securely and tie over the wire with a broad "ribbon" bow of green cellophane.

As the brandy butter keeps indefinitely the cellophane tent protects it from any dust. This is one item which can be made up, dressed up and put away in a cool place well ahead of final Christmas preparations for which **any** Sociable cook should be thankful!

Christmas cake

The **Christmas Cake** is of course made as soon after each Christmas as possible **for the following one.** Fanny's grandmother had vintage cakes, one year, two year and three year aged in swathings of holland. These were kept on a shelf, carefully dated and eaten throughout the year as well as around Christmas. They were also very carefully cut into large or small **thick** slices, for it was this redoubtable grandmother who regularly informed her old parlourmaid, at teatime, "You may cut me a piece of cake, Clarkson, but pray do not cut it tasting of the knife", thereby exemplifying the golden rule that a thin piece of cake is an abomination.

Save for the fact that we wrap our cakes in kitchen foil, we use the same recipe as Gran first used when Queen Victoria was still a comparatively young woman. First the ingredients, 8 oz. sifted flour, 1 flat coffeespoonful each of nutmeg, ginger, cloves and cinnamon, grated rind and strained juice of 1 small orange and 1 small lemon, 2 oz. ground almonds, 1 oz. shelled chopped walnuts, 4 oz. *glacé* cherries, 4 oz. mixed diced peel, ¾ lb. currants, ¾ lb. sultanas, 4 oz. seeded raisins, 8 oz. butter, 8 oz. soft brown ("pieces") sugar, 3 standard eggs, ¼ gill each of brandy, Madeira or Marsala, and port, 1 oz. black treacle, 1 oz. golden syrup, 1 coffeespoonful orange flower water, 1 coffeespoonful rose water, and if possible the same of Noyaux.

Now for the method. Cream butter thoroughly in a very large bowl. Cream in sugar. Mix flour, spices, dried fruits and nuts in a smaller bowl. Whip eggs with brandy and fortified wines, rose and orange flower waters, fruit juices and rinds in a third bowl. Warm treacle and syrup (mixed) and add to egg mixture. Then add fruit and flour mixture gradually to butter cream mixture, with gradual additions of the fluid mixture and then beat and beat with well-scrubbed hands. Turn into lined and oiled tins and bake at gas 3 (335°F) for the first hour, then reduce to gas 2 (310°F) and continue to bake until mixture ceases to "sing".

After this recipe appeared in **The Daily Telegraph** a great number of people wrote in asking how much mixture filled what sized cake tin. So we tested the next batch that we made and came up with the following figures which will, we hope, help in the future; provided of course you bear in mind that raw cake mixture is filled to a maximum three-quarters of the tin's overall height. All given sizes are for round tins.

| Tin | Mixture |
|---|---|
| $7\frac{1}{2}$ inch by 3 inch | 3 lb. 4 oz. |
| 9 inch by 3 inch | 3 lb. 14 oz. |
| 12 inch by 3 inch | 5 lb. 3 oz. |
| 15 inch by 3 inch | 6 lb. 8 oz. |

Gran's
pound
cake

The same quantity scale can be applied when baking **Gran's Pound Cake.** Neither this nor the preceding Christmas Cake mixture deteriorates by being kept waiting for a few moments before baking. So you can reverse the normal procedure of lining and oiling cake tins beforehand by doing so after you have weighed out the finished raw mixtures. Then you can estimate exactly what sizes to use. If you prefer to get a rough picture before you start work, then you will need to tot up the ingredients to arrive at a rough total. This pound cake mixture totals either an approximate 8 or 9 lb. depending whether you use the everyday version or the special one. Thus you will realise straight away that you would get three 7-7½ inch diameter cake tins of cake out of the "special" one or about two 7-7½ inch and one 6 inch out of the everyday one.

The everyday mixture is 1 lb. each of butter, flour (or 8 oz. cornflour and 8 oz. flour), eggs weighed in shell, castor sugar, currants, sultanas and mixed peel. For the special version add 1 lb. of a mixture which is made up of 6 oz. chopped *glacé* cherries, 2 oz. diced angelica, 4 oz. chopped or flaked sweet almonds, and 4 oz. chopped seeded raisins. Add milk very sparingly to the everyday version—just enough to achieve a mixture which flops very slowly off a lifted spatula.

For the special, use Madeira and brandy instead of milk and in the proportions 2 tablespoonsful Madeira (Bual or Malmsey) to 1 scant tablespoonful brandy.

The method is constant. Cream the butter, cream in the sugar. Break the eggs into a bowl and whip them up. Sift flour and corn-flour together and add a little at a time with gradual additions of the whipped eggs. Then stop whipping and fold in the fruits by hand. Then give the mixture a thorough beating adding either milk or brandy and Madeira in sparing little dollops.

Turn into prepared tins and bake at gas 4 (355°F) one shelf below centre for approximately 1¼ hours. Immediately you take the cakes from the oven and cut away paper walls until they are level with the tops of the cake tins, invert cakes-in-tins on a rack. Remove tins when these have cooled to blood heat.

These are the sort of cakes at which the English excel. In fact very few other nations even like them. If they are not available at tea and bed-time there is a monumental moan from the French and English in this house while the Spanish and Portuguese who work for us look at us all wonderingly and say "no thank you" just managing to conceal their shudders!

We on the other hand are very partial to a number of their specialities including Portuguese **Torta d'Amondoa,** a most attractive almond tart.

torta
d'amondoa

Line a flan ring or Victoria sponge tin with scant ¼ inch thickness of sweet short paste*. The given quantity for one batch will leave you ample for the lid. Make up the filling by putting 6 oz. ground almonds and 6½ oz. sifted icing sugar into a bowl and working them well together. Beat in 3 eggs singly with the grated rind of 1 lemon, 2 oz. softened butter and a teaspoonful of *crème de noyaux* liqueur. Fill into the prepared flan case. Push the pastry edges over the filling so that they form an enclosing inner border. Brush the top surface of this border with a pastry brush dipped into cold water. Press an exactly matching circle of sweet short paste on top, pinch the top edges lightly together between finger and thumb all the way round to flute them. Brush the top with ½ of an extra raw beaten egg and bake at gas 5 (380°F) until the paste is a very light golden brown. Dust thickly with icing sugar before serving.

chocolate soufflé omelette

Now let us continue globe trotting—this time to Austria for an oven-baked **Chocolate Soufflé Omelette.** Butter a 6½ inch *soufflé* mould, sprinkle base and sides with castor sugar and put together in a bowl 1 rounded tablespoonful flour, 2 rounded teaspoonsful sweetened chocolate powder, 3 egg yolks, 2 oz. vanilla-flavoured castor sugar and ½ gill of cold milk. Whip to a smooth batter. Pour on 1 gill of milk heated with 1½ oz. butter, stir mixture well, scrape into the top of a double saucepan over hot water and continue stirring until it coats the back of a wooden spoon thickly. Remove from the heat and beat a little until cool. Fold in 3 stiffly whipped egg whites, turn into the prepared *soufflé* mould and bake in a pre-heated oven at gas 7 (425°F) one shelf above centre for 18-19 minutes.

French bread and butter pudding

And now come with us to France for a French version of **Bread and Butter Pudding.** It was created by an Englishman and a Pole for service at Maxims in Paris!

Butter a small pie dish. Cut up 3 *brioches* thinly. Lay them in the pie dish. Whip 2 eggs and 1½ oz. vanilla-flavoured sugar together. Pour on ¾ pint of scalding milk, stir well, scrape mixture into the top of a double saucepan over hot water and just as in the previous recipe stir until this custard coats the back of the wooden spoon. Thin down with ¼ pint double cream. Pour over the *brioche* bread, leave for 15 minutes, then bake in a pre-heated oven at gas 4 (355°F) one shelf above centre until the top is crisp and golden brown.

terre goule

We remain in France for a while to give you some more family favourites including Normandy **Terre Goule,** a rice pudding which has about the same relationship to English rice pudding as real white sauce does to wallpaper paste! Classically, **Terre Goule** should be made in an earthenware *terrine* which is shaped like an inverted Chinese coolie's hat, but unless you are a purist, you can make yours in any large earthenware casserole or *pâté terrine*.

You begin with 8 oz. rice, 2 pints milk, a vanilla pod and 3 oz. castor sugar. Tip the whole lot into your chosen container. Stir it up and then put it in the oven, uncovered, on the centre shelf and at gas 1 (290°F). Let it cook to a sort of pap between runny and thick. Take it out. Give it a jolly good stir, return to the oven, cover it lightly with foil and let it cook till it is doughy and much too thick. Take it out again and beat in

1 pint of single or coffee cream. Taste it and increase the quantity of castor sugar until the flavour pleases you. Then back with it into the oven under the foil and let it cook until it is thick and rather yellowy in colour. Serve it with double cream. Remember, this is a Normandy recipe and the Normans wallow in cream. Serve it with calvados and expect to sleep for the rest of the afternoon.

So many people find difficulty in making another good old standby of almost all French restaurants—**Crème Caramel**—which is our reason for recording one which really works every time.

Dissolve and brown 3 oz. of castor sugar in a thick, small pan over miniscule heat. When really dark pour into a *soufflé* mould or pie dish and swirl it around until the caramel coats the base and sides. Stand the now prepared container in a meat-baking tin which has been one-third filled with cold water. Scald 1 pint milk with a vanilla pod. Whisk together in a bowl 2 whole shell eggs and 2 extra yolks with 3 rounded tablespoonsful castor sugar. Whisk in the hot milk and then pour three times from pan to bowl and back again. This pouring "cooks" the mixture a little before it is **really** cooked. All that remains is to pour it into the *soufflé* mould over the caramel lining and put it one shelf below centre in its meat baking tin and at gas 2 (310°F). Leave it until it is set which will take approximately 1 hour.

303

For a plain **Baked Custard** you merely omit the caramel altogether and do everything else exactly as we have explained for **Crème Caramel** except that when you have finished and the mixture is in a *soufflé* mould or pie dish, cover the top lightly with grated nutmeg.

With this basic baked custard mixture you can produce an excellent **Macaroon Custard Pudding** if you first butter the base of a *soufflé* mould or pie dish, cover it with macaroons—using broken bits to fill the spaces—moisten these with about 4 tablespoonsful of Bual or Malmsey Madeira and leave to macerate for about 1 hour before pouring the given custard mixture on top and baking as instructed.

During the latter part of the war we found out that as none of us ever took sugar in our tea, we were always able to hoard sufficient to make jam. Dishes which used jam instead of sugar were therefore very valuable. As a family winter pudding we used to make a modest and rather unsuitably named **Apple Charlotte** for which there are not any given quantities but just an assembly of peeled cooking apples, shredded suet, fine soft breadcrumbs and jam. Butter a medium-sized pie dish. Put in a fairly thin layer of jam, cover with about $\frac{1}{4}$ inch layer of breadcrumbs, then a thin layer of suet and then a layer of extremely thinly sliced apples. Finish with a layer of jam and repeat until the pie dish is filled ending with a layer of bread-crumbs. Bake one shelf above centre at gas 4 (355°F) for about 30 minutes and ideally serve this hot goo with cream, though it can be served plain or indeed with custard.

beestings

Just in case there are any readers with dairy farms we decided to add a recipe for **Beestings.** This does not require a herd of cattle but just one cow which has newly calved and come to the **third milking\*.** If you try to make **Beestings** with the fourth milking, it will not set. If you do it with the first or second milking you will be able to dig it out of the pie dish, throw it on the floor and it will bounce! So only use the third milking please.

Fill a large pie dish with it. Stir in a $\frac{1}{2}$ egg-spoonful of salt and put the pie dish on the bottom shelf of an oven set at gas 1 (290°F). Leave for 3-4 hours or until as firm as a baked custard. Take out, score across and across to liberate the whey from the firm curds. Pour off the whey.

Serve with sugar and fresh or stewed fruit with cream whenever possible.

mum's
fruit
salad

And lastly, here is one which refutes the fattening orgies of this chapter, for when even the most starch and sugar omniverous begin to wilt. We have always called it **Mum's Fruit Salad** and without for an instant recommending one recollection concerning it, this is so **professional** in the

\*Authors' Note: The Oxford Dictionary definition of Beestings is 'first milk after parturition'—on their own head may it bounce say we.

305

behind-the-catering-scenes connotation that it may serve as a vivid illustration. The occasion was a party—following a slightly smaller party. Fanny's Mum had made far too big a batch, explaining, "it will do for both parties if we keep it nice and cool!" On the morning of the second party the over-matter was examined. Unmistakably it was in the fringe-state of fermentation. There were the first minute bubbles breaking on the top. This condition was pointed out. "That won't hurt them" said Mum briskly, pouring on a generous extra libation of (cooking) brandy. "Better than laxatives." And everyone seemed to enjoy it.

Ideally then this salad should be put not more than 36 hours before it is to be enjoyed without fringe benefits. All fruits which discolour—like segments of pear and apple and sliced bananas—may be used if, after preparing, they are sprinkled with lemon juice in separate bowls before laying them with other, less temperamental, fruits. This will stop them blackening. Whatever the selection the method then becomes constant. Place a layer of one fruit in the bottom of your chosen container. Sprinkle with sifted icing sugar. Cover with a second layer, then more sugar and so proceed till the container is almost filled. Cover with a scrap of kitchen foil and refrigerate. Just before serving, stir well, and stir in liqueurs which are complementary to the chosen fruits (pages 233-4)—and to the approbation of your palate.

# How many housewives have crowns?

We can't tell, exactly. Last year alone, over 20 million pieces of 'Pyrex' glassware were sold — and each one embossed with the 'Pyrex' crown and the maker's initials — J A J for James A. Jobling.

'Pyrex' oven-to-table ware is so versatile and so attractive. There are many, many designs, both in clear glass and decorated opalware. Casseroles, plates, platters, bowls and many others. All heat resistant — and all good to look at.

And have you discovered 'Pyrosil Ware'? Saucepans, frying pans and coffee pots, that look like pretty porcelain, yet are so tough they can withstand a naked flame or electric ring. Wonderful to cook with — beautiful to serve from.

## PYREX   PYROSIL♛WARE®
Regd. Trade Mark

James A. Jobling & Co. Ltd., Wear Glass works, Sunderland.

# Chapter 14

# *Dark brown study*

| | |
|---|---|
| Chocolate Birds | Mum's Chocolate Trifle |
| Chocolate Swans | Petits Pots de Chocolat |
| Chocolate Leaves | Crème Marie Louise |
| Chocolate Cases | Gâteau l'Ambassadeur |
| Square Chocolate Gâteaux | Ganache |
| Chocolate Dobos Sponge | Ganache Chocolates |
| Chocolate Dobos Torte | Ganache Pyramids |
| Chocolate Soufflé | Ganache Cream Puddings |
| Gâteau au Chocolat | Ganache Layer Cake |
| Chocolate Meringues | Ganache Petits Gâteaux |
| Chocolate Ice Cream | Chocolate Truffles |
| Mocha Ice Cream | Florentines |

*Question: The family always praises the things I make with chocolate powder but when I work with the best milk, plain or bitter chocolate I can buy—it always seems to go wrong. Why?*

*Answer:*

Although we are going to devote an entire chapter to this problem there is a very short answer indeed . . . because you use milk, plain or bitter chocolate.

The chocolate situation in this country in relation to home cooks presents a most curious anomaly. Everyone wants to cook with chocolate. Chocolate cookery is a synonym for Top of the Culinary Pops or Instant Success at Table. Let any cook so much as murmur "Now my chocolate mousse . . . " and all other cooks are on her like a cloud of vultures. Everyone wants new chocolate recipes, yet for a very long time indeed home chocolate cookery has been severely handicapped.

Only cooking chocolate (*couverture*) can be used successfully for a great many items which people want to make for themselves; but *couverture* is sold wholesale in bulk to professionals and only very rarely retailed in domestic quantities to housewives. Indeed very few housewives know of *couverture's* existence and assume that when they buy a half-pound slab of eating chocolate they are buying exactly the same as the professional chocolate maker, only in smaller quantities. This they try to soften. It goes into a lumpy goo, then they add water to it which is absolutely fatal, so they become furious because the expensive stuff is wasted and very reasonably assume that the whole thing is far too difficult and needs professional experience. None of which is in fact true at all.

So first let us clear the air. Using **eating** chocolate as a substitute for **cooking** chocolate is just a prime example of trying to fit a square culinary peg into a round culinary hole. Eating chocolate is meant for eating. It will not reheat successfully to be used thereafter as a smooth, well-coloured coating or moulding agent.

At this point you may very well mutter crossly, "Well, how are they going to get a chapter out of something we can't do?" So let us quickly tell you that at last cooking chocolate has been put up in the form of chocolate chips which can be bought in very small bags, softened and used to make chocolates, Easter eggs, the chocolate swans we invented and a great many other things as well. From this point, therefore, we will talk of chocolate chips in precisely the same breath as *couverture* and all the things we tell you for one can be used for the other.

Whichever you are using, chips or *couverture*, your No. 1 enemy is over-heating. Cooking chocolate must always be reduced to a smooth creamy consistency at very low heat and must always be given a very thorough beating indeed before using it. Like a woman, a dog and a walnut tree, the more you beat it, the better it be! The next thing you must know is how to thin cooking chocolate if it is too thick for, say, the top of a cake or for using as a layer in a chocolate trifle. For this purpose there is only one way—with sugar syrup.*

Cooking chocolate can be softened either over hot water in a double or porage saucepan or in a heat-resistant container in the oven; but neither way should be this be done quickly. We learned how to soften chocolate from M. Jean Sabat, the very famous *pâtissier* and *chocolatier* of Tours. A huge block would be placed in a bowl and put into the warming drawer of an oven (at lowest heat) overnight. When taken out the following morning the block still held its shape but as soon as it was touched with a wooden spoon, it collapsed creamily. This was when it had its beating. After beating and if it is too thick for its intended use, add small spoonfuls of sugar syrup* **sparingly** beating each addition into the mixture until it reaches the required consistency.

When you have used the amount of undiluted cooking chocolate you require you can cover any residue with a scrap of foil and store it in a dry place in complete confidence that it can be re-heated almost indefinitely, thereafter.

Quite apart from standard chocolate work, we have invented a very simple way of making chocolate ornaments and containers. These are enormous fun to do, they can be advance-made and stored in an airtight tin in a dry place to draw on at speed for parties. We are confident that once you have caught the idea you will be able to go on and invent a great many shapes of your own. So here we go— together.

For this Bon Viveur Invention you will need prepared cooking chocolate, greaseproof paper, a pencil and 2 knives, one round-tipped and the other one small and pointed-tipped. Then you decide on an outline shape —a silhouette in fact. Let us say a Gull in Flight as a basic example, as this is easy to draw or trace from an illustration. Draw it in pencil on greaseproof paper, then, having turned the paper over so that outline shows through, use one or other of the two knives to spread softened chocolate to the edges of your chosen design. You will need the pointed knife for pushing the chocolate into fine wing tips, beak and such like. The round-tipped one does for the central part of each spread.

chocolate
bird

Leave the chocolate to set, then peel off the paper and you will find that you are then holding a **Chocolate Bird** in your hand! This can be used to enhance either a simple or an elaborate dish. Say you merely put a dollop of coffee ice cream into a *coupe* and top it with *crème Chantilly** or whipped cream. Just push a chocolate bird on top of each portion to give it a "lift" and make it charming and impressive instead of dull and ordinary. The bird of course is eaten in the fingers like a *petits fours* biscuit or a wafer.

312

The particular elaboration of this theme which we have found effective can be followed by you from the diagram of **Chocolate Swan** components (page 383). Trace them in greaseproof, fill them in, peel off and store between layers of greaseproof or wax paper, to draw on when needed. Pray remember, however, that chocolate will turn whitey-grey if stored in a damp place. Then you will have to either recoat it or brush it with the professional chocolate varnish which we do not recommend. It is harmless but has a silicone base! Try to avoid using it please. Indeed, if the Sabats found us using it, they would probably murder us!

If you make the ovals of our swan diagram in sponge and then pipe the edge all round with suitably flavoured butter cream, you can put ice cream or ice cream scoop-cut domes of any cream pudding into the centre, press the wings and tail into the chosen cream to hold them securely and anchor the base of the head and neck piece with a couple of rosettes of butter or whipped cream. Decorate the dome tops with little feathery squiggles of whipped cream or *crème Chantilly*\* and scatter the tops with milled pistachio nuts.

A chocolate cake looks really something if you put a large **Chocolate Swan,** filled with chocolate butter cream or whipped cream, in the centre and make a small flotilla of cygnets to swim round the top edge.

Do you begin to grasp the idea? Now skim

313

through the pages of a few illustrated magazines and find your tracing subjects from these unless you are fortunate enough to be able to draw freehand—which we cannot! Illustrations of flowers, fruit, birds, fish,— are all ideal subjects for such tracings.

There is another gorgeous piece of chocolate garnish one-up-man-ship, which completely foxes the uninitiated. Assemble a few well-shaped unblemished rose leaves with each leaf carefully cut from the main stem but leaving a little bit of stalk on itself. Wipe them in case there is any fly but do not wash. Now tow the upper side of each leaf carefully across some softened chocolate. Lay aside to set with the uncoated side downwards.

chocolate
leaves

You will find that after a few minutes you will be able to peel away the actual leaf leaving a perfect **Chocolate Leaf** with every bit of delicate veining reproduced on its upper surface. These can be pushed into spirals of cream on individual portions of pudding or ice cream. A whole iced cake can be covered with them so the top looks like a flat Victorian (chocolate) nosegay. They can be used as a border for a trifle in a large, round dish or to decorate the tops of individual *gâteaux*, *petits fours* or chocolate or coffee-iced *choux* buns.

chocolate
cases

It is possible you have not thought of making your own edible **Chocolate Cases.** They look wildly professional and you scarcely need us to tell you that you can fill them with almost any kind of creamy, jelly, mousse or sponge fruit and custard pudding. For them, you must have those straight-sided, crimped-edged waxed paper cases which are sold by most large stationers for picnics. Just pour in softened chocolate, swirl it around until base and sides are well coated and leave until set. These cases all have a little rim, pull out one little bit very gently which stretches the case as it pulls at the fluting, go on doing this all round and you will be able to remove the case, leaving the little chocolate container ready for you to use. Remember that no oiling or greasing is necessary for any of the above.

If you want us to suggest some special "chocolate case" fillings for you, we would start by saying that the most gorgeous of all chocolate puddings *Crème Marie Louise* (page 323) is the perfect one, but there are many more which are a good deal less elaborate and expensive. Slip a base circle of fatless sponge into each chocolate case, two-thirds fill with confectioners' custard flavoured with a few drops of either Tia Maria or Crème de Cacao (liqueurs) and push a spiral of whipped cream through an icing bag and pipe down into this custard, so that it is four-fifths submerged like an iceberg and only a small cream peak rises above it centrally. Then just scatter coarsely grated milk chocolate overall.

Alternatively you can use the *Petits Pots de Chocolat* mixture (page 322); or small

portions of *Gâteau L'Ambassadeur* (page 324).
If you really want to be a show-off with these
little puddings and whatever the filling, you
can top them with rounded triangles of
chocolate trellising made to the same size
and shape as the Pompadour Ice Cream
Fan Wafers sold in packets by the grander
grocers (page 369). Trace the outline on
greaseproof, turn the paper over, fill a paper
icing bag* with softened chocolate and then
just doodle in thin chocolate wiggles inside
the outline you have drawn. When set, you
can peel off these lacy sections and drive one
point uppermost into each filled chocolate
case.

square
chocolate
gâteaux

You can also use the paper treatment for
making individual **Square Chocolate
Gâteaux.** You need 4 squares of chocolate
for each, so draw and fill in the required
number of squares leaving spaces in between
on your greaseproof, with each square
measuring $2\frac{1}{4}$ inch. Now leave them to set
while you make your cake.

dobos
sponge

First you will need a batch of **Dobos
Sponge.** Assemble 3 standard eggs, 2 oz.
twice sifted self-raising flour and $2\frac{1}{2}$ oz.
sifted icing sugar. Separate the yolks from
the whites. Put about half the sugar with
the yolks and whisk until they double their
bulk and become foamy and light in colour.
Fold in the remaining sugar. Whip up the
egg whites very stiffly and fold these into
the batter alternately with the flour. When
smoothly blended, level off into a standard

Swiss roll tin which has been lined with oiled greaseproof paper. Bake in a pre-heated oven at gas 5 (380°F) until very pale golden and just set. Baking time depends upon mixture's thickness but they only need a few minutes. Cool on a sheet of greaseproof paper on a rack.

Cut into squares when cold. Now spread an equal thickness of chocolate butter cream between these squares to make three-tiered cakes. Spread the sides with the same butter cream. Peel the chocolate squares off their paper and press round the four sides. Decorate the top of each with a piped squiggle of butter cream, or you can spread the tops thinly with the butter cream instead and then sprinkle thickly with browned flaked almonds.

chocolate dobos torte

We must be honest at this stage and admit that this is not the proper way to use **Dobos Sponge.** The recipe is right but if you are going to make it into a classic **Chocolate Dobos Torte** you should bake **very thin** layers on oiled greaseproof paper in 6 inch diameter cake tins. Then on removing from the oven and cooling them on greaseproof, as we have already explained, you must go one step further by mounding them one above the other with papers in between and putting them under a weight for one hour. Then you assemble these with an equal depth of filling between each layer.

For the filling soften 2 oz. cooking chocolate and beat it into 2 oz. of well whipped butter,

into which you have whipped 1 egg yolk and
continued beating while adding 2 oz. of
sifted icing sugar.

When the cake is assembled, spread top and
sides with cooking chocolate which has been
thinned down with a little sugar syrup so
that it will not be so hard as to crack when
cut. As it begins to set, press a knife around
the top to mark off individual sections.
Alternatively it can be dusted with sifted
icing sugar before service.

chocolate
soufflé

There is a rather splendid hot **Chocolate
Soufflé,** in which we deviate from standard
practice by using egg yolks. You will need
to soften $1\frac{1}{2}$ oz. butter in a thick pan. Stir in
$1\frac{1}{2}$ oz. self-raising flour and gradually beat
in a scant $\frac{3}{4}$ pint of milk, which has been
mixed over a low heat with 4 oz. cooking
chocolate, 1 vanilla pod (removed after
heating milk) and 3 oz. castor sugar. When
you have added half this milk mixture, get
someone else to whip 6 egg whites stiffly for
you or use an electric mixture while you finish
the sauce. When all the milk mixture is
incorporated, pour on to the lightly whipped
egg yolks, scrape back into the pan and beat
very thoroughly away from the heat. Pour
this mixture gradually on to the stiff egg
whites beating all the time. Pour into a
well buttered *soufflé* mould. Level off the top.
Sprinkle thickly with castor sugar. Bake one
shelf above centre in a pre-heated oven at
gas $7\frac{1}{2}$ (435°F) for 15-16 minutes. If desired,
you may further enhance the delicacy of this

*soufflé's* flavour by stirring $1\frac{1}{2}$ tablespoonsful of either Tia Maria or Crème de Cacao into the milk mixture and yolks before adding it to the egg whites.

If you should want the kind of Chocolate Cake that we like best—one which is dark and moist underneath and has a thin crust on top, you can repose your confidence in our **Gâteau au Chocolat.**

gâteau au chocolat

Assemble 3 standard eggs and an extra egg yolk, 5 oz. castor sugar, $2\frac{1}{2}$ oz. sifted flour and either $4\frac{1}{2}$ oz. of cooking chocolate, if you agree that the slightly bitter tang is attractive, or the same quantity of sweetened dessert chocolate if the bitterness does not appeal to you.

Place eggs, extra yolk and castor sugar in a bowl and stand this in an outer container half filled with boiling water. Now whip relentlessly until the mixture becomes thick, pale and fluffy. Remove the inner bowl and fold in the flour. Add the softened (over hot water) chocolate but be careful—beat it well and thus diminish its temperature before adding it to the cake mixture. Pour the mixture into a buttered and floured standard Victoria sponge tin and cook in a pre-heated oven at gas 4 (355°F). The cake is moist at 25 minutes and well cooked at 30—you choose.

It may then be served plain under a thick dusting of sifted icing sugar, or split and filled. For the filling, soften $2\frac{1}{2}$ oz. cooking chocolate over hot water, beat in 2 egg yolks and $1\frac{1}{4}$

oz. softened butter. Continue beating until the mixture cools. Add a scant ½ oz. of sifted icing sugar and a teaspoonful of Tia Maria or Crème de Cacao.

Spread over one half of the cake, clap the second on top, press together and spread any that oozes out around the sides. Then pick up the cake like a wheel between the palms of your hands and trundle the sides through finely chopped nuts. Cover the top with softened cooking chocolate, thinned down with a little stock sugar syrup* and decorate either with walnuts or with little sections cut from chocolate coffee creams.

If you have enjoyed this recipe, you might like to go on to an even more moist and much richer version, which merely replaces 2 oz. of the flour with 2 oz. of ground almonds. When baked this cake is turned out, cooled and piped thickly on top with Tia Maria or Crème de Cacao-flavoured *crème Chantilly**.

chocolate meringue

You can play tricks like this with meringue mixture too, if you just make up the standard no-weep basic meringue by whipping 5 egg whites stiffly, whipping in 2 oz. castor sugar and continuing to whip unceasingly for 3 minutes thereafter. You then just fold in— with a plastic or metal spatula—a further 6 oz. of castor sugar and 1½ oz. sifted sweetened chocolate powder as well. Then to fox everyone, stir in about 1½ oz. of chocolate chips. Drop in rough blobs on an oiled greaseproof-paper-lined baking sheet and bake at gas 1 (290°F) until you can lift them off easily, (¾-1 hour according to the size of the blobs). The curious thing about this recipe is that though the meringue bakes perfectly the little chocolate chips retain their shape inside.

One such **Chocolate Meringue** over a slice of home-made chocolate ice cream decorated with whipped cream makes a very good party pudding, so you will next want to know how to make the **Chocolate Ice Cream.**

chocolate ice cream

Soften 2½ oz. of cooking chocolate with 2 tablespoonsful of stock syrup*, stir into 1½ pints confectioners' custard* and beat well. Pour into refrigerator ice cube trays, freeze until the mixture begins to set, then scrape into a bowl and beat until mixture is loose and creamy. Fold in 6 fl. oz. of fairly stiffly whipped cream and re-freeze until required.

mocha ice cream

Remember that you can turn this into **Mocha Ice Cream** very easily if the confectioners' custard is made up with 50 per cent. coffee and 50 per cent. milk instead of all milk.

Once again you can play tricks with it if you have used cooking chocolate. Whether it is the plain chocolate version or the mocha one, you can streak it with plain chocolate, so that the effect is of faint chocolate marbling when the ice cream is finally set.

You follow the recipe right through until the second freezing is completed, i.e. after the cream has been added. Then you re-scrape it into a bowl and just beat it down until it is no longer lumpy. Ladle in a little syrup-diluted chocolate with one hand, while drawing it down with a fork with the other. This can then be refrozen in the freezing trays but is better reset in a mould.

mum's
chocolate
trifle

Now it is time to share with you what Fanny has always passed on as **Mum's Chocolate Trifle.** Line out a wide shallow bowl with 24 roughly broken Savoy fingers. Pour a small teacupful of sweet Madeira (Bual or Malmsey) on top. Stir in ½ lb. of warmed, sieved, bought or home-made peach or apricot jam and 2 rounded tablespoonsful of shredded almonds. Stir together and press down so that mixture presents a flat surface. Put 4 oz. cooking chocolate into the top of a double saucepan over hot water with 2 tablespoonsful of single cream or top of the milk. Stir until smooth and creamy. Beat in 3 egg yolks and remove from heat. Add 3 stiffly whipped egg whites, beat again and set aside.

petits pots
de chocolat

This is to be used as a layer of sauce in your trifle but while it is put to this purpose in Mum's Chocolate Trifle, it is nothing more or less than **Petits Pots de Chocolat** which can be served as a pudding on its own if it is filled into little custard glasses, left to set and topped with stiffly whipped cream.

Before we use it in the trifle, however, we must cover the sponge mixture with $1\frac{1}{2}$ pints of standard confectioners' custard*, into which 6 macaroons are crumbled. Chill the bowlful until it is almost set. Cover with the **Petits Pots de Chocolat** mixture. Pipe rosettes of whipped cream on top. Sprinkle with coarsely grated milk chocolate and decorate all round the edge with Chocolate Rose Leaves (page 314) which brings us to the point we must tell you a fairy story.

Once upon a time there was a little Austrian princess who married an emperor of France whose name was Napoleon. The little Princess soon became homesick for the rich chocolate confections of her native land, so Napoleon commanded his *chef* to create a new one in her honour and it was called after her, **Crème Marie Louise.** Some years ago we made an elaborate presentation of this when we cooked at the Royal Albert Hall in front of 6,750 people. Here is a slightly smaller version.

crème
Marie
Louise

Soften $\frac{3}{4}$ lb. of cooking chocolate in the warming drawer of your oven at the very lowest possible heat. Beat up $\frac{1}{2}$ pint double cream until it holds a peak. Take the chocolate from the oven and beat it very thoroughly until it is cool and creamy. Beat it into the cream quickly and equally quickly beat in 4 egg yolks. As it starts thickening add 1 tablespoonful of rum and 1 small teaspoonful each of orange flower and rose waters. Serve in little glasses with *crème*

*Chantilly*\*—on top or give it the same treatment in little chocolate cases as we explained on page 314 of this chapter.

gâteau
l'ambassa-
deur

We have long debated whether this pudding or **Gâteau l'Ambassadeur** should take pride of place at the top of our chocolate pudding list. Certainly when we made the *gâteau* on television, we had more demands for it than anything we have ever shown, and equally certainly it is a boon for a home cook because it will keep for at least a week in mild refrigeration and therefore can be got well out of the way when a large batch of cooking lies ahead. One or two of the thousands to whom we have given this recipe have written saying it does not work but we can assure you that if you leave nothing out and do exactly what we have described, **it does, every time!** After we had received these little moans, we gave the recipe to a pupil-trainee aged 16, who had never made it in his life and he did so perfectly with no assistance from us.

Alas we cannot take the credit for this either! It was filched for us by the proprietress of a small hotel in Paris which had been recommended to us as being "clean, quiet, inexpensive, very respectable and only five minutes from the Folies Bergères!" Madame stole it from an embassy and we became the grateful receivers of stolen goods!

The ingredients are precise and must on no account be varied. The container in which it is set must be an oiled, sliding-based $7\frac{1}{2}$ inch

324

diameter cake tin. You assemble $\frac{1}{4}$ lb. of cooking chocolate, $3\frac{1}{2}$ oz. crumbled *petit beurre* biscuits, $3\frac{1}{2}$ oz. best unsalted butter, $3\frac{1}{2}$ oz. sifted icing sugar, 3 tablespoonsful double cream, 3 tablespoonsful cooking kirsch, 2 egg yolks, 2 stiffly whipped egg whites and 2 oz. peeled fresh white grapes.

Soak the biscuits in 2 tablespoonsful of kirsch and add the third spoonful to the peeled grapes. Soften the chocolate to a smooth paste over a low heat with 2 tablespoonsful warm water. Meanwhile shave the butter into small flakes. Then scrape softened chocolate into a bowl and beat in the butter until it is perfectly smooth. Fold in the egg yolks and beat again. Stir in the sugar until it vanishes. Now fold in all remaining ingredients. Turn into prepared cake tin and allow to set in mild refrigeration. Unmould and garnish the top with *crème Chantilly*\* lightly flavoured with kirsch.

If we have succeeded in wooing you this far into the exciting realms of professional chocolate work, which we have carefully translated into domestic terms, we are confident you will boldly tackle something very special indeed. Its professional name is ganache **Ganache.** It is wildly adaptable, marvellously rich, makes ideal sweetmeats for gifts and is completely unsuited to very small children! Please do not try sloshing this mixture up when you are in a hurry. Follow the instructions unswervingly when you have an uncluttered mind.

Begin by putting 12 oz. cooking chocolate to soften. Meanwhile oil a square or rectangular, maximum 1 inch deep tin or set up a professional wooden frame. Fanny's hands are about as handy with a hammer as a dog's paws with a finger bowl, but she has never had any difficulty in making these frames. You simply saw 4 inch, 9 inch, 12 inch or 15 inch long strips of ordinary planed wood slatting and nail them together with panel pins and a nice light hammer, which will not blacken the finger nails when you make a bosh shot. With a new frame it is advisable to leave it soaking overnight in a shallow pan of oil to "season" the wood. After this you merely brush the inside of the frame and the marble or Formica surface on which you will set it, with oil.

Having got that off our chests let us tackle the remaining ingredients for basic **Ganache.** They are $2\frac{3}{4}$ oz. castor sugar, 2 egg yolks, $3\frac{1}{4}$ fl. oz. of boiling double cream and 1 generous tablespoonful of Tia Maria or Crème de Cacao. Only when the softened *couverture* is collapsible enough to be beaten down to a smooth thick cream, do you start the actual making. Then you whip egg yolks and sugar together in a bowl until they are transformed into a thick, pale batter. Pour the boiling cream on to this and whip very thoroughly indeed. Scrape the mixture into the top of a double saucepan over hot water. Then stir over a low heat with a wooden spoon until it clings thickly to the back of the spoon. Now remove from heat and beat in softened *couverture* again very thoroughly. Finally beat in the chosen liqueur, scrape into the oiled frame or tin, level off and leave until set. Then either cut into squares or stamp out into fancy shapes with ornamental metal cutters. Store between layers of waxed paper in an air-tight tin.

Once having tasted this, we are reasonably confident you will want some variations on the theme. Firstly, you can turn these into **Ganache Chocolates** by dipping them into more softened *couverture* and slipping them into paper sweet cases. Decorate the tops with split almonds, halved walnuts, sprinklings of chopped nuts, crystallised rose petals, violets or little leaves of angelica, *glacé* ginger or pineapple.

Secondly, you can fold into the mixture chopped mixed nuts and *glacé* fruits, in which case you drop rough blobs on to an oiled surface and put them into paper cases when they are set.

Thirdly you can fold whipped double cream into the hot **Ganache** and thus make a fabulous party pudding.

Fourthly, you can spread it between layers of our *Gâteau au Chocolat* (page 319). When doing this we suggest you bake the given cake quantity for a shorter period, dividing the mixture between two oiled, greaseproof-paper lined Victoria sponge tins.

ganache chocolates

Fifthly, you can make one and a half times the given amount of *Gâteau au Chocolat*, bake in two thin layers in two standard Swiss roll tins and clap the two together with a thick spreading of hot **Ganache** in between. When cold cut into either fingers or squares for serving under a thick dusting of sifted icing sugar. Or you can coat the sides of each little cake lightly with softened chocolate, dip these moist sides into chopped nuts or chocolat vermicelli, coat the tops with syrup-diluted cooking chocolate and top-decorate with tiny rosettes, spirals or criss-cross trellising using a No. 43 or 44 icing pipe —these are the little ones which you put into paper icing bags.

There are thousands more variations but just to start you thinking we will finish on our chocolate truffles sixth variant—**Chocolate Truffles.** For these you allow the **Ganache** to set in a bowl to the point where you can roll it into little balls, which you then roll in chocolate vermicelli until each one is thickly coated. The rather slummy alternative, if you are in a hurry, is to roll them in sweetened chocolate powder. Both these sweetmeats can be made and stored successfully.

Florentines So can **Florentines.**
Our recipe for these was given to us by Noreen Prichard-Carr. When we tested this recipe we found that although they are just a bit tricky to make, the end product justifies the care demanded. The only problem is that the mixture gets messy and a bit spread

during baking time. We, frankly, thought they would be a failure, and rather unhopefully worked sides to middle with a small knife. The result as the mixture cooled, was that they held together impeccably and kept well thereafter in a foil-lined tin.

Prepare your flat baking sheets first, lining each out with greaseproof and brushing with oil. Then put together in a saucepan $2\frac{1}{2}$ fl. oz. of milk, 4 oz. butter, 6 oz. castor sugar and set over a very scant heat for the sugar to dissolve, making sure the last grain has disappeared before the mixture nears boiling point. Meanwhile assemble 6 oz. flaked almonds, $1\frac{1}{2}$ oz. flour and $1\frac{1}{2}$ oz. each of chopped *glacé* cherries, sultanas, mixed peel and seeded raisins all mixed together. As the sugar mixture approaches boiling point give it a very thorough stir, then stir in (a) flour, (b) almonds and (c) mixed fruits and peel. Now work it up well until distribution is even.

Drop heaped dessertspoonsful fairly wide apart on the prepared baking sheets. Pat them down, then bake on centre shelf in the oven at gas $3\frac{1}{2}$ ($345°$F) for 20 minutes.

Remove and tidy up the edges as already explained. By this time they will have cooled sufficiently for you to trim them round neatly with a pair of scissors. This done, set them upside down on a rack and spread the under-sides with softened cooking chocolate or chocolate chips (page 365). As the chosen chocolate sets, streak across with a fork to achieve the professional surface.

# Chapter 15

# *Outlaw damp flannel !*

Brown Bread
Individual Bread Rolls
Bread Plait
White Bread Dough
Walnut Bread
Sweet Walnut Bread
Sweet Fruit Bread
Pain de Fruits
Swedish Christmas Bread
Dutch Easter Bread
Waffles
Saindoux

Flapjacks
Southern Spoon Bread
Talahassee Hush Puppies
Saffron Bread
Saffron Buns
Hot Cross Buns
Sweet Scones
Cornflour Scones
Wholemeal Scone Mixture
Wholemeal Sultana Scones
Gran's Quick Bread

*Question: I'm sick to death of the shop loaf, and want to make my own bread; but I certainly cannot cope with making it every other day, and mine seems to get stale so quickly—do you bake three times a week? Is it beyond the scope of a modest home cook and are there any special things I need to know?*

*Answer:*

There **are** special things you need to know, very simple ones which we will explain. We bake at most twice a week. Our bread keeps splendidly. We are guilty of a slight terminological inexactitude in saying **we** bake, because in the last 18 months all the items in this chapter have been made by 16-year-old beginner cooks.

Now let us go back to the very beginning and talk about the "special things." The very first thing you must do is to separate the culinary sheep from the goats. A great gulf divides the professional baker from the home bread maker.

The experienced professional baker will be meticulous at all times about the strength or weakness of the flour from which he makes his selections. All further premises are based upon this first one: that the flour must be perfect for the job! Having coped with every other contingency the baker must then work to stringent rules and regulations concerning size and weight and the burning necessity to show a profit on everything he makes.

All **we** home cooks have to do is to avoid a few standard pitfalls for the unwary in order to produce the kind of bread that we, our family and friends enjoy—with a fig for the cost, or weight, provided all is within our budget.

What we must do is be a good deal more careful than a great many of us are about what flour we buy. Those of us who are passionately opposed to artificial fertilisers, artificial bleaching agents and artificial sprays used to combat the mildew dangers of stored grain, will go to health food departments of large stores, or health food or pure food shops and buy compost-grown stone-ground flour. Those of us who merely wish to avoid feeding our families to white bread made with flour which is riddled with chalk or artificial bleaching agents will studiously court myopia by peering closely at the smallest print on every bag of white flour that we bring into our homes. When we see "This flour contains no artificial bleaching agent whatever" printed on the packs, we buy and take home contentedly. We store our flour in a very dry place; we do not keep large quantities in stock so that residues become ageing breeding grounds for weevils and we sift our chosen, strong as possible flour, three times before using. Since the strength of flour is rarely indicated on the label, ingratiate yourself with your local baker and get him to sell you a little of the flour he uses for making bread.

Just to complete the picture let us list a few of the smaller essential rules for good home baking.

Never scrimp the kneading.

Try whenever possible to buy live bakers' yeast and not the dried varieties.

Always warm the container in which the dough will be made.

Never scrimp on proving time—if the dough has not risen to the top of the tins when proved, it will quite definitely not rise any more during baking.

Never fill tins more than just over half full of raw dough before proving.

Always rap baked bread with the knuckles when testing to see if it is properly baked. Give the top of each loaf a sharp tap. If it emits a hollow sound, the bread is done. If it gives off a dull heavy sound, it is insufficiently cooked and will be soggy and heavy.

Cool the bread on racks.

When perfectly cold, wrap loaves tightly in kitchen foil and (ideally) store in a wooden khiver or bread chest. Failing this, store in a wooden kitchen drawer or do what we have done in the absence of a khiver or a large enough drawer—buy an unpainted wood chest for about £4 9s. 6d. (stockists page 370) and paint it to suit your kitchen décor. We have painted ours in bold stripes and locked the paint in with a final overcoat of colourless varnish. It is not a bad plan to give the inside a lining of kitchen foil, shiny side outwards.

You can also use a traditional earthenware crock for storage. This will be less attractive but equally functional.

Now we can go ahead with our baking. We can ignore the nastiness of much of today's mass-produced bread and we can fill our homes with the sweet fragrant aroma of baking bread which more than any other food smell sets the gastric juices working, the taste buds quivering and evokes an almost painful craving. As so many of us have to watch our waistlines we will begin by reminding you that the more healthful and brown bread slimming **Brown Bread** is made with 3 lbs. of fine brown flour and all the remaining ingredients we have given in Basic Home made Bread*.

When we have made up some of a batch into loaves, we can use small quantities to individual make **Individual Bread Rolls.** Scale off bread rolls the dough into 2 oz. pieces. Roll these out on a lightly floured surface into neat fat sausages about 4 inch long. Pinch the ends into points so that the finished effect is of small ovals. Take a pair of scissors and nick a series of large "vees" along the centre of the top of each roll. Give these their second proving, brush them with strained beaten egg and salt in the proportion 1 egg to 1 level teaspoonful salt and bake at gas 8 (445°F) as for bread loaves.

If you want to turn these very effectively into individual **Knots** or **Plaits,** scale off the dough into 2 to 3 oz. pieces for the knots or 9 inch pieces for the simple 3-strand plaits, then turn to page 162 for knotting and plaiting instructions, and bake after final proving at gas 8 (445°F).

bread plait If you really want to be a show off, you can make an impressive 5-strand **Bread Plait.** Follow the diagram and instructions on page 390, but please be wise before the event and follow our instructions until you are familiar with this five strand plait!

white bread dough Whether you want to make large loaves of white bread or plaits, knots or oval rolls, you will find that nothing is very different from making up the **White Bread Dough.** For a good family batch weigh out and sift two separate 2 lb. quantities of white flour tipping one into the warmed mixing container. Stir 4 flat dessertspoonsful of both bakers' yeast and castor sugar together until dissolved. Hollow the flour in the mixing crock, tip in the yeast fluid. Heat 21 fl. oz. of milk and 21 fl. oz. of water to blood temperature, add them to the yeast fluid and work all up by hand to a loose paste. Work 1¼ oz. salt in with the hand. Put several tea towels or preferably a piece of clean blanket or felt over the top and if you have no suitable warming drawer or cupboard, stand on top of a cooker with the oven on at gas 4 (355°F). Leave for 20 minutes. Remove cloths, draw in the remaining 2 lb. of flour by hand, beat up to a smooth dough and then knead it for at least 10 minutes on a lightly floured board or other wooden surface. Remember to come right down on the dough from above and not go at it sideways as if

335

pushing a garden roller. Bread dough dislikes being tickled and is happiest when given a good strong handling with the heel of the hand. Brush the inside of your chosen bread tins with oil, dust them with flour and tap off any surplus into the flour bin. Put in the dough and re-prove as explained for 45-50 minutes, pre-heating the oven to gas 8 (445°F). Egg wash the tops of each loaf and bake as explained.

The above recipe is not the same as our previous one* because recent experience with students has shown that a high percentage of white dough absorbs less moisture than brown dough, so for one thing we are giving a slightly lower fluid content per pound of flour. If you think your dough is coming up too thick, you then can add 1 extra fl. oz. of water and 1 extra fl. oz. of milk after tipping the second lot of flour into the crock.

Emboldened by the inevitable success of your simple breadmaking, go on to make special breads. Try **Walnut Bread** for serving with summer salads and other savoury items. Assemble 1 lb. Scofa flour, ½ lb. salted butter, ½ pint milk, 2 level teaspoonsful salt, 2 generous pinches nutmeg and 1 pinch of cinnamon, 8 oz. roughly-chopped walnuts and 2 standard eggs. Sift flour with spices and salt into a large bowl. Rub in the butter very finely. Work in the walnuts. Beat eggs and milk together. Make a well in the centre of the dry mixture, tip in the egg and milk and work up to rather a wet mixture. Only

walnut
bread

336

half-fill the resultant dough into well-buttered rectangular bread tins and bake in a pre-heated oven, middle shelf, at gas 4 (355°F) for 1 hour or until baked bread gives off a hollow sound when rapped with the knuckles. Cool on a rack and wrap in kitchen foil for storage.

sweet
walnut
bread

If you want a **Sweet Walnut Bread** work 12 oz. of soft brown ("pieces") sugar into the flour and spice mixture given for the **Walnut Bread,** but **with only a generous pinch of salt.** For the extra bulk made by the sugar, give an additional 15 minutes baking time i.e. 1 hour 15 minutes instead of 1 hour.

sweet fruit
bread

If, for special occasions, you hanker after a **Sweet Fruit Bread,** you will need to allow for it when making up a batch of plain white dough (page 335). Weigh off 1½ lb. of the dough and shape it into a ball. Pull it apart gently from top centre until you have achieved a rough bowl shape. In a separate basin cream 3 oz. of lard and work in 2 oz. crushed loaf sugar, 2 oz. sultanas, 1 oz. currants, 1 oz. peel and 1 raw egg. Place this mixture into the hollowed out dough, draw the pulled-out edges back over the top, press one half over the other and press down gently with the heel of the hand. Pull out, fold over and press down, repeating these three movements until the fruit mixture is fairly evenly distributed. Half fill oiled and floured tins with the dough, prove till the mixture has risen to the top of

337

the tins and then bake for 15 minutes at gas 7½ (435°F). Brush liberally with raw beaten egg, sprinkle crushed loaf sugar over the top and continue baking until the loaf is firm, springy and gives off a hollow sound when knuckle-rapped.

When we make up a batch of bread on Christmas Eve for the holiday or at Easter, we not only wrap the cold **Fruit Bread** in foil but on Christmas morning or Easter Day we loosen the wrapping without removing it all, warm the bread through at gas 1 (290°F) for about 12 minutes, and then serve sliced and hot with lashings of Normandy butter when no farm butter is available.

This **Fruit Bread** is one of a small company of W.G.F.F. (Worth Getting Fat For) which we cherish. With it goes **Pain de Fruits,** an extremely delicate and distinctly luxurious waist ruining bread from Alsace.

pain de
fruits

Begin by buttering and flouring an 8 inch diameter solid (not sliding based) cake tin. Put 7 oz. flour, 1 oz. potato flour and ½ oz. powdered cinnamon into a sieve and sift into a large mixing bowl. Add 4 oz. sultanas, 2 oz. chopped almonds, 2 oz. chopped hazelnuts and 4 oz. mixed peel. In another bowl whip 8 oz. castor sugar with 6 standard eggs until very light and frothy. Work the mixture up by dolloping handsful of the mixed flours and fruits on to the batter and beating between each dollop. Finally beat in 2 tablespoonsful of rum and 1 teaspoonful of strained lemon juice. Bake on the centre shelf

at gas $3\frac{1}{2}$ (345°F) for approximately 1 hour
5 minutes.

Swedish
Christmas
bread

Yet another W.G.F.F. is **Swedish Christmas Bread** which reverses all our ambitions
about other home-made breads since it is
wrapped after baking and cooling in linen
cloths **to keep the crusts soft.** Nor is it
for strictly teetotal maiden aunts as it is
launched in the kitchen with stout!

Pour $4\frac{1}{2}$ gills of stout on to 2 oz. of hot
melted butter. Then stand and beat it
patiently until it descends to blood heat,
after this it must be poured into a large bowl
and be given $1\frac{1}{2}$ gills corn syrup (page 367)
which is also beaten in. Sift together 1 lb.
11 oz. of rye flour and 13 oz. of white flour
which makes a total of 2 lb. 8 oz. of mixed
flours. Weigh these off into three lots of 1 lb.
4 oz., $15\frac{1}{2}$ oz. and $4\frac{1}{2}$ oz.

Tip the 1 lb. 4 oz. onto the stout mixture and
mix it very thoroughly with a wooden spoon
if you are fussy about using your hand—which
is always better if you can bring yourself to do
so. Mix 3 oz. bakers' yeast with 1 teaspoonful
of castor sugar. If it does not liquefy, add a
second teaspoonful. Pour the resultant fluid
on top of the flour and stout mixtures and
beat thoroughly, adding in as you do so 1
level teaspoonful salt, the grated rind of 4
small or 2 large oranges, 4 level dessertspoonsful caraway seeds (optional) and the
$15\frac{1}{2}$ oz. flour. When the dough is so blended
that it has a shiny, "polished" appearance,
prove it under a thick covering of cloths or

339

blanket until it has almost doubled in bulk. Spread the third (4½ oz.) flours over a wooden surface. Tip the proved dough on top and knead it up steadily until it has taken in all the flour, leaving the wooden surface cleared by which time it should look smoothly glossy. Divide it into three equal parts—shape these into three long round-ended loaves. Lay these on well-buttered baking sheets, cover them again and prove until they have once more very nearly doubled their bulk.

Bake at gas 3½-4 (345-355°F) for about 40 minutes. At half-time (20 minutes) brush the tops with a tablespoonful of black treacle or molasses (stockists page 368) dissolved in 4 tablespoonsful of water. When baked, removed from the oven and set on racks to cool, brush them again with the molasses mixture and wrap up when **cold.**

Yet a third—Johnnie's favourite to the point of making fantastic excuses for (a) flying over to Holland at Eastertide and (b) arguing that it is an **essential** part of the weekly baking plan is **Dutch Easter Bread.**

Dutch Easter bread

When you make up ordinary white bread dough (page 335) and are of the same mind as Johnnie, always weigh off 1½ lb. of the dough, roll out rather gently to a ½ inch thick rectangle, and brush the top surface liberally with (cooled) melted butter.

Put 4 oz. ground almonds and 4 oz. sifted icing sugar into a bowl. Add 1 oz. chopped *glacé* cherries, 2 oz. sultanas and 1 oz. finely diced angelica. Bind with sufficient raw, unbeaten egg-white to make a paste firm enough to shape into a sausage. Shape this "sausage" to the length of the rolled out dough, place in position on one dough edge and roll up like a Swiss roll.

Score the top with $\frac{1}{4}$ inch deep cuts made slantwise down the whole length. Brush liberally with raw egg-yolk, sprinkle very thickly with crushed loaf sugar and bake at gas 8 (445°F) until bread gives off the usual hollow sound when rapped.

waffles

We have argued ourselves out of the plain fact that **Waffles** are not bread and do not contain yeast on the grounds that they can be made to take the place of toasted bread, if the sugar is omitted from the mixture. Anyway they taste so good that we must give you our special recipe! You will need a waffle iron (page 370). The most sensible domestic one that we know is 8 inch in diameter in four sections which can be divided after cooking, unless—like this household—you can account for a complete circle on your own.

Sift 11 oz. of flour into a roomy bowl with 1 level teaspoonful soda bicarbonate and 1 level teaspoonful baking powder. Make a well in the centre. Drop in 2 standard eggs and just enough from $\frac{1}{2}$ pint milk or milk and water to enable you to stir the mixture to a thick springy dough. When fairly smooth, beat in the remaining milk gradually and steadily, but on no account whisk it. When it is smooth, stir in 4 oz. of softened butter with a wooden spoon.

Use this mixture in a waffle iron which has been **heated dry** on both sides over a low heat and then brushed inside on both sides with melted butter or oil or better still, with *saindoux*. This we give you on page 343.

This **Waffle Batter** keeps for 48 hours in mild refrigeration so it does not have to be used up immediately after making. Thus, you can make up waffles for family supper on one evening, to serve classically with a jug of melted butter and a jug of maple syrup (page 368).

Then in summer you can mound each waffle or section of a waffle with fresh raspberries or strawberries, dust thickly with sifted icing sugar and top with whipped cream.

Alternatively, you can serve waffles for breakfast with crisp bacon rashers on top, provided these are cut very thinly (no. 3 cut) and you remember to pour bacon fat on to each waffle afterwards.

Now a word or two about the one place where you can go wrong—the cooking of the mixture. Firstly, the waffle iron must smoke viciously and sizzle as you brush on whatever fat you choose; secondly, the heat underneath must only be moderate and thirdly, you must be careful about the amount of mixture that you put in: for the size of waffle iron we have cited, we reckon 2 large dollops from a tablespoon is enough to fill the iron. Ease the dollops out lightly from the centre with the back of the spoon, so that the mixture is about $1\frac{1}{4}$ inch from the indented edge before you press the second half of the iron upon it.

If you overdo it, the surplus mixture will come oozing and bubbling out of the sides, making a fearful mess. If this does happen, have a knife handy and cut the surplus away as it oozes.

Always remember to turn the iron over before looking to see if the underside is done. If, when you lift the lid, this is a pale golden brown, leave it to cook on the second side as is, but if it is a rather disconsolate beige, turn it back again to brown before you cook the second side.

If you want to make waffles when you have no maple syrup in the house, golden syrup makes a very good substitute—in fact some people prefer it.

saindoux

Now for the **Saindoux.** Some years ago when we were in Brittany gorging ourselves on *crêpes dentelles* we wormed our way as usual into the kitchens of a celebrated *crêperie* owned and run—as an addition to her hotel—by a beautiful cook and most enchanting human being **Madame l'Helgoual'ch.**

These pancakes which are made on a griddle get their name from the fact they look like lace. They are not easy to make. You have to have a special black wheat flour and a special wooden skimmer for spreading the batter transparently thinly. Consequently the greasing agent is of paramount importance; hence **Saindoux.**

It is made by melting down enough raw unsalted pork fat in the oven at gas 1 (290°F) to yield 1 lb. Strain this off into a bowl.

Leave it out of refrigeration until it is soft, cold and opaque. Then beat in 2 raw egg yolks very thoroughly indeed. Scooped into a jar and stored in mild refrigeration it keeps indefinitely. Every time you want to make waffles or use a griddle, take out your **Saindoux** and use it instead of oil or butter.

This brings us to the inescapable fact that we must continue deviating long enough to share with you our cherished recipe for **Flapjacks.** Like the national loaf they can be like little bits of innersole when in fact they should be as light as air, so here is the way to ensure that essential lightness every time.

flapjacks

Sift ¾ lb. self-raising flour into a large bowl. Beat 13 fl. oz. of milk with 2 standard eggs. Sprinkle 1 dessertspoonful of sugar on top, stir into the flour and gradually work up to a thick batter. Sprinkle 1 level teaspoonful of cream of tartar over the surface, cut it in swiftly and gently with the side of a wooden spoon and leave for 3 minutes or until tiny bubbles break on the top surface.

Heat a griddle or thick iron frying pan over a fairly low flame. Brush with **Saindoux,** drop large dessertspoon-sized blobs of batter on to the griddle, spacing them widely apart. Wait until the mixture rises and, again, little bubbles break on top. Lift flapjacks up with a spatula and smack them down rather hard on to the underside. When a very smooth golden brown on each side, cool them on a rack and if not serving them immediately,

store them in an earthenware, lidded container.

southern
spoon
bread

From the Deep South we wangled a family
recipe for **Southern Spoon Bread** for which
you will need 1 lb. of white corn meal which
you sift into a bowl and stir in 1 pint boiling
water, working this mixture up until it is
smooth and free from lumps. Beat in 1
teaspoonful of salt, then 3 tablespoonsful
melted lard and as this begins to thicken up
the mixture, beat in $\frac{3}{4}$ pint milk and 3 well
beaten, separated egg yolks. Whip 3 egg
whites until they are just stiff. Cut them in
with the side of a spatula or the side of a
wooden spoon. Pour into a well-buttered
baking dish and bake at gas 5 (380°F) for
45 minutes. Serve hot in the baking tin.

Talahassee
hush
puppies

You can also show off with something as new
over here and as "different" as our recipe for
Spoon Bread—**Talahassee Hush Puppies.**
This also calls for corn meal—$1\frac{1}{2}$ lb. of it
sifted with 1 teaspoonful of salt and 2 heaped
teaspoonsful of baking powder into a large
bowl. Mix together $\frac{3}{4}$ pint of milk with $\frac{1}{4}$ pint
of water and stir it gradually into the flour
with small additions from 1 large Spanish
onion chopped very finely. Then sift in a
little extra cornmeal until you have a soft but
workable dough.
Tip on to a floured wooden surface, dip the
hands in flour, pull off and shape up pieces
of dough into "pones". These are in fact
oblong cakes about $\frac{3}{4}$ inch thick, 3 inch wide

345

and 5 inch long. When these are all made up, heat a deep pan of oil or lard until just below slightly smoking stage. Slide in the "pones" a few at a time, fry until they are well-browned all over and serve piping hot like **Spoon Bread.**

saffron
bread

Except in Cornwall there are very few people who know much about **Saffron Bread** yet it can be excellent if carefully made. Somehow the whole idea of saffron is so fascinating that we went so far as to plant the *crocus sativus* in order to harvest our own saffron, but unfortunately the birds got there first and pulled the flowers to bits. We are trying again—having found a "safe" bird-repellent (page 365).

Begin by dissolving 1 oz. bakers' yeast in ¾ gill of lukewarm milk. Weigh off and sift 12 oz. of flour. Put ½ rounded teaspoonful of saffron on a plate and warm it in the oven and then pound it with 1 teaspoonful of castor sugar and stir in 1 dessertspoonful of brandy. Then mix this with 3 oz. castor sugar. Add 1 small egg, whisk well. Whisk in 4 oz. softened butter and about 2 oz. of the given quantity of flour. Add the yeast mixture and the remaining flour. Beat the mixture thoroughly until it is smooth and firm. Sprinkle a little extra flour on top, cover thickly, and prove until the bulk is doubled which will take between 1½ and 2 hours. Turn on to a lightly floured wooden surface, knead well for about 5 minutes and then make up into plaits as in diagram page 390.

Prove these for the second time and when half as big again, brush the tops with beaten raw egg and salt, sprinkle thickly with crushed loaf sugar, then with chopped almonds and bake at gas 5 (380°F) for 15-20 minutes.

saffron buns This is also an excellent mixture for making into individual **Saffron Buns.** Just scale off the mixture into balls, pat the tops down slightly and make three or four sharp deep cuts across them. Prove for the second time and treat the tops before baking exactly as for the large loaves.

hot cross
buns
We have always held the opinion—and indeed have aired it in **The Daily Telegraph** —that home-made **Hot Cross Buns** are inevitably inferior to bought ones because of the lack of specialised plant for steam proving. We have, however, been experimenting with our yeast ferment* as used for *babas* and *savarins**, and have found that the given quantity, made up after its four beatings with a further ¼ pint of water produces surprisingly good **Hot Cross Bun** results.

Cream 6 oz. butter, add 6 oz. soft brown sugar and cream together. Gradually work in 1 lb. flour with the ½ pint of yeast ferment and 1 well beaten egg. Lastly add the pinch of salt. Cover and prove for 15 minutes.

Add a further 1 lb. flour, 5 oz. sultanas, 6½ oz. currants and a few drops of oiled bun spice which you can obtain from your nearest home baker **in small quantities.** Work up to a smooth firm dough adding a little more warm water as required to obtain a good kneading consistency. Prove again for 30 minutes, turn on to a lightly floured wooden surface and "knock back" till the dough subsides.

Divide into $2\frac{1}{4}$-$2\frac{1}{2}$ oz. pieces. Roll into balls. Set wide apart on lightly floured baking sheets. Prove until well risen and either mark across on the top of each, using the flat side of a kebab skewer, or lay very thin strips of almond paste in crosses on the top. Bake at about gas 7 (425°F) for 8 minutes. Brush the tops with a sugar glaze made by dissolving a dozen lumps of sugar in a gill of warm water. Try to apply this glaze to the four sections between whichever form of cross you have chosen. This way the cross shows up much more boldly on the finished bun. Then complete the baking.

If, however, you want to make the mixture up overnight and do the final proving and baking in the morning, add the second lot of flour and the remaining ingredients as itemised above without the intermediate stage of proving. Cover the mixture (in a deep container) with a light cloth only and, last thing before you go to bed, put in an outhouse or shed, which is just frost proof but not heated. In the morning you will find the proving is well ahead. Finish it in the usual way until the mixture is nearly doubled and then proceed as instructed for knocking back, kneading, scaling, final proving and baking.

After this somewhat complicated recipe let
us refresh ourselves with some very simple
ones. Not only do we restrict our breadmaking to a maximum twice per week and
keep the breads perfectly moist and edible in
their jackets of kitchen foil, but we make a
weekly batch of one or more kinds of scones,
parcel these up in foil and keep them in mild
domestic refrigeration.

In fact some years ago when we were testing
this use of foil we parcelled up a number of
items and packed them together in a refrigerator—kippers next to cream cake,
butter and cheese alongside. Among our
tested items was a parcel of simple home-
made scones. Somehow they got overlooked
and were not found for three weeks. Believe
it or not they were still edible—but of course
they were made with Swiss flour. We would
not advocate more than a week at most with
any flour we have found over here—it seems
to mildew so fast!

Whatever it is that is put into bought scones,
we find they taste of soda bicarbonate—or
so it seems to us.

There is one packet scone mix (page 369)
which is excellent, but as this is a Cook's
Book we will stick to our own! However
sweet scones many **Sweet Scones** we make for family
consumption they never seem to have a
chance of even getting cold so we no longer
try to keep them—it is hopeless!

For these put 10 oz. sifted self-raising flour
into a howl and rub in 2 oz. lard and the

same of butter until the mixture is very fine grained. Then add a small handful of sultanas and 2 oz. castor sugar. Bind with milk (sometimes) yoghourt (sometimes) or sour milk when you can succeed in souring modern combine milk!

The dough is then rolled out very lightly to a minimum $\frac{3}{4}$ inch thickness, stamped into rounds or cut into squares—this is purely a matter of preference—which are set on a lightly floured baking sheet to bake one shelf above centre at gas 5 (380°F) for from 15 to 20 minutes depending on their size. Split and recklessly buttered they may be no good at all to the waistline but they are highly appetising.

cornflour
scones

So are simple **Cornflour Scones** for using instead of bread with soups and *hors d'oeuvre*. Just sift 5 oz. of both flour and cornflour together, rub in 2 oz. lard and 2 oz. butter, add a generous pinch of salt and bind with milk, sour milk or yoghourt. Bake as explained for **Sweet Scones** and serve whole for folk to butter themselves.

wholemeal
scone
mixture

For a **Wholemeal Scone Mixture** use 100 per cent stone-ground wholewheat flour (page 370). Put 8 oz. of it in a bowl, add 1 heaped teaspoonful of baking powder and mix well together with 1 level teaspoonful of salt. Then rub in 3 oz. of butter. Bind the mixture to a firm dough with milk, roll out to a $\frac{3}{4}$ inch thickness, stamp into rounds or ovals and bake one shelf above centre at gas 8 (445°F) for about 16 minutes.

If you want to turn these into **Wholemeal Sultana Scones,** you just omit the salt and add 2 oz. "pieces" sugar and 3 oz. sultanas.

With the exception of these two stone-ground recipes, the references on pages 341 and 345

**Gran's Quick Bread,** baking powder moulders unused in our kitchen. **Gran's Quick Bread** was immensely popular when we were children and used to be devoured in vast quantities by hungry men coming in at dusk after a day's hunting or shooting. In fact even the most sophisticated were prepared to bypass the almost obligatory brandy and soda of those days, in favour of these simple breads served piping hot in napkin-lined baskets for splitting open and mounding with butter, home-made jams and thick cream and washing down with huge cups of scalding hot tea. All you do—a maximum 20 minutes before serving—is pre-heat an oven at gas 5 (380°F). Sift 1 lb. self-raising flour and a generous heaped tablespoonful of baking powder into a bowl and cut in, with a knife, sufficient cold water to bind up swiftly to a dough, which can then be dolloped on to a floured baking sheet in the shape of rather enormous rock buns. After about 15 minutes baking. they have crusty outsides and soft innards. They **must** be eaten up immediately as they are quite revolting when they are cold!

There are one or two ends in this chapter that we would like to tie up before moving on to something else. They concern the fact that members of the bread family sometimes turn mouldy during storage. The shop loaf is, of course, the worst offender, partially due to underbaking, partially because there are too great quantities of water in the mixtures and partially as a result of the flours used. If you buy the best flour you can possibly get, if it is always kept perfectly dry and never put anywhere where it can be a victim of even fractional humidity and if you are meticulous about baking everything thoroughly, you should be perfectly safe for 5-6 days, with the proviso that you never wrap bread and store it until it is absolutely cold.

It is scarcely surprising that the Sociable Cook aims to make her own breads, buns, scones, flapjacks and waffles.

She knows she is then superbly well-equipped for hungry young "Mum I'm starving, is there anything in the 'fridge-cupboard-pantry?'", for cutting the costly fish and meat consumption-edges from adult family appetites and for coping with the unexpected poppers-in.

This is when the Sociable Cook puts on kettle or percolator, or stands the pot of cooling coffee *au bain marie* to re-heat without deleterious boilings-up and butters slices of very sociable breads, or heats up a waffle iron and helps herself from a bowl of waffle mixture in the refrigerator, or ekes out a meat course which is just enough for the family by supporting it with **Hot Spoon Bread** or **Talahassee Hush Puppies.**

# *Bon Viveur* *makes the most of* **HIGH SPEED GAS**

*by using*

## PRINCE *TWO*
## MAGITROL *by*
# PARKINSON COWAN

# Chapter 16

# *Squirrels hoard and so should you*

In support of our urge (page 48) that you resolve to start or add to your store cupboard we have listed what we regard as Very Important Items. These may help you to decide what you still need or would very much like to acquire.

## Setting up from the beginning

anchovy *purée* (in bottle)
angelica
bicarbonate of soda
cochineal (this is not a vegetable colouring; it comes from an insect)
coffee beans (never store ground coffee)
concentrated tomato *purée* (in tube, in tin)
cooking chocolate (*couverture*) and/or chocolate chips
cornflour
cream of tartar
desiccated coconut
dried fruits: apricots, currants, peel, prunes, seeded raisins, sultanas

dried herbs and spices (if you have no fresh herbs available):
basil; bay leaves; borage; cayenne; carraway (ground
and seed); celery (salt ands eed); chervil; chilis (ground
and whole); chives; cinnamon (ground and sticks);
cloves (ground and whole); coriander seed; cummin
seed; dill seed; fennel seed; garlic (powder and salt);
ginger (ground, whole and root); mace (ground and
blade); marjoram; mint; mustard (powder and seed);
nutmeg (ground and whole); onion (powder and salt);
paprika (ground—try for rose paprika; it is the best);
parsley; pepper (black, ground and whole, white,
ground and whole, mignonette, pimento, ground and
whole); rosemary; sage; tarragon; thyme; turmeric,
(ground)

drinking chocolate

flour (we find self-raising adequate for **everything** unless
you are anti-white flour in which case substitute stone
ground)

French mustard

garlic heads

gelatine (powdered)

*glacé* cherries

ground almonds

harmless vegetable colourings: blue, caramel (brown),
carmine, green, mauve, saffron (yellow)

masala paste (this is far and away better than curry powder)

olive oil

orange flower water (indispensable for cakes and puddings)

Parmesan cheese (the hard, keeping one)

pastas (omnibus name for spaghetti family): The main
ones are *macaroni* (thick): *spaghetti* (medium): *vermicelli*
(fine); *tagliatelle*, or *fettucine* (narrow strips or ribbands);
*lasagne rosa* and *verde* (like *tagliatelle*, pink and green,
sold in little nests); *tirtellini* (like ears); *pastine* (like giant
rice grains); *ravioli* (flute-edged baby packets containing

meat mixture); *farfalle* (flute-edged bows); *stellete* (baby stars); *rigatoni* (like baby lengths of drain-pipe awaiting stuffing); and minute soup-ones in miniature alphabet shapes—we do not know the proper name for them!

potato flour (*fécule de pomme* for thickening without clouding)

rennet (in bottle for junkets and certain cheeses)

rice (for boiling—the long grained Patna variety)

rice (risotto—short fat-grained one, ask for Italian rice)

rose water (indispensable for cakes and puddings)

salt (*gros sel* or Maldon)

semolina

suet (packaged)

sugars: brown coffee crystals; castor; domino dark brown; domino dots; domino hostess; granulated (for sugar syrup work and some kinds of crystallisation—not for general cooking); icing; lump; rainbow coffee crystals; rock and rye candy sugar; soft brown or "pieces"

vanilla pods (black sticks—the true flavour—never use essence)

wine vinegar (white and/or red)

Worcestershire sauce (only Lea and Perrins)

### Inedible Essentials

aluminium kitchen foil

fine strong string

greaseproof paper

tissue paper (for emergency fat-skimming)

### Adding to an existing store cupboard

almond dragees

anchovy fillets†

artichoke bottoms (*fonds d'artichauts*)†

asparagus spears†

Bath Oliver biscuits and Dorset Knobs (for cheese)

bean sprouts (excellent for winter salads)†
black treacle or "molasses"
capers
caviare (Danish-type)
cherries (in maraschino and in Curaçao)
chestnut *purée* (sweetened and unsweetened)†
chestnuts (whole in syrup)†
chocolate Bath Oliver biscuits
chocolate buttons
chocolate vermicelli
cooking wines and liqueurs
corm powder (for Mexican *tortillina*)
corn†
corned beef (for **Corned Beef Hash**)†
*Crêpes dentelles*
crystallised fruits
crystallised ginger
crystallised peel cups
crystallised rose petals
crystallised violets
cum-quats†
diet breads
dried beans
dried members of mushroom family in packets (*cèpes* and
    *morilles* are best)
flour: brown and 100% wholewheat stone-ground (for
    home-made bread, scones, etc.)
garlic salt
gherkins
ginger (preserved)
*glacé* pineapple
golden syrup
hearts of palm†
honey
hundreds and thousands (for the children)

lentils

lycheest†

maple syrup

*marrons glacés*

marshmallows

milk (unsweetened for emergencies)†

"mimosa" garnish

mole powder, red and green (for Mexican dishes)

Nuts: bitter almonds; Brazil kernels; cashew; flaked
almonds (for browning); ground almonds; hazelnuts
(grind as substitute for almonds); Jordan almonds; pecan;
pistachio (for pudding and cake garnish); Valencia
almonds (whole, unskinned for general use); walnuts
(for bread, cakes and puddings)

okra†

olives: green (French and Spanish); green (stuffed); black
(dry pack or in brine)

orange juice (unsweetened)†

*pâté*†

*Patum Peperium*

peanut-butter

petit beurre or digestives (for biscuit-cakes)

pimentoes (for stuffing and for garnish)†

poppy seeds

ratafias

red kidney beans†

sago

Sakura Oriental cocktail biscuits

sardines†

savoy finger biscuits (for *charlottes*)

silver and gold balls for garnish

smoked oysters

snails†

soups: bird's nest; *bisque de homard* (excellent); green turtle;
kangaroo tail; shark's fin†

split, dried peas
stringed sugar crystals for wine-making
sugar, preserving
Tea: China, Indian, green and the Virgin Tea of China
for punches
tomatoes†
truffles or truffle trimmings (when feeling very rich!)†
tuna†
vine leaves†
water chestnuts (excellent for winter salads)†
yams†
**†Items sold in tins**

## These things are far better put up by you than acquired over the counter

*bouquets aromatiques** (from your own dried herbs)
Christmas cakes (page 296)
Christmas puddings (page 294)
coffee syrup*
dried herbs*
frozen fruit and vegetables (see pages 54-56)
fruit *purées*, notably for *sorbets* but also for perfect winter
fools. Cook fruit dry in slow oven. Rub every possible
scrap through a sieve, sweeten to taste, bottle, sterilise
and store.
fruit syrups, notably strawberry—there is always more
syrup than fruit in cooked strawberry jam. Ladle off the
syrup into bottling jars, sterilise for long-keeping and use
over ice cream, as sauces, etc. Cook other fruit dry in oven
gas 2 (310°F) till purged, press through a sieve, bottle,
with sweetening to taste, and sterilize for long-keeping.
golden breadcrumbs, the fine crisp ones are just crusts
dried off in the oven gas 1 (290°F), smashed down with
a meat batter or rolling pin inside a fold of brown paper,
then sieved and stored in a screw top jar.

herb vinegars, with wine vinegar of course—you just thrust whatever fresh herb you need—basil, tarragon, chives, shallots, thyme, marjoram, chervil or peeled, cut garlic cloves—into small bottles of wine vinegar, seal them up and let them seep their aromatic flavours in.

jams, jellies, fruit cheeses (preserve with brandy)

mincemeat (page 239)

orange and lemon essences*

orange and lemon sugar (page 52)

Oxford sauce (page 258)

pickles, chutnies, bottled fruit and vegetables

praline*

seasoned flour*

stock sugar syrup*

tomato *coulis*\* (it is far and away superior to any bottled tomato sauce)

vanilla sugars*


## These you can make and store for 3-4 weeks

anchovy butter*

apricot jam *purée*\*

basic butter cream*

*beurre Chivry*\*

chocolate cases (page 314)

chocolate leaves (page 314)

confectioners' custard*

doodled chocolate trellises

Florentines (page 328)

*ganache* (page 325)

garlic butter*

green butter*

mayonnaise*

meringues*

*vinaigrette*\*

### These items keep for a week to 10 days

close-textured sponge*
croissant dough*
*gâteau l'ambassadeur* (page 324)
pancakes* (5 days in refrigerator; 10 in deep freeze)
*petits pots de chocolat* (page 322)
savoury short paste*
sweet short paste*

### SPECIALS

smoked buckling  (keeps 7-10 days in refrigeration) page 365
    ,,    cod's roe    ,,   ,,    ,, ,,     ,,
    ,,    salmon
    (from Ireland)   ,,   ,,    ,, ,,     ,,
smoked trout        ,,   ,,    ,, ,,     ,,

## FASHION

"Fashion is what one wears oneself. What is unfashionable is what other people wear."

Yes, yes, Oscar Wilde. But in that case one must study the Laws and Precepts of Fashion to make sure of breaking them—which is just as hard work as studying to observe.

There is no escape: to keep in the swim—or out of it—you have got to read the Acknowledged Authorities. They write for the Woman's Feature in *The Daily Telegraph*. There you will read all about Fashion—not only in clothes but also food, entertaining, home decorating, beauty culture. And you will find it most interesting—an individualist like you.

# The Daily Telegraph

is the paper you can trust

*Chapter 17*

# Shopper's guide

**Bean Slicer**
> Leon Jaeggi & Sons Ltd., 232, Tottenham Court Road, London, W.1.
> Staines Kitchen Equipment Co. Ltd., 122 Victoria Street, London S.W.1.

**Bird Repellent Powder** (Morkit)
> E. J. Woodman & Son Ltd., High Street, Pinner, Middlesex.

**Buckling**
> Harrods, Knightsbridge, London S.W.1.

**Butter Stamp with Acorn Design**
> Betty Hope, 19 Beauchamp Place, London S.W.3.

**Chrysal** (flower reviver)
> Carters Tested Seeds Ltd., Raynes Park, London, S.W.20.

**Chocolate Chips** (Polka Dots)
> Name of local stockist obtainable from Symbol Biscuits Ltd., Sunya House, Scrubs Lane, London, N.W.10.

**Cod's Roe**

Fortnum and Mason, Piccadilly, London W.1.

**Cooking Chocolate** (*couverture*)

Harrods, Knightsbridge, London S.W.1.

John Barker & Co. Ltd., Kensington High Street, London W.8.

Selfridges, Oxford Street, London W.1.

**Cooper Meat Thermometer**

Leon Jaeggi & Sons Ltd., 232 Tottenham Court Road, London W.1.

Staines Kitchen Equipment Co. Ltd., 122 Victoria Street, London S.W.1.

**Corn Syrup**

Selfridges, Oxford Street, London W.1.

**Crab Meat**

Selfridges, Oxford Street, London W.1.

Branches of Mac Fisheries.

**Danish Caviare type**

Selfridges, Oxford Street, London W.1.

**Dried Cèpes**

Louis Roche Ltd., 14 Old Compton Street, London W.1.

**Dried Cod**

Lina Stores, 18 Brewer Street, London W.1.

**Dried Morilles**

Louis Roche Ltd., 14 Old Compton Street, London W.1.

**Fécule de Pomme** (Potato flour)

Selfridges, Oxford Street, London W.1.

**Filtres** (coffee)

Leon Jaeggi & Sons Ltd., 232 Tottenham Court Road, London W.1.

Staines Kitchen Equipment Co. Ltd., 122 Victoria Street, London S.W.1.

**Fine Florists Wire**
>Cocquerel's Sundries Ltd., 28 Wellington Street, London W.C.2.

**Flaked Almonds**
>Selfridges, Oxford Street, London W.1.

**Grapefruit Cutter**
>Leon Jaeggi & Sons Ltd., 232 Tottenham Court Road, London W.1.
>Staines Kitchen Equipment Co. Ltd., 122 Victoria Street, London S.W.1.

**Heat Resistant China Pans** (Pyrosil)
>Name of local stockists obtainable from James A. Jobling & Co. Ltd., Wear Glass Works, Sunderland.

**Icing Bag and Pipes** (miscellaneous) and
>**Individual Moulds** (*oeufs en gelée*)
>Leon Jaeggi & Sons Ltd., 232 Tottenham Court Road, London W.1.
>Staines Kitchen Equipment Co. Ltd., 122 Victoria Street, London S.W.1.

**Jelly Bag and Stand**
>George Fowler Lee, 42-44 Queen Street, Reading.

**Larding Needle**
>Leon Jaeggi & Sons Ltd., 232 Tottenham Court Road, London W.1.
>Staines Kitchen Equipment Co. Ltd., 122 Victoria Street, London S.W.1.

**Maldon Salt, Maple Syrup, Molasses**
>Selfridges, Oxford Street, London W.1.

**Mandoline**
>Bon Viveur (Cuisine) Ltd., 19 Meerbrook Road, Kidbrooke, London S.E.3.

**Maraschino Cherries**
>Fortnum & Mason, Piccadilly, London W.1.

**Masala Paste**
> Spice Box, 8 Bute Street, South Kensington, London S.W.7.

**Mincer**
> Name of local stockist obtainable from Andrews Housewares Ltd., 137 Kirkdale, Sydenham, London S.E.26.

**Packet Scone Mix**
> Name of local stockist obtainable from Allinson Ltd., 210 Cambridge Heath Road, London E.2.

**Parisian Cutter, Parsley Mill, Potato Shaver**
> Leon Jaeggi & Sons Ltd., 232 Tottenham Court Road, London W.1.
> Staines Kitchen Equipment Co. Ltd., 122 Victoria Street, London S.W.1.

**Pâté de Foie** (type recommended is Le Parfait)
> Generally available throughout the country.

**Pompadour Fan Wafers**
> Selfridges, Oxford Street, London W.1.

**Powder Colouring**
> Hartley Smith School of Cake Decorating, 34 Hampstead Road, London N.W.1.

**Puff Pastry** (Jus-Rol)
> Obtainable throughout the country at good stores which sell frozen foods.

**Real Olive Oil** (La Véritable Huile de Provence)
> Peter Dominic Ltd., Aux Caves de France, Horsham, Sussex.

**Ribbon Noodles**
> Lina Stores, 18 Brewer Street, London W.1.

**Silicagel**
> Obtainable from branches of Boots the Chemists.

**Smoked Salmon**
> Thos. Murphy (Dublin) Ltd., Wholesale Division, Wholesale Fish Market, Dublin 7.

**Smoked Trout**
>   Fortnum & Mason, Piccadilly, London W.1.

**Soy Sauce**
>   Hong Kong Emporium, 53 Rupert Street, London
>   W.1.

**Square Flan Case**
>   Leon Jaeggi & Sons Ltd., 232 Tottenham Court
>   Road, London W.1.
>   Staines Kitchen Equipment Co. Ltd., 122 Victoria
>   Street, London S.W.1.

**Truffle Peelings**
>   J. Bourbon Ltd., 81 Wardour Street, London W.1.

**Trussing Needle**
>   Leon Jaeggi & Sons Ltd., 232 Tottenham Court
>   Road, London W.1.
>   Staines Kitchen Equipment Co. Ltd., 122 Victoria
>   Street, London S.W.1.

**Unpainted Wooden Chest**
>   Woodwork Centre, 7a Deptford Broadway, London
>   S.E.8.

**Waffle Iron**
>   Leon Jaeggi & Sons Ltd., 232 Tottenham Court
>   Road, London W.1.
>   Staines Kitchen Equipment Co. Ltd., 122 Victoria
>   Street, London S.W.1.

**Water Chestnuts**
>   Hong Kong Emporium, 53 Rupert Street, London
>   W.1.

**Whole Wheat Flour**
>   Name of local stockist obtainable from Allinson Ltd.,
>   210 Cambridge Heath Road, London E.2.

# GARNISH

Left hand drawing shows how a citrus fruit is grooved in a continuous ribband with a canelle knife. Right hand drawing shows the use of four canelled oranges and a plain kebab skewer as garnish for poultry. The cut ends of each orange ribband are threaded through the skewer ring and allowed to float out.

*Fig.1* *Fig.2* *Fig.3*

## HOW TO CUT A LEMON BASKET
Cut from left and right of lemon tip as shown by dotted lines in fig. 1. Remove these two sections. Cut away flesh and skin to make 'handle' (fig. 2). Cut deep 'vees' around top of 'basket' below handle as shown in figs. 2 and 3.

## ORANGE WATER LILY—HOW TO PREPARE

Make cuts through skin and pith as shown in Diagram 1
and as far down as the beginning of the dotted lines.
Diagram 2. Ease back 'petals' leaving the orange standing
free in the centre. Separate the orange segments gently so
each one may be removed easily.

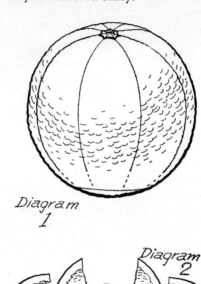

Diagram
1

Diagram
2

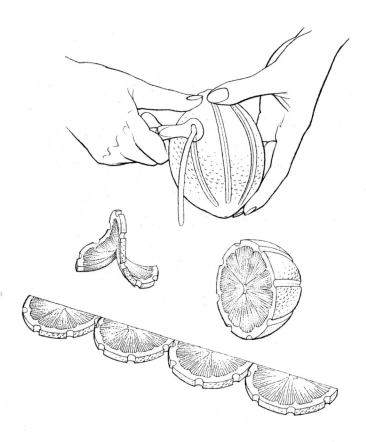

Shows how to use a canelle knife to prepare slices of decorative lemon or other citrus fruit. Draw as shown on lemon held in pair of hands a series of ribband strips of pith away with canelle knife. Slice lemon in rounds and cut each round in halves. Lay flat round edge of chosen dish. For upright treatment nip skin through in one place at edge of each slice and give it a twist and it will stand quite securely when placed in position.

Shows a whole, cold ham skinned and seared in a criss-cross trellis over its whole upper or fat surface. This searing which looks very effective is done with an ordinary metal skewer heated over a naked flame. Each 'square' is decorated centrally with a cube of yellow pineapple and a red or green glacé cherry held in position with half a wooden cocktail stick. The ham bone is concealed by a ham frill. The edge of the dish is bordered with piped *duchesse* potatoes, garnished with stuffed olives and the space on the dish between border and ham is filled alternately with little mounds of *pommes pailles* (straw potatoes) and sliced mushrooms.

A simple garnish for a whole salmon, or salmon trout. The same flower and leaf design spread more widely can be used over a whole turbot or any other large fish.

1. Border shows cannelled, halved slices of unpeeled lemon with small tufts of parsley between.

2. The flower heads are made of five thin, overlapping slices of unskinned cucumber with four crescents of unskinned tomato and half a stoned black olive set in each centre. The bud uses only a petal of black olive and two crescents of tomato. The narrow leaves are tarragon. The stems are cut and curled from onion, shallot or thick chives stems, as are the little diamond-shaped pieces down the main stem.

3. The fish is first skinned to the beginning of both head and tail as shown. A tuft of parsley is thrust into the mouth.

# FINISHING THE CAKE

## HOW TO USE A PLAIN PAPER ICING BAG

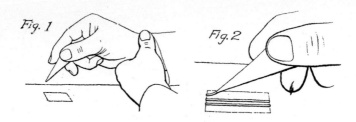

*Fig.* 1 shows position of hand holding pipe and opposite hand supporting and steadying wrist.

*Fig.* 2 shows position of pipe above plastic or glass practice board to start laying down a straight line of piping.

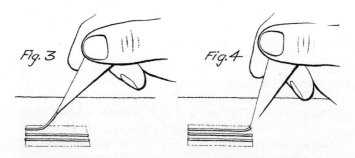

*Fig.* 3 shows how pipe is raised as the thread progresses.

*Fig.* 4 shows position of pipe at the end of a single line or thread.

An easy treatment of royal icing to decorate top and sides
of a round, rich fruit cake. All the work is done with a
plain ⅛ inch writing pipe and it is recommended that the
inexperienced practice first on a small piece of glass or
perspex. A little practice will show that it is not necessary
to have a pipe at all but just to cut a fraction from the tip
of an ordinary paper icing bag and use this instead.

How to apply almond paste to a rich fruit cake. When almond paste is made and rolled out to required thickness on a surface dusted lightly with cornflour, the base of the fruit cake is brushed thickly with sieved apricot jam or warmed redcurrant jelly and then pressed down lightly but firmly on to the almond paste. Then cut the surplus almond paste away neatly with a sharp knife (see illustration

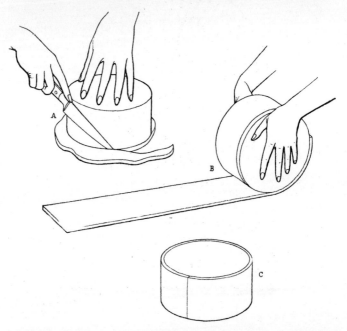

(A)). Roll out a long strip of almond paste the exact length of the circumference of the cake and the exact width of the cake's sides. Brush the sides all round liberally with jam or jelly and trundle the cake over the almond paste strip (B), placing the hands on top and bottom as they would otherwise be covered with jam! Illustration (C) exemplifies the perfect neatness and precision of the finished result.

# TYING UP

## THE BARDING OF POULTRY OR GAME

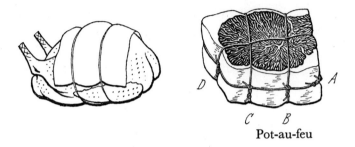

Pot-au-feu

Showing size of strip of raw, unsalted pork fat and positions of string for tying securely in place.

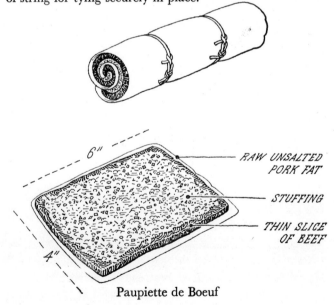

Paupiette de Boeuf

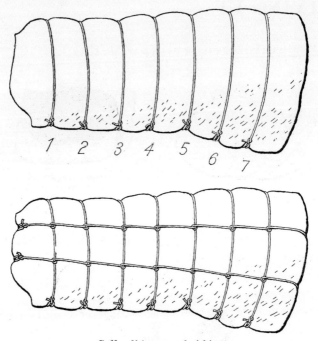

Selle d'Agneau bridée

## CROWN ROAST

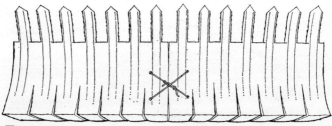

Fig. 1

*Fig.* 1 shows two trimmed best end necks with skin and flesh cut down between each cutlet bone and tips of bones

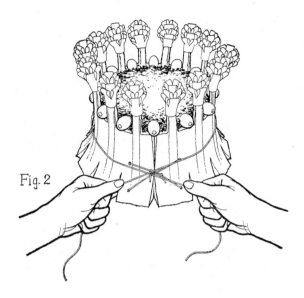

Fig. 2

snipped to sharp points (to receive stuffed olives or mara-schino cherries) with a pair of strong kitchen scissors. Centre of Fig. 1 shows position of string securing the two best end necks together.

*Fig.* 2 shows how when string has been tied on opposing side, exactly as in Fig. 1, it is brought round the two up-standing, joined best ends to form and secure a crown. This diagram shows little cutlet frills placed on the bone tips and stuffed olives driven through the interstices be-tween the cutlet bones into the central stuffing after roasting. Note how the chining (the severing at regular intervals) in both diagrams along the length of the best end necks enables the crown to stand steadily on the baking tin or dish.

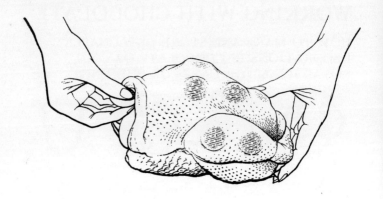

Having loosened the upper part of the skin of an uncooked chicken, push circles of truffles (for the very rich) or small, de-stalked mushroom cups under the skin, under-side uppermost.

# WORKING WITH CHOCOLATE

HOW TO MAKE AND STORE DETACHABLE
DECORATIONS IN CHOCOLATE OR
ROYAL ICING FOR CAKES OR PUDDINGS

In either case trace the designs on to a sheet of paper. Set
this on the table, cover with a sheet of greaseproof and
copy with a plain writing pipe in a nylon icing bag filled
with either chocolate or royal icing. Detach when set and
store in layers between waxed papers in an airtight tin
in a dry place.

HOW TO ASSEMBLE
CHOCOLATE SWAN COMPONENTS

Showing head, wings and tail secured to chocolate or
sponge oval base with rosettes of butter cream or royal
icing, leaving room in the centre of each for a ball of ice
cream.

383

## MUM'S CHOCOLATE TRIFLE

Rosettes and fingers of Crème Chantilly are piped over chocolate covering to trifle and over the chocolate leaves which decorate the border of the dish. Halved green glacé cherries are set round the inner ring of cream rosettes and in the centre. Little diamonds of softened angelica are put into the next outer ring of cream rosettes.

## SIMPLE DECORATION FOR A RECTANGULAR OR PANEL CAKE

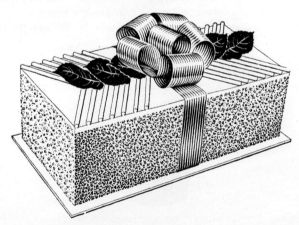

The sides of this cake are spread neatly with butter cream before the top is iced. Then the cake is held firmly between the palms of the hands at top and base and the sides are pressed into either chocolate vermicelli, coarsely grated chocolate or milled nuts. Then the top is covered with royal icing and before it is set, the strip of ribband is laid centrally across the top and down the sides with the ends tucked just under the base. When the royal icing is set, the echelons are piped in royal icing with a $\frac{1}{4}$ inch writing pipe as shown. Each end is lopped off neatly with a knife dipped in cold water. Then the chocolate leaves (page 314) are placed in position with dabs of royal icing to hold them securely and the bow is affixed to the centre of the top of the ribband also with royal icing.

## PIGS IN CHOCOLATE OR ROYAL ICING

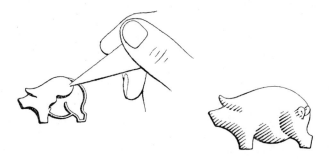

Trace the outline of pig (right hand drawing) on to grease-proof paper, reverse the paper, use a plain writing pipe to pipe outline on the reverse side. Fill in as shown using either chocolate or royal icing. When dry and set, pigs can be pulled off the paper for use flat, or clapped together in pairs (remember to reverse an equal number for these) and stuck together with dabs of either chocolate or royal icing for using the pigs standing.

# CHOCOLATE HOUSE ASSEMBLY

Begin by drawing the outlines as shown in Chocolate House assembly (diagram A) on sheets of greaseproof paper, remembering to do two for front and back, two sides, two roofs, one base and one chimney. Then spread these fairly thickly with softened cooking chocolate (*couverture*) or softened chocolate chips. When set peel paper from backs gently. Place base at the back of a large pastry board and

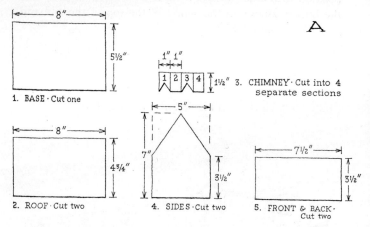

1. BASE · Cut one

2. ROOF · Cut two

3. CHIMNEY · Cut into 4 separate sections

4. SIDES · Cut two

5. FRONT & BACK · Cut two

for position look at the illustration of Chocolate House and Garden (Diagram B). You will see that a narrow strip for pathway has been left, left and right of house and the larger part of the board remains uncovered in front to make the garden. Affix sides by coating the base of each side piece with softened chocolate. Press each into position and hold firmly for a moment or two until set. Repeat the process with front and back remembering this time to coat both sides and base of each piece so that it grips the edges of the side pieces which have already been affixed. When all this is securely set, go over the interior with a small knife and a little softened chocolate to seal the joins where the sections are joined and make them completely secure. Follow the same chocolate coating process all round the edges of the two roof pieces, press these securely in position and go over the central top join with a little chocolate on the tip of the knife to seal these completely. To affix chimney place the four sections, having coated the edges with softened chocloate, in position singly sticking each one to the next and then securing them inside and after putting in position on the house (diagram B) with a little chocolate on the tip of a knife.

B

You are now ready to start the decorations. Tease out a scrap of cotton wool and push it into the hollow chimney to simulate smoke. Use white royal icing in a small paper icing bag to pipe little peaks around the roof edges to simulate icicles and the same material in a writing pipe for the door and windows. Add icicles to either roof or chimney or both as desired. Then rough up with white royal icing all over the remaining board area flattening down the piece from the door of the house to the front rim of the board to simulate a path. Chocolate finger biscuits with one end lopped off each have been used to make the fence posts. More ambitious decorators can add a gate and a closer fencing of posts. Finally place four little miniature trees as shown in diagram B.

Note: If liked the interior of the house can be filled with sweets or biscuits before affixing the roof and a miniature Father Christmas can be pushed into the cotton wool at the top of the chimney.

# MISCELLANEOUS

## BRICKS

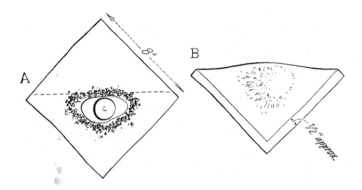

*Diagram A* showing position of fillings on paste square
*Diagram B* showing first fold with overlapping paste leaving a small border on lower half.

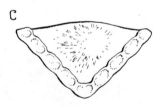

*Diagram C* showing how under flap of paste is pinched into position having been brushed with raw, beaten egg or cold water.

## PLAIT LOAF

Take a piece of dough about ¾-1 inch thick, 4 ins. wide and 18 ins. long: cut into five strips—each about ¼ inch wide—within ½ inch of end of dough (illustration 1).

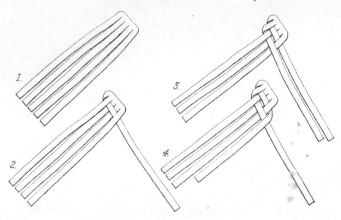

Take the LEFT strip, pass it to the right, under one strip, over two strips and under one strip (illustration 2).

Take the next LEFT strip, pass it to the right under one strip and over two strips (illustration 3).

Take the TOP RIGHT strip and fold down over the LOWER strip (illustration 4).

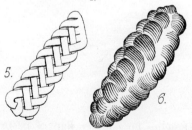

Repeat as in illustration 3 and 4 until the plait is completed as in illustration 5. Baked plait is shown in illustration 6.

# HOW TO PREPARE A COOKED ARTICHOKE
## FOR SERVING

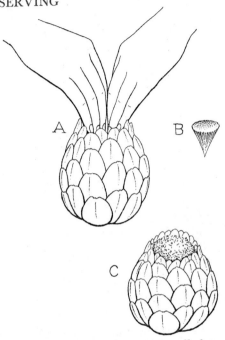

(A) shows how uppermost leaves are pulled apart centrally until the fingers can reach half way down the artichoke. Here the remaining leaves sitting over the "choke" form a cone. Grip this firmly between thumb and first two fingers, twist round and the little cone will come away easily (see (B) showing cone inverted). Having removed this cone, the seed pad or 'choke' is then pulled away gently. It will always come away easily if the artichoke is cooked. This leaves the *fond* or artichoke bottom clear. Allow the top leaves to fall back slightly. Invert cone as shown in (C) over the top, sprinkle with milled or chopped parsley and serve with *vinaigrée* or *vinaigrette*.

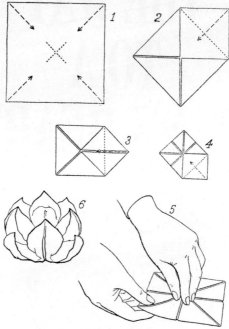

Diagrams 1 and 2 show how a plain, square table napkin in kitchen foil, linen, paper or tissue paper is folded four corners to centre.

Diagram 3 repeats this folding a second time to reduce the square still further in size. Turn the napkin over so that the four corners are underneath and repeat the folding a third time on the reverse side or base as shown in Diagram 4. Hold these last four points firmly together with the finger tips and pull up the four folded points which are now underneath. This will reveal to the searching fingers four single points which lie in between, pull these up and you will find they form the locking pieces which hold the complete water lily together.

# THE WAY TO A MAN'S HEART

Read Jean Robertson's cookery notes regularly in the SUNDAY TELEGRAPH! You'll find out how to make anything from Sauce Bearnaise to scrambled eggs, you'll know all about the week's best food buys, and you'll get ideas for new and exciting menus. Jean Robertson in the

## SUNDAY TELEGRAPH

# Index

397

398